'60s SPEED
THE GOLDEN AGE OF MOTORCYCLE
GRAND PRIX RACING
CHRIS PEREIRA
FOREWORD BY TOMMY ROBB

A VELOCE BOOK


Veloce is an imprint of David and Charles, Ltd
Email: info@veloce.co.uk | web: www.veloce.co.uk | tel: 01305 260068



First published in March 2014 by Veloce Publishing Limited as *Motorcycle GP Racing in the 1960s*.
This edition published in the UK and USA in 2026.



A catalogue record for this book is available from the British Library.

ISBN-13: 9781836440758 hardback
ISBN-13: 9781836440765 ebook

Layout of the digital edition of this book may vary depending on reader hardware and display settings.

Printed in China through Asia Pacific Offset Group, Ltd for:
David and Charles, Ltd
Suite A, Tourism House, Pynes Hill, Exeter, EX2 5WS

Veloce production team:
General Manager: Kevin Quinn
Commissioning Editor: Kizzy Taylor-Richelieu
Senior Book Editor: Becky Martin
Head of Design: Kevin Atkins
Production Manager: Sam Childs

David and Charles publishes high-quality books on a wide range of subjects. For more information visit www.davidandcharles.com.

Follow Veloce on social media: **Facebook:** Veloce Publishing | **Instagram:** @velocebooks | **X (Twitter):** @VeloceBooks
Subscribe to our monthly newsletter ***On the Grid***, details on our website www.veloce.co.uk

# '60s SPEED

## THE GOLDEN AGE OF MOTORCYCLE GRAND PRIX RACING

CHRIS PEREIRA

FOREWORD BY TOMMY ROBB

# Contents

# Foreword by Tommy Robb

**THIS BOOK** is a must for all dedicated fans of grand prix motorcycle racing as it was in the 1960s, a time when there were five individual World Champions, one in each class from 50cc, 125cc, 250cc, 350cc and 500cc, not just a Moto GP Champion and a WSB Champ.

Those were the heady days, when men like Mike Hailwood, Giacomo Agostini, Phil Read, Tarquinio Provini, and many, many more like them ruled the World Championships, and left a memory of an era never to be forgotten.

Chris Pereira has an almost encyclopaedic knowledge of grand prix racing during the '50s and '60s. He was himself a club racer in the '60s, and more recently in Classic Racing on his Ducati and various other makes. He has produced a memorable book that will allow the classic '60s fan to wallow, deep in the comfort of their armchair, in memories that will still excite.

Those were also the days when the saying "falling off doesn't hurt, but the sudden stop at the end is what causes the pain and problems" was coined. It's worth remembering that in those days, before thickly-padded leathers and state of the art crash helmets and gloves, the rider owed his survival to the protection provided by a couple of millimetres of soft goatskin or horsehide skin-tight leathers, which would have looked more fashionable on a ballet dancer than on a high speed sportsman.

No high-tech protection bags in those days, only the odd straw bale placed delicately in front of a protruding tree, gatepost or telephone pole meant the difference between life and death or permanent disability.

As one of the World Championship contenders of the '50s, '60s and '70s, my own severe osteoarthritis of today, instigated by previous high-speed mishaps, serves as a stark reminder that, exciting though the era was, a rider was lucky if he walked away at the end of each rigorous grand prix season, when many of his pals never made it.

As you settle down to indulge yourself (without pain) in that comfortable armchair for this enjoyable read, remember that today's 'fewer deaths' are due to those riders way back in the '60s who battled with the organisers, week in and week out, for safer tracks.

This book gives an insight into those truly wonderful days of long ago, when mobile phones, computers and iPods were still a long way in the future.

**Tommy Robb**

# Acknowledgements

**FIRSTLY, I** have to thank Rod Grainger of Veloce Publishing for taking a leap of faith and agreeing to publish this book. Thanks are also due to my good friend Tommy Robb for adding his illustrious name and credibility to this book.

Books on motorcycle racing history are of little value without photographs. I would, therefore, like to thank 1960s motorcycle sport photographer Malcolm Carling, who is a major contributor to this book, and allowed me free use of photographs from his vast library. Thanks are also due to Franz Besendorfer and Karl-Heinz Reiger for their excellent contributions. Other photographic material came from Luigi Taveri, Elwyn Roberts' collection and Karl-Gunter Peters.

I am particularly indebted to my friend Martyn Harris for putting me in touch with Malcolm Carling and for providing photographs from his own collection. Thanks also to my friend Roger Oliver for providing valuable research material.

Last, but by no means least, I must thank my wife Sondra for her unstinting support, tolerance, and understanding during the inevitable traumas and tantrums while this work was being compiled.

This book is dedicated to my father who introduced me to the joys of motorcycling when I was still a young teenager, and whose prewar TT scrapbooks first aroused my life-long interest in motorcycle racing.

While every effort has been made to ensure historical accuracy, errors will no doubt come to light. I would therefore welcome any authenticated corrections so that any future editions may be revised.

**Chris Pereira, Bracknell, Berkshire**

# Introduction

**IT'S DIFFICULT** to define in simple terms exactly what it is about the 1960s that evokes such emotion amongst ex-riders, historians, and classic racing enthusiasts, and the coining of such emotive terms as the 'Glorious Sixties'. Is it purely a yearning for what is past and memories dimmed by the passage of time? Or, was there something unique about this era? In the context of motorcycle racing history, it was undoubtedly a period that saw a great variety of makes and types of machine. There was also a much greater depth of riding talent concentrated in one Championship series. It was also, arguably, the last decade of grand prix road racing in the time-honoured Western European tradition, which produced the truly great exponents of pure road racing; the likes of Mike Hailwood, Giacomo Agostini, Jim Redman, and Phil Read, not forgetting all the brave riders who followed in their tracks.

During the 1960s, great advances were made in motorcycle racing technology, creating fierce competition between the major bike manufacturers. This inevitably produced some epic battles between riders on rival factory machines. Such a diversity of makes and technologies had never been seen before, and probably never will again. A survey of the grand prix results between 1960 and 1969 reveals that at least 50 different makes of machine, from over half a dozen countries, were involved. Even more remarkable was the variety and technical complexity of the machines that were produced. Four-strokes with one, two, three, four, five and six cylinders, ranging from 50cc to 500cc, did battle with two-strokes comprising piston-ported singles, air- and water-cooled disc-valve singles and twins, disc-valve water-cooled V-fours, and square-fours. In combination, these elements created what is probably one of the most exciting decades in motorcycle racing history.

Individual solo Championships were run in five separate solo classes: 50cc, 125cc, 250cc, 350cc and 500cc, usually with grids of 30 or more riders. Consequently, riding talent, too, was spread across a much broader spectrum of GP racing, and specialisation in one particular class was the exception rather than the rule. Most GP riders of the 1960s rode in at least two classes, while many rode in three or more, which involved riding in several long races on the same day. For example, in the course of winning two World Championships in 1966, Mike Hailwood rode in four solo classes, winning ten 250cc, six 350cc, and three 500cc grands prix, making a total of 19 GP wins in one season; a record that probably still stands today.

As the 1950s drew to a close, grand prix racing and the World Championship series faced an uncertain future. Economic recession and falling sales had taken their toll on the motorcycle industry. By the mid-1950s, the once successful British factory teams – Norton, Velocette and AJS – had already withdrawn from racing. They were soon followed by the German NSU and DKW teams. At the end of 1957 came the shock withdrawal of the Italian Gilera, Moto Guzzi and Mondial factories. These events had a devastating effect on the sport. Racing had suddenly been deprived of the essential support from factory-backed teams with their specially-developed and often exotic machines. Many world class riders, too, became redundant, and some went into retirement while others choose to continue racing as 'Privateers'. Consequently, interest in the sport began to wane, and the future of World Championship racing seemed very uncertain.

During 1958 and 1959 the World Championships struggled on, with only MV Agusta and the riding talents of John Surtees providing any degree of interest in the two premier solo classes. Technically, too, it was a period of relative stagnation, with MV maintaining its superiority using existing 350 and 500cc four-cylinder machines. The only spark of interest during these two years was in the smaller capacity classes, where MV domination of the 125 and 250cc classes was challenged by the 125cc Desmodromic Ducati in 1958, and the East German MZ two-strokes in 1959.

Quite clearly, grand prix racing at the start of the 1960s was in dire need of a new stimulus. One event, which took place in 1959, proved to be of much greater significance than anyone realised at the time. The arrival of a team of Japanese riders and machines at the TT races only caused mild curiosity, mingled with scepticism and even derision. With the benefit of hindsight, the European debut of the virtually unknown Honda team in 1959 must now be regarded as *the* defining moment in the postwar history of motorcycle racing. One that proved crucial to the recovery of World Championship grand prix racing. It is also the reason for a noticeable Honda bias in this book.

The return of the Honda team to participate in the World Championships in 1960 marked the beginning of a new era. Honda was joined initially by Suzuki and then by Yamaha to form the Oriental Triumvirate, and the stage was set for the battle for supremacy between the three. This evolved into a battle between the four-stroke and two-stroke technologies. Since this struggle took place initially in the lightweight categories, and the 125 and 250cc classes in particular; it was these two classes that generated the most interest until well into the 1960s.

The 350 and 500cc classes were relatively uninteresting, being dominated by the four-cylinder MVs ridden by John Surtees, and his successors Gary Hocking and Mike Hailwood. It was not until the arrival of the three-cylinder MVs in 1965, and Honda's expansion into these two classes, that they regained some of their former prestige. The only spark of interest in the 350 and 500cc classes was probably the battles between the private riders, mainly on classic British single-cylinder Manx Nortons, 7R AJSs, and Matchless G50s, for the honour of being the highest placed privateer, with the occasional podium finish behind the works machines.

Although production of the aforementioned British machines had virtually come to an end in 1962, they remained as much a part of grand prix racing as they had been during the 1950s, by helping to fill the grids in the 350 and 500cc classes. Essential to their continuation were some of the dedicated engine specialists, such as Ray Petty, Francis Beart, Steve Lancefield, Bill Lacey, AMC development engineer Jack Williams, as well as enthusiastic racing dealers like Tom Kirby, Tom Arter, Geoff Monty and Reg Dearden. Colin Seeley's initiative in taking over the production of the 7R and G50 machines using his own frame designs was also important.

By about the mid-60s, updated components for these machines were also being produced by specialist manufacturers such as Austrian Michael Schafleitner, who began producing five- and six-speed gear clusters, and Italian Danielle Fontana, who manufactured bigger and more efficient front brakes, all of which helped to improve the performance and prolong the useful life of the classic British machines.

Grand prix racing in the 1960s had yet to come under the influence of the self-styled 'Supremos'; big money sponsorship and business interests from outside the motorcycle industry. The sport was governed by the somewhat autocratic Federation Internationale de Motocyclisme (FIM), which consisted of many powerful race organisers who were frequently unsympathetic to the needs of the riders themselves.

Unlike modern purpose-built circuits with built-in safety features and large run-off areas, many of the GPs in the 1960s took place on traditional public road circuits, surrounded by hedges and ditches, buildings and street furniture. These hazards left little room for riding errors, the consequences of which were often tragic. In contrast to today's technical circuits, where riders spend 90 per cent of the time in the intermediate gears, many of the 1960s circuits were much longer than today and featured long fast sections, where riders would have been flat-out in top gear and an off-road excursion could prove disastrous. Average speeds were also much higher in the '60s and the races were often much longer. Death or serious injury were a constant threat, and as many as 11 riders are known to have lost their lives while riding in the World Championships during the ten-year period. Many of the circuits had been used prewar, and had altered very little since. The exceptions were the Dutch TT, which had moved to the shorter Van Drenthe circuit in 1955, and the Ulster GP, which had moved from the Clady circuit to Dundrod in 1953. The TT Races were still considered the most prestigious event in the calendar, and despite being run on the demanding and potentially dangerous Isle of Man Mountain circuit, the event was virtually obligatory for any aspiring World Championship contender.

Track safety was fairly basic, and by their very nature, the tracks did not lend themselves to safety modifications. The attitude of some race organisers towards track safety was pretty cynical, too, and safety measures usually consisted of a few strategically placed straw bales. Requests by the riders for additional safety measures were often ignored. At some circuits it was quite common to see spectators standing within a few feet of the track, separated from it by a simple rope barrier. Later in the 1960s, the dreaded metal Armco barriers lining the circuits began to appear, to meet the demands of Formula One car racing. These so-called safety barriers, proved to be lethal to motorcycle riders unfortunate enough to come into contact with them during a crash, and were the cause of many fatalities. Medical facilities, too, varied considerably, and were often relatively rudimentary compared to today. Many injured riders are known to have died trackside due to exposure and lack of medical attention.

Protective equipment for the riders consisted of the classic 'pudding basin' crash helmet, basically a compressed cork shell, often painted with an individual colour or design. Racing leathers were black and close-fitting, sometimes with some additional padding in vital areas. Boots were usually very light, with glove-leather uppers. Body armour had not yet been invented. The days of massive transporters and luxury motorhomes were still a long way off. Even the affluent Honda team used three small Nissan vans in which to transport its machines and technicians during the early 1960s. Race transport and accommodation were quite basic, usually consisting of the ubiquitous Thames van. Some of the more enterprising riders, like Paddy Driver, used cut-down Jaguar saloons with a pick-up body that carried two racing machines.

Tyre technology, too, was still in its infancy. The age of special compounds for different conditions was still a long way off, and everybody raced on the same tyres wet or dry. However, in the early 1960s, Dunlop introduced tyres with a triangular profile with better adhesive qualities. The thinking behind the concept was to provide a larger contact patch when the machine was leaning over in a corner. The tyres were developed by Bob McIntyre, and were thought to have evolved from his particular riding style that involved a sudden change from upright to maximum lean. Following the retirement from racing of the Avon tyre company at the end of 1963, the use of 'triangular' tyres became virtually universal, although some riders disliked them because of their tendency to break away without warning.

Tyres with a triangular profile encouraged greater lean angles, and were partly responsible for a major change in riding styles that developed during the 1960s. The earlier very neat 'at one with the machine, knees and elbows tucked in' style, as epitomised by Geoff Duke in the 1950s, gave way to a much more aggressive style in which riders began to stick out their inside knee and used some degree of inward body lean while cornering. This style was arguably pioneered by John Surtees, when he switched from Nortons to the MV fours in 1956 – he probably used inward body lean to compensate for the MV's lack of ground clearance. Another rider conspicuous in his use of inward body lean in the late 1950s was the well-known short-circuit rider Alan Rutherford, riding the Duke BSAs. During the 1960s, this style evolved further, leading to the 'dangly,' almost off-the-machine style of John Cooper.

A general description of the period would be incomplete without examining the vitally important economic aspects. The arrival of the Japanese factories, with their vast financial resources, inevitably helped in the economic recovery of grand prix racing. They were also willing to invest heavily in riding talent to achieve success. Consequently, riders lucky enough to secure contracts with a Japanese manufacturer found themselves earning previously undreamt-of retaining fees. In the early 1960s a Japanese factory contract was worth on average between £1200 and £1500 – a paltry sum by today's standards, but quite considerable at the time. By the end of the decade, though, figures not far short of £10,000 were fairly common. Of course, fees varied depending on the rider, and World Championship contenders like Mike Hailwood and Jim Redman could command higher than average fees. The major factory teams also had relatively lucrative contracts with the fuel and oil companies. Consequently, the 'trade barons' as they were called had considerable influence with the factory teams to whom they could often recommend talented riders. Accessory manufacturers, such as tyre and sparkplug companies, also played a supporting role, paying out bonuses. Mainly due to the ban on advertising appearing on machines, financial support, such as it was, came mainly from within the motorcycle industry, and big money sponsorship as we know it today was virtually unheard of.

In addition to prize money, all riders received 'appearance money' or 'start money' from the organisers, which again depended on their status. In the case of the factory teams, this was usually negotiated by the team leader, which often led to disagreements among the team riders. Some GP race organisers, however, were quite miserly with start money, relying on the fact that the riders were obliged to race for Championship points, and even major Championship contenders had no choice but to race for ridiculously low sums. Professional 'privateers' competing in the Championships were less fortunate than their factory contracted counterparts. However, many of them also received some assistance, either in cash or in kind from the fuel/oil, tyre and sparkplug companies. They were also able to supplement their incomes by earning 'start money' in the many non-Championship national races that took place, mainly in France, Belgium, Holland and Germany. Known as the 'Continental Circus,' these events supported a small army of nomadic privateers, mostly from Britain, Australia, South Africa and New Zealand, who spent the racing season travelling around Europe, and relied on the start money and prize money from these events to earn a living.

It's interesting to record that the somewhat 'hand-to-mouth' existence of the privateers sometimes led to mild acts of deception. A rider faced with a blown up 350cc machine, for example, would substitute his 500cc machine fitted with 350cc numbers, tank, and exhaust system, etc (a relatively easy task with the 350/500cc AMC and Norton machines), in order to make a token start. It was not unknown for a rider to arrive on the startline with a dead machine, which would be pushed off at the start only to retire almost immediately. These acts, however, were never used to gain an unfair advantage over a fellow rider.

Despite the obvious differences in circumstances between the factory riders and the privateers, the massive financial gulf that would eventually develop much later between them had not yet manifested itself to any great degree, and participation in World Championship grand prix racing during the 1960s was still within the reach of the average private rider. Furthermore, the general nomadic existence created a much friendlier paddock atmosphere, when riders mixed much more freely and were ready to help each other out. The unsung heroes of the GP paddocks were undoubtedly the factory mechanics, who worked long hours under difficult conditions, often pandering to unnecessary demands made by the riders. The privateers, on the other hand, had to rely on their own mechanical skills to keep their machines running throughout the season. Their wives and girlfriends also played an important part, and often looked after the paperwork, race entries and suchlike, helped with keeping the bikes clean, and shared the driving on the long journeys between circuits.

There's no doubt that the arrival of the Japanese factories during the 1960s changed established perceptions of grand prix racing, and Japanese machines and technology successfully challenged the hitherto Western European domination of the sport. By 1967, grand prix participation by the main Japanese manufacturers had reached its peak, and an inevitable downturn began. The final blow was delivered by the FIM, which introduced new rules at the end of 1967, which at a stroke outlawed many of the then current grand prix machines from 1969 onwards. By the end of the decade, further significant changes had already begun to take place that would eventually change the nature of grand prix racing forever; many of them for the better; some arguably not.

# 1960 Recovery

**AT FIRST,** prospects for the 1960s didn't look very promising. Only the MV Agusta factory had decided to continue racing in 1960, and John Surtees duly completed his hat-trick of double World Championships before announcing his retirement from motorcycle racing. An element of unreliability had plagued the Italian machines during the season, and spoiled John's previous unbroken run of grand prix wins. In the Junior TT he was slowed with mechanical problems, and John Hartle, who was having a one-off ride for MV, scored his first TT win.

At the Dutch TT, Surtees' 500 was slowed by carburation problems and, while trying to make up time, he fell off, handing victory to his team-mate Remo Venturi. In the 350 Ulster, Surtees was hounded by Alan Shepherd on a 7R AJS until it expired with a broken timing chain, and in the 500 race he lost time in a lengthy pit stop, allowing John Hartle on a Norton to pull off a well deserved win. History was made in the Senior TT when Derek Minter became the first rider to lap the TT circuit at over 100mph on a single-cylinder machine, with a lap of 101.05mph on his Lancefield-tuned Norton. He was followed a few seconds later by Mike Hailwood who, also on a Norton, lapped at 100.37mph.

During most of the season, and throughout most of the 1960s, in fact, the battles for minor places were fought out by a group of British and Commonwealth riders. The usual suspects were Dickie Dale, Paddy Driver, Alan Shepherd, Jack Ahearn, Jack Findlay, Mike Duff, Frank Perris, John Hartle, and Fred Stevens, to name but a few. Another rider, Australian Bob Brown, finished third in the 500cc World Championship in 1959. In 1960 he put in some fine rides on his Nortons to take a well deserved second in the Dutch TT, splitting the MVs of Remo Venturi and Emilio Mendogni, plus two third places in France and Belgium. Sadly, Bob lost his life during practice for the German GP, but still posthumously took fourth place in the 500cc World Championships.

Bob Brown (Brownie), who came from Sydney, was 30 years old in 1960, and had been racing in Europe since 1955. His reputation for being a quick but safe rider had earned him a place in the Gilera team in 1957, deputizing for the injured Geoff Duke. Bob had justified his selection with third places in the Junior and Senior TTs. In 1959, riding his private Nortons, he was third in both the 350 and 500cc World Championships, beaten only by the works MVs. Because of his experience with the four-cylinder Gileras in 1957, Bob was offered 250cc works Hondas in 1960, on a race-by-race basis. In the TT he rode the highest placed Honda to fourth in the 250 Lightweight TT. On July 23, the German GP had returned to the Solitude circuit after a lapse of three years, and was being run in conjunction with Formula Two car races. It's thought that a combination of tar and grit, dragged onto the road surface by the cars, was the cause of several crashes during motorcycle practice. The most serious of which was that of Bob Brown, who crashed his 250 Honda at the notorious 'sand pit' corner in the twisty Mahdenthal section, and sustained head injuries to which he later succumbed.

The first indication of the extent of future Japanese involvement in grand prix racing took place in the Isle of Man in June. Honda had returned with completely new machines, and a large team consisting of five riders, 15 race machines, and several technicians. On the basis of their performance in 1959, the Hondas were not expected to offer a serious threat to the established European machines. The completely redesigned (46x37.5mm) 125cc RC143 was still a twin-cylinder, with vertical-shaft-driven double overhead camshafts, four valves per cylinder, wet-sump lubrication, and an integral six-speed gearbox, mounted in a spine-type frame. The earlier, clumsy-looking NSU-type leading-link front forks had been replaced by telescopics. Claimed power output was 18ps at 13,500rpm. The original four-cylinder 250cc RC160 of 1959 had also been completely redesigned by Mr Kawashima. Appearing in Europe for the first time, the new (44x41mm) 250cc four-cylinder RC161 now had a central gear train driving the double overhead camshafts and four valves per cylinder, with a power output of 38ps at 13,500rpm. The wet-sump, six-speed gearbox and engine unit was mounted in a spine frame, with telescopic front forks. The RC161 proved to be the first in a long line of gear-driven, double overhead cam, four-cylinder machines, from 125cc to 500cc, used by Honda between 1960 and 1967.

Initially relying on Japanese riders, Honda fielded two separate teams that changed places halfway through the season. The first team of Giichi Suzuki, Naomi Taniguchi, Teisuke Tanaka, Sadao Shimazaki and Gen Kitano were replaced after the Belgian GP by Sadao Fukuda, Kenjiro Tanaka, Yukio Sato and Kunimitsu Takahashi. Realising the need for riders with European GP experience, Honda had also recruited Australians Tom Phillis and Bob Brown. Unfortunately, plans to recruit John Hartle fell through due to conflicting oil contracts. At the Dutch TT, Tom Phillis and Naomi Taniguchi were sidelined due to practice crashes, and Honda suddenly found itself short of riders. Faced with a rush of volunteers all eager for a works ride; Honda team manager Mr Kawashima selected Rhodesian Jim Redman, who'd been recommended to him by Tom Phillis. Later, when Bob Brown was refused permission to take over Phillis' 250, it was offered to Redman. This proved to be the turning point in Jim Redman's career and the start of his long and successful association with Honda.

At first the Hondas seemed unable to match the performance of their Italian rivals, and although three of the new 250s finished fourth, fifth and sixth in the TT, they were withdrawn from the Belgian GP for serious modification. They returned for the German GP at Solitude in much better fettle, where first-timer Kenjiro Tanaka took advantage of a tow from the fast recovering Ubbiali to hoist himself up to third place. From then on the Hondas seemed to improve steadily, and, at the Ulster, Phillis and Redman were second and third behind Ubbiali's MV. It was at the final GP of the season, at Monza, that Honda demonstrated its true potential. In the 125 race Redman and Takahashi were fourth and sixth. In the 250 race the dashing Kunimitsu Takahashi pressed the leading MVs of Ubbiali and Hocking very hard, until Hocking retired. Despite his lack of experience, the young Japanese rider grimly held on to second place ahead of Degner and Hempleman on MZs. On the last lap Redman came storming through after a bad start dragging Degner along in his slipstream, both of them passing the unfortunate Takahashi within inches of the finishing line. The performance of the Hondas had taken many people by surprise, and John Surtees was so impressed that he tipped them, somewhat prophetically, as future World Championship winners.

In retrospect, another significant event was the arrival in the Isle of Man of a new Japanese team from the Suzuki factory making its European debut. The all-Japanese team of Mitsuo Itoh, Michio Ichino and T Matsumoto had 125cc twin-cylinder, air-cooled, piston-ported RT60 two-strokes, which had been mistakenly entered as Colledas. The (44x41mm) machines were producing a very modest 13ps at 11,000rpm, and were very much in the early stage of development. Unfortunately, their principal rider, Mitsuo Itoh, was injured in a practice crash and his machine was eventually ridden by regular TT exponent, Liverpudlian Ray Fay. Although the riders achieved quite low finishing positions, the Suzuki team was obviously very dedicated, and gave every indication that it was committed to a long-term development programme aimed at producing World Championship-winning machines.

MV regained its supremacy in the 125 and 250cc classes with its double overhead cam 125cc (53x56mm) single-cylinder, and 250cc (53x56.2mm) twin-cylinder machines. The seven-speed 250 weighed only 109kg (238lb), and was reputed to be producing 36bhp at 12,000rpm, which made it nearly as fast as the 350-four. While winning back-to-back double world titles, Carlo Ubbiali was seriously challenged by his new team-mate, Rhodesian Gary Hocking. Riding the East German MZs in 1959, Hocking had posed a serious threat to MV, who subsequently lured him away from the MZ team in 1960. This led to some serious rivalry, and produced some memorable battles between the success-hungry Hocking and his new team-mate Ubbiali. The reigning double World Champion, however, rose to the challenge, displaying his mastery of the lightweight classes with some superb riding. A typical example was in the 250cc German GP at Solitude. Ubbiali crashed at the Glemseck corner soon after the start, and was passed by the entire field. Picking up his damaged machine he proceeded to fight his way back through the field to finish a close second behind Hocking.

Other Continental involvement came mainly from the East German MZ team, which was unable to match its 1959 performance, and so it was left to Ernst Degner, supported by New Zealander John Hempleman, to uphold the honours. The two of them trounced the MV team on the fast Spa Francorchamps circuit to take first and second place in the 125cc race, with Degner eventually finishing third in the 125cc World Championship. Czech stalwart Frantisek (Frankie) Stastny did his best with the twin-cylinder 350 Jawa, scoring a couple of second places in the French and Italian GPs. With Ducati having withdrawn from racing, another Italian marque, Aermacchi, made its GP debut with a roadster-based, 250cc, single-cylinder machine on which Alberto Pagani finished fifth in the Belgian GP. This was a prelude to the introduction of the proper racing versions that became available later.

BMW's domination of the sidecar class, which had begun in 1955, was set to continue. The almost universal adoption of the RS54 Rennsport engine, which lent itself admirably to sidecar use, led to a remarkable 19 year domination of the World Championships by BMW. The horizontally-opposed, twin-cylinder, double overhead camshaft production engines were originally 66x72mm long-stroke units, although some special works 70x64mm short-stroke engines were made available to select drivers. The 1960 Championship was won by the gifted German engineer Helmut Fath, partnered by Alfred Wohlgemuth, using a modified Rennsport unit, with his own fuel-injection system. Runner-up in the Championship was the Swiss pairing of Fritz Scheidegger and passenger Horst Burkhardt. In third place were Britons Pip Harris and Ray Campbell, with their BMW outfit. Harris and Campbell had a superb win in the Dutch TT with the same BMW outfit, trouncing their Continental rivals Fath and Scheidegger.

# 1961
# Honda domination

**IN A** determined bid for World Championship honours in 1961, Honda deployed the full extent of its vast financial and technological resources in a campaign of unprecedented proportions. Such was the scale and intensity of the Honda attack, that the focus of interest inevitably centred on the 125 and 250cc classes. Faced with the prospect of boring run-away wins in the 350 and 500cc classes by MV, spectator numbers had previously fallen. Now, however, race goers found themselves lured back to the circuits, stirred by the sight and sound of dozens of high-revving Hondas being ridden by some of the best riders of the day, all scrapping furiously for the win. The crowds came flocking back, and the revival of grand prix racing was well under way.

The 1961 Hondas had undergone further improvements. The new 250cc RC162 that appeared for the first time at the West German GP, was producing 45ps at 14,000rpm, and now had dry-sump lubrication. Initially, this did cause some problems with over-heating at some circuits, particularly Spa Francorchamps, where some of the works bikes ran without front mudguards, while some had the belly pan removed. The earlier spine frame had been replaced by a new semi-duplex cradle frame, with the usual Honda practice of suspending the engine from the front, to act as a stressed frame member. New Ceriani-type front forks replaced the old exposed spring type, together with a new larger double front brake with large twin air scoops. The 250s also had a new three-piece fairing, incorporating a belly pan that enclosed the underside of the engine. The new 125cc 2RC143 introduced at the TT had a revised bore and stroke (of 44x41mm), but still had vertical-shaft and bevel gear-driven camshafts, and was producing 23ps at 14,000rpm. It also had the new semi-duplex cradle frame, new front forks, and the new three-piece fairing with belly pan.

Honda was able to field an exceptionally strong mixed team of Japanese and European riders. Foremost amongst the Japanese was the dashing and somewhat fiery Kunimitsu Takahashi, who was certainly the most promising of this first generation of Japanese riders. The other Japanese riders were Sadao Shimazaki, Naomi Taniguchi, and Moto Kitano who was replaced at the TT by Teisuke Tanaka. Diminutive Swiss ace Luigi Taveri was also recruited because of his undisputed talents as a lightweight jockey. In 1960, Tom Phillis and Jim Redman were rewarded with full-time works contracts for their efforts. In addition to this, Honda also loaned a 'works' 250 to Irish importer Reg Armstrong (to be ridden by Bob McIntyre) and another to British dealer Bill Smith, whose machine was intended for John Hartle. Stan Hailwood was also able to use the bargaining power of his Kings of Oxford chain of dealerships to secure machines for his son Mike. The policy of loaning machines to non-factory riders was understandably not popular with some of the works riders, particularly Jim Redman, who was openly critical of this situation.

Honda's racing policy could, therefore, be described as 'saturation'. In addition to its five Japanese riders, Honda could also rely on the services of at least 6 top class European riders at any given time. This was clearly demonstrated at the Belgian GP, when the entire front row of the 250cc grid was made up of the Hondas of Hailwood, McIntyre, Redman, Phillis, Hartle and Shimazaki. Back then, Honda seemed quite unconcerned about the inherent dangers of such a free-for-all, and consequently, during the season, the World Championship leader often found himself under attack from his own team-mates. Apparently, it did not seem to matter to Honda who won as long as it was on a Honda (a situation all too familiar to followers of Moto GP today). Despite the possibility that rivalry within the team could have led to self-destruction, Honda consistently achieved a high percentage of finishers amongst the first six, particularly in the 250cc class, when it frequently filled the first four places.

In winning his and Honda's first World Championship, Mike Hailwood's 250cc title was achieved with a total of four wins against opposition only from his fellow Honda riders. The rest of the wins being shared out between McIntyre, Redman, Phillis and Takahashi. Although Gary Hocking won the season opener in Spain against Phillis and Redman on 1960 models, MV realised it was out-classed, and wisely withdrew from the 250cc class. During the rest of the year the Continental opposition was simply overwhelmed by the sheer number of Hondas. At the early-season German GP on the very fast Hockenheim circuit, Jim Redman and Kunimitsu Takahashi on two of the new RC162s had a race-long scrap for the lead, in which Takahashi just beat Redman to the line to record the first grand prix win by a Japanese rider.

Bob McIntyre was particularly unlucky in the TT. He led the race from the start and, on the second lap, had set a new lap record of 99.58mph, which exceeded John Surtees' lap record on the 350 MV. However, Bob's Honda developed an oil leak that spread to the rear tyre, causing him to ease the pace, which gradually whittled away his 30-odd second lead over Mike Hailwood, who, at this stage, was riding one of the borrowed 1960 Hondas. Inevitably, on the last lap, Bob's Honda ran out of oil and seized up near Quarry Bends. It was not Bob Mac's year; he suffered several DNFs, and crashed in the Italian GP breaking his collarbone, but had the consolation of winning the Ulster GP, setting new race and lap records. At the final round in Sweden, that was attended by Mr Honda himself, Mike Hailwood led the 250cc Championship by just six points from Jim Redman. Hailwood led from the start, but Redman was in determined mood, and fought his way past into the lead – but tried a bit too hard and slid off an a corner. Although he re-mounted to finish fourth, Hailwood went on to win and take the Championship.

The situation in the 125cc class was not so clear cut. Honda faced fierce opposition from the single-cylinder (54x54mm), disc-valve MZ. Despite being seriously disadvantaged by a lack of resources, Dr Walter Kaaden had painstakingly developed his machine until it was producing 25hp at 10,800rpm and had achieved the remarkable figure of 200bhp per litre. The performance of the MZs was clearly demonstrated on the fast Hockenheim circuit, when they out-ran the entire Honda team to take the first four places. In the Isle of Man, Mike Hailwood won his and Honda's first TT, riding what was allegedly Luigi Taveri's practice machine, on which, ironically, he was involved in a last lap scrap on the roads with Taveri himself.

During most of the season, Degner and Phillis were involved in some fierce battles for the title, a typical example being the French GP. On the twisty Clermont Ferrand circuit, with its ascending and descending succession of sharp curves and banked corners, Phillis and Degner engaged in a race-long, fairing-bashing encounter, during which the lead changed several times and was only resolved in an out-braking contest at the final hairpin. With Phillis in the lead, Degner dived up the inside, but Phillis grimly stuck to his line; Degner was forced to back off or hit the Honda's rear wheel, and so Phillis won the sprint to the line by less than a wheel's length.

Both riders had suffered their share of minor injuries. Degner crashed in the 250cc Belgian GP, injuring an elbow, and missed the crucial 125cc race, while Tom Phillis suffered severe cuts and abrasions when his 500 Norton Domiracer tangled with Roy Ingram's Norton in the Ulster.

In 1961, the East German GP had been granted World Championship status for the first time, being run on the prewar 5.3-mile (8.6km) Sachsenring circuit – in wooded undulating terrain, and passing through the small town of Hohenstein Ernstthal. It featured a variety of corners and a very fast twisty downhill section, which passed the memorial to Jimmy Guthrie, at the spot where he was killed in 1937. The MZ team from nearby Zschopau was anxious to do well, and Walter Kaaden provided a new 125 for Degner with rearward facing exhaust ports and a high level exhaust system. The new machine was a flier on which Degner had a convincing win over Tom Phillis, reducing the Honda rider's lead in the Championship to nine points. In the same race, Luigi Taveri had an anxious moment when the right hand clip-on on his Honda gave way while braking for the final Queckenberg corner on the last lap, forcing him to take the slip road. Being unable to turn round, he carried on through a tunnel under the grandstand and back onto the circuit, crossing the line ahead of his nearest rival, Takahashi, but was later disqualified.

After nine rounds Phillis and Degner had three wins each and Degner led the Championship by two points going into the penultimate round in Sweden. Then the unthinkable happened. Degner and MZ virtually had the 125cc title in their pockets. His machine was really flying and he led the race comfortably for a couple of laps but then suddenly disappeared. Having abandoned his machine somewhere out on the circuit, and with the alleged assistance of the Suzuki team, he defected to the West to join his wife and family who had already been smuggled out of East Germany. A last ditch attempt by Degner to ride Joe Ehrlich's EMC at the final round in Argentina failed to materialise. Tom Phillis duly won unchallenged in Buenos Aires to take the title. It was a tragedy for MZ, losing its one and only chance of winning a World Championship. To add to its misery, Degner eventually joined Suzuki, and used his knowledge gained at MZ to help it develop World Championship-winning machines. This was clearly a case of industrial espionage, and the full extent of Degner's betrayal and the entire conspiracy surrounding his defection were only revealed many years later.

### WALTER KAADEN

It's now universally acknowledged that Dr Walter Kaaden is the father of the modern racing two-stroke, a fact for which he never received his just rewards. The young Walter Kaaden grew up in Zschopau, home of the DKW motorcycle factory, and later studied at the Technical Academy in nearby Chemnitz. During the war he worked at the rocket research establishment in Peenemunde. After the war he returned to Zschopau and, during the late 1940s, raced his own two-stroke machines. In the early 1950s he went to work for the new IFA concern, later to become MZ, which was located on the site of the prewar DKW factory. He then took charge of the racing department and began developing the 125cc disc-valve engine. It was Kaaden's pioneering work on pressure waves in two-stroke exhaust systems – leading to the use of expansion chambers – that revolutionised racing two-stroke technology. He also reintroduced the use of additional transfer ports, with significant increases in power output, and was responsible for such innovations as rearward facing exhaust ports and the now universal spring retaining system for securing exhaust pipes to exhaust stubs. It was, therefore, a tragedy and a travesty of justice that when poised to see his work rewarded with a World Championship win, this achievement was cruelly denied him at the eleventh hour. To add to this, he could only watch helplessly while the results of all his work later flourished in Japan with the benefit of resources he could only have dreamed of. The rapid development in two-stroke technology that subsequently took place in Japan, and which led to the two-stroke domination of grand prix racing, clearly owes its origins to Dr Walter Kaaden.

The Japanese invasion had gathered momentum. Suzuki returned with a new twin-cylinder, disc-valve 125cc RT61, and a similar 250cc called the RV61. In addition to its Japanese riders (Itoh, Ichino, Matsumoto and newcomer Masuda), it had engaged Paddy Driver as a development rider, and spare machines were also provided for Hugh Anderson and Alastair King in the Isle of Man. According to Paddy Driver, the Suzukis suffered from plug failures and engine seizures, as well as a lack of spares back-up. Many of the machines had to be withdrawn during TT practice, and the team was eventually forced to return to Japan early in the season.

A new Japanese team, from the Yamaha factory, made its European debut at the French GP. Its bikes were the disc-valve two-stroke (56x50mm) 125cc single-cylinder RA41, turning out 20ps at 10,000rpm, and a doubled-up 250cc twin-cylinder RD48 producing 35ps at 10,000rpm. The Yamahas were ridden by Fumio Ito, who had gained some notoriety in 1960 riding a Rennsport BMW in some of the GPs, and T Noguchi. Machines were also loaned out to Tony Godfrey and New Zealander Peter Pawson to try out during TT practice. The RD48, in particular, showed some promise, with Fumio Ito finishing sixth in the Isle of Man and the Dutch TT, and fifth in the Belgian GP, after which the team returned to Japan.

Although MV had officially retired from racing, it entered Gary Hocking in the 350 and 500cc classes on the thinly disguised 'Privat' machines; Gary duly winning both Championships. The MV fours were beginning to show their age, though, and Hocking was beset with mechanical problems on several occasions. Once again, the British single-cylinder machines fulfilled their supporting role admirably, providing a race within a race. Mike Hailwood won the Senior TT on his special Bill Lacey-prepared Norton, becoming the first rider of a single-cylinder machine to average over 100mph for the race. Gary Hocking had led initially, with Mike pushing him hard, but in his efforts to stay in front, Gary over-stressed the MV, which then went off-song and eventually stopped. Mike followed up his TT win with a string of runner-up places to Hocking, before joining MV at the end of the season with a win at Monza, to finish second in the World Championships. Norton, in fact, enjoyed something of a renaissance in the Isle of Man when Phil Read took advantage of Hocking's ailing MV to win the Junior TT. Mike Hailwood had been leading the race until the last lap when his 7R AJS expired, spoiling his chance of winning four TTs in one week. One other remarkable performance was put up by Tom Phillis, who finished third in the Senior TT, with a lap at over 100mph – on a works Norton with a much-modified Dominator 88 engine, prepared by Doug Hele. During the race Tom had been involved in a battle on the road with the very able Liverpool rider Ralph Rensen, which unfortunately had tragic consequences when Ralph crashed just beyond the 11th milestone and was killed instantly.

Surprise runner-up in the 350cc Championship was the ever-popular Czech veteran Frankie Stastny, on the twin-cylinder Jawa. Two wins in West Germany and Sweden were backed up by some solid podium finishes in the Dutch TT, East German GP, and Ulster GP. Stastny's team-mate Gustav Havel took second in West Germany and Sweden, and thus earned third place in the Championship. An expected challenge from Bob McIntyre on a (65x52.5mm) 350cc twin-cylinder Bianchi failed to materialise due to persistent mechanical unreliability. Producing 48bhp at 10,600rpm, the machine, designed by Lino Tonti, had started life as a 250cc and was considered to be slightly over-engineered, with its gear drive to the double overhead cams and a multiplicity of ball and needle roller bearings. However, at the Dutch TT, McIntyre demonstrated the machine's true potential in a race-long battle with Hocking's MV, in which he was beaten into second place by only a matter of yards. Other Bianchi riders were Alastair King, second in the Ulster, and Alan Shepherd in a one-off ride who was fourth in the Italian GP at Monza.

### FRANTISEK STASTNY

Frantisek Stastny, or Frankie as he was affectionately known, came from Kochanek, Prague. He started racing in 1949 on Velocette and Norton machines before joining the Jawa factory as a test rider in 1953. He spent his early career riding the early Jawa racing machines in eastern Europe before making his TT debut in the 1957 250 Lightweight race. He started riding regularly in the World Championships in 1961, backed by team-mate Gustav Havel, and for several years they were usually the best of the rest behind the works MVs and Hondas. He was third in the Junior TT in 1962 and 1963. His career was interrupted by crash injuries in 1963 and 1964, but he won the 350 Ulster in 1965, albeit from a somewhat decimated field. He recorded his fourth GP win in the 500cc East German in 1966 on the 440cc Jawa. During 1967 and 1968 he was involved in the development of the new 350cc V4 two-stroke Jawa, and despite several crashes caused by that machine's temperamental nature, he rode it to third place in the 1968 Czech GP, and fourth in the Ulster. His racing career virtually came to an end after being involved in a multiple pile-up at a Czech national meeting in 1970. Always cheerful and jovial, Frankie was popular at post-race celebrations. Before he started racing he had been a racing cyclist, an ice hockey player, and speed skater, and was married to an Olympic speed skater. Following his retirement he made occasional appearances with his 350 Jawa at Historic revival meetings in England and Europe. He died in April 2000 following a heart attack.

In the usual BMW-dominated sidecar class, Max Deubel, partnered by Emil Horner, proceeded to established a new generation of successful German drivers. Using what was reputed to be an ex-works Walter Schneider outfit, Max won the first of his many World Championship titles. He faced fierce opposition throughout the season from the Swiss pairing of Fritz Scheidegger and Horst Burkhardt, but claimed the title with three wins against two by the Swiss. Upholding British prestige, Pip Harris and Ray Campbell scored two third places in the TT and the Belgian GP on their BMW, and veteran Jackie Beeton and Eddy Bulgin were third in the Dutch TT, also with a BMW.

After winning the first round in Spain, the reigning World Champion Helmut Fath was involved in a serious accident at a national meeting on the notorious Nürburgring south loop circuit; in which he received serious injuries, and his passenger Alfred Wohlgemuth was killed. At the same meeting, former Norton and Moto Guzzi works rider Dickie Dale, who had just won the 350cc race, crashed his 500 Norton near Mullenbach, and, though not seriously injured, he suffered a fatal heart attack while being transported to hospital by helicopter. Florian Camathias, too, was involved in another tragic crash at Modena in April, putting him out of action for a while, and claiming the life of his passenger Hilmar Cecco.

*John Surtees – who dominated the 350 and 500cc World Championships in 1960 – seen here leaping Ballaugh Bridge on his MV, in the 1959 Senior TT.*

*Below: Popular Australian Bob Brown, who rode works Hondas in 1960, and posthumously finished fourth in the 500cc World Championships on his Norton. (Courtesy Malcolm Carling)*

*Double World Champion in the 125 and 250cc classes in 1960: Carlo Ubbiali on his 125 MV.*

*Team-mate to John Surtees and runner-up in the 500cc World Championship, Remo Venturi (MV) in the 1960 Belgian GP. (Courtesy Karl-Gunter Peters)*

*New Zealander John Hempleman on a 250 MZ at the Sachsenring in 1960. (Elwyn Roberts Collection)*

*Naomi Taniguchi on his works 125cc Honda at Ramsey Hairpin in the 1960 TT. (Elwyn Roberts Collection)*

*Giichi Suzuki on his 250cc works Honda in the 1960 Lightweight TT. (Elwyn Roberts Collection)*

*Double World Champion in 1961, Gary Hocking on the 350 MV at the Sachsenring. (Elwyn Roberts Collection)*

*1961 125cc World Champion Tom Phillis on the 125 Honda in the Ulster Grand Prix. (Courtesy Malcolm Carling)*

*Tom Phillis on a 250 Honda in the 1961 Lightweight TT. (Elwyn Roberts Collection)*

*Bob McIntyre on the 350 Bianchi in the 1961 Ulster Grand Prix. (Courtesy Karl-Heinz Reiger)*

*Sadao Shimazaki working on his 125cc Works Honda in the Isle of Man, 1961.*

*Japanese riders.*

*Left to right, top row: Giichi Suzuki, Isao Morishita, Michio Ichino.*

*Second row: Mitsuo Ito, Moto Kitano, Naomi Taniguchi.*

*Third row: Sadao Shimazaki, Teisuki Tanaka, Yukio Sato.*

*Bob McIntyre (Honda) at White Gates in the 1961 250cc TT, where he set a new lap record at 99.58mph before retiring with mechanical problems.*

# 1962
# Triumph & tragedy

**MIKE HAILWOOD,** who had joined MV at the end of 1961, won his first 500cc World Championship in 1962 virtually unchallenged, but still managed to set new race and lap records in the process. His team-mate Gary Hocking won the Senior TT, and then announced his retirement, following the death of his friend Tom Phillis in the Junior TT. Once again, it was mainly the British single-cylinder Nortons and Matchless machines that filled the top six places behind Hailwood's MV. Runner-up in the Championship was privateer Alan Shepherd on a Tom Kirby G50 Matchless, with a win in the Finnish GP and three second places in Belgium, Ulster and East Germany. Phil Read was third by virtue of two third places in the Dutch TT and the Ulster on his Norton. Austrian Bert Schneider, also on a Norton, was fourth.

For the first time since 1957 there was some fresh interest in the premier classes, when Honda decided to extend its GP involvement into the 350cc class. Honda's entry was at first rather tentative, with a four-cylinder 250 bored out from 44 to 47mm (285cc) called the RC170. Bob McIntyre rode one of these machines at a couple of minor British meetings early in the year, and a second machine was provided for Jim Redman. However, at the TT, Tom Phillis, who was always ready to accept a challenge, persuaded Redman, who really did not need much persuading, to stand down and let him ride the new machine; with tragic consequences as it turned out.

Tom Phillis, from Sydney, Australia, was 28 years old. He'd been racing Nortons as a 'privateer' in Europe since 1958, and had earned a reputation as a talented and much respected rider. Selected by Honda in 1960, he became the first non-Japanese rider to race one of the four-cylinder machines, and gave Honda its first grand prix win in Spain in 1961. Tom was eager to do battle with the MVs in the Junior TT, and took part in 1962. Starting at number one, he was passed on the first lap by Hailwood, number three, and Hocking, number six. The two MVs flashed past together to start their second lap, followed a couple of seconds later by Phillis, chasing after them and obviously trying hard to stay in contention. On the right/left approach to Laurel Bank, through the leafy tunnel with a forbidding rock face on the left and a stone wall on the right, he crashed and received fatal injuries. Tom was likeable and popular, and his loss was felt deeply by the whole Honda team, not least of all by his good friends Jim Redman and Gary Hocking, both of whom contemplated retiring from racing. In fact, Hocking felt he was in some way responsible for having put Tom under too much pressure in the Junior TT. Consequently, after winning the Senior TT, Gary announced his retirement from motorcycle racing and returned to Rhodesia (Zimbabwe). Later that year, he himself lost his life when his Lotus Climax car mysteriously went off the road during practice for the Natal GP near Durban. It was a sad end at the age of only 25, for a brilliant but rather enigmatic rider, whose short career yielded just a fraction of his great potential.

Jim Redman gave the ill-fated RC170 Honda its first win, at the Dutch TT, where he convincingly beat Hailwood on the rather fragile and outdated MV. At the Ulster GP, due to the untimely deaths of Phillis and McIntyre, Honda found itself seriously short of riders. A plan to recruit Alan Shepherd fell through, and Tommy Robb joined Jim Redman on the 350cc machines. Honda had obviously decided to get more serious, and brought out a new (49x45mm) 340cc RC171, turning out 50ps at 12,500rpm, that Redman took to a debut win in the Ulster. As anticipated on a circuit like Dundrod, Mike Hailwood kept his MV glued to Redman's rear wheel for five laps, until the fragile valvegear on the MV failed and dropped a valve. Tommy Robb on the second Honda had problems with a serious oil leak and lost his second place to Frankie Stastny's Jawa. With two more convincing wins in East Germany and the Italian GP, Redman finally wrapped up the 350cc Championship.

At the final round of the 350cc Championship at Tampere in Finland, Tommy Robb needed a win to take second place in the Championship. With second place within his grasp, Tommy approached team leader Jim Redman requesting the use of one of the earlier 285cc machines, which would be more suitable in the prevailing wet conditions, giving Tommy a better chance of winning the race. Jim was a hardened professional who had come up the hard way to become Honda team leader, a position he, quite naturally, guarded jealously. Consequently, he was not always sympathetic towards his team-mates, a situation that allegedly led to a certain amount of conflict and clash of personalities. His reply to Tommy Robb's request was typically non-committal, and when the flag dropped Jim made his intentions clear by streaking off into the lead. Despite his small stature, the normally affable Tommy could be a tough customer when riled, and, with his Irish dander well and truly aroused, he set off in pursuit of Redman. Riding like a demon in the slippery conditions, slipping and sliding, and using all his early moto-cross skills, he caught and passed Redman and pulled away to take the win and secure his second place in the Championship.

---

### TOMMY ROBB

Belfast-born Tommy Robb had started racing in 1954, and cut his teeth on the Irish road circuits before moving on to the British short-circuit scene where he soon established himself as one of the elite class. In 1961, he was engaged by the Bultaco factory to help promote its new 125cc racers, and was also riding 250, 350 and 500cc machines for Geoff Monty. It was early in 1962 when he received a call from Irish Honda importer Reg Armstrong that was to change his life. He was offered a place in the Honda team to ride the 125cc machines and also spearhead the company's entry into the new 50cc class. Later, when the Honda team found itself short of riders due to the deaths of Tom Phillis and Bob McIntyre, Tommy found himself promoted into the 250cc class, when he achieved one of his greatest ambitions by winning his first grand prix on his home circuit in Ulster. One of the nice guys in racing, Tommy was very popular with his fellow riders as well as with the spectators; a popularity that extended long after his retirement from racing and well into the 21st century. He rode in Historic events quite recently, until health problems forced him to stop.

---

To add to the international flavour, Russian machines appeared for the first time in a World Championship grand prix. One of these had, in fact, appeared briefly at the Sachsenring the previous year. The SKEB S-259 (55x52mm) 248cc and S-360 (62x57.6mm) 349cc, twin-cylinder, double overhead cam machines were designed by Evgeni Mathiushin and produced by the Serpuchov Central Construction & Experimental Bureau. Claimed power outputs were 38hp at 11,500rpm for the 250, and a rather optimistic 50bhp at 10,100rpm for the 350 version. For 1962 the S-360 had been built-in collaboration with the Jawa factory, which resulted in machines that bore a strong resemblance to the current Jawa racers. The leading Soviet rider was Nikolai Sevostianov from Moscow, a 33-year-old officer in the Red Army. Originally a motocross rider, he rode in the ISDT and started road racing in 1952. He scored Russia's first World Championship points at the East German GP, with fifth place in the 250 race and sixth in the 350 race.

As a result of some additional Continental involvement, the classic British singles were now finding themselves pushed out of the top six in the 350cc class by the Jawas of Stastny and Havel, the Bianchi of Silvio Grassetti, and a bored-out 250cc MZ ridden by Alan Shepherd. The twin-cylinder double overhead camshaft Jawas had a bore and stroke of 59x63.6mm, respectively, and produced 49bhp at 10,600rpm, giving the Czech riders some fairly consistent top six places, with Stastny finishing fifth in the 350cc Championship.

Yamaha who'd shown some promise with its 250cc RD48 the previous year, was absent in 1962, having decided to spend the year developing new machines. Suzuki was having problems with its twin-cylinder RV62s, and these were withdrawn from the first two rounds.

The 250cc class was, therefore, more-or-less dominated by Honda. The 1962 RC163 Hondas were only slightly improved versions of the previous year's models, with minor modifications that included a new 210mm double-sided, two leading-shoe front brake. Redman, McIntyre and Phillis took the first three places in the Spanish and French GPs. Bob McIntyre's TT jinx struck again, and, after setting a new lap record of 99.06mph from a standing start, he was forced to retire with engine failure on the second lap.

Derek Minter temporarily stole factory rider Jim Redman's thunder by winning the 250cc Lightweight TT on a 1961 ex-works machine, supplied to and entered by British concessionaire Hondis Ltd. According to Minter, he was approached on the start line by Honda team manager Reg Armstrong; a former TT winner and Norton and Gilera works rider, who reminded Derek that Redman was leading the Championship. Derek, however, choose to ignore the implication and raced to win. The incident did not go down too well with the Honda hierarchy, and undoubtedly affected Minter's future chances of a factory contract.

Following McIntyre's retirement, Redman and Minter took it in turn to lead, and, at one stage were on the road together, when Minter passed Redman on the tricky Ginger Hall to Ramsey section to lead up the mountain. Redman was a canny rider, who never stuck his neck out unnecessarily, particular in the TT, but he was also having problems with a loose filler cap and was losing precious fuel. After Jim's second fuel stop, Minter regained the lead and went on to win, although he was lucky to do so, because his Honda started vibrating badly on the last lap and finished with a broken crankshaft.

At the Dutch TT, the ever popular Tommy Robb, who had been recruited by Honda mainly as a 50cc and 125cc rider, made his debut on one of the 250cc, four-cylinder machines, taking the place of Tom Phillis. Unfortunately, due to his unfamiliarity with the machine, Tommy missed a gear going into a corner and fell off, causing an irate Tarquinio Provini on a Morini to fall off as well. Redman eventually won, with McIntyre second, and the places were reversed in Belgium where McIntyre took the win. Redman won again in the West German at Solitude, backed up by Bob McIntyre who had agreed to help him win the Championship. At the Ulster, Tommy Robb was back in action, and he and Redman kept swapping places at the front, until the penultimate lap when Redman's Honda went onto two cylinders and Tommy achieved a life-long ambition to win his home Grand Prix.

Between the West German and the Ulster, the Honda team, and indeed the world of motorcycle racing, suffered yet another tragedy, when on the sixth of August, the popular 33-year-old Scot Bob McIntyre crashed at Oulton Park and suffered injuries to which he succumbed a few days later in hospital. Bob was leading the very wet 500cc British Championship race on his Potts Norton when he went off the road at the fast left kink at the top of Clay Hill. It's thought that in lapping a slower rider he was on a slightly wider line and hit a patch of standing water that caused him to lose control. Although best known for setting the first 100mph laps on a Gilera in the 1957 Senior TT, as a courageous and determined rider, Bob's career was marked by several outstanding performances on his private machines against superior opposition. He is remembered today with the running of the annual 'Bob McIntyre Memorial' classic race meeting at the Knockhill circuit in Scotland.

The 250cc race at the East German GP on the Sachsenring road circuit was the scene of one of the most memorable races of the 1960s. The MZ team, now under severe travel restrictions since Degner's defection, was having to rely on Alan Shepherd to keep the flag flying. For its home GP, however, Walter Kaaden offered one of his new, specially-prepared twin-cylinder 250s to Mike Hailwood. Mike, no doubt somewhat bored by his relatively easy rides on the 500 MV, readily accepted the opportunity for a good scrap. Alan Shepherd's MZ was really flying, and he held the lead until his engine just stopped. This left Hailwood and Jim Redman locked in a wheel-to-wheel battle for the lead that lasted the whole race, during the course of which Hailwood set the first 100mph lap for the circuit. At the final Queckenberg corner on the last lap, while trying to get past a lapped rider, the Honda and the MZ touched fairings momentarily, Redman recovered fractionally quicker and beat Hailwood to the line by less than a wheel. With six wins to his credit Redman eventually wrapped up the 250cc Championship and his first 250/350 double world title.

A very worthy third place in the 250cc Championship went to that grand old man of racing, and, for many years, a well-known Epsom motorcycle dealer, Arthur Wheeler, in his final year of grand prix racing. Arthur's racing career spanned over seven decades, during which he competed regularly on short-circuits, the TT, and the World Championships. He is mostly associated with Moto Guzzis, on which he recorded several fourth places in the 250 Lightweight TT, and won the 250cc Italian GP at Monza in

1954. After finishing fourth in the Lightweight TT in 1962, he went on to record consistent top six places in the Dutch, Belgian, West German, and Ulster GPs on his private Guzzi, and then travelled all the way to the final round in Argentina, where he duly won the 250 race to clinch third place in the Championship. After a period of retirement, and never one to let age stand in his way, the evergreen Arthur returned to racing in classic events during the 1980s, and renewed his acquaintance with his favourite TT course by riding in the Classic Manx GP. He was still racing in 2000 at the age of 84, until he tragically succumbed to septicaemia in 2001, caused by a minor, non-racing injury.

After its narrow win over MZ in 1961, Honda brought out an entirely new 125cc in 1962. The new RC145 produced 24ps at 14,000rpm, had the same bore and stroke as the earlier model, but now had the camshafts driven by a central gear train, as on the four-cylinder models. The crank throws were set at 180 degrees, and magnesium was used for the engine castings to reduce weight. With this machine the popular Swiss rider Luigi Taveri took his first World Championship title with six straight wins, also winning his first TT and setting the first 90mph lap by a 125cc machine. Initially, however, it was the fiery Japanese rider Kunimitsu Takahashi who led the race for the title, with wins in the first two rounds in Spain and France. His win at Clermont Ferrand was particularly commendable, when he rode with considerable verve on the wet and twisty circuit to beat his much more experienced European team-mates.

Twenty-year-old Takahashi was being groomed by Honda to become Japan's first World Champion, and his forceful riding certainly made him a suitable candidate. He was, however, inclined to be a bit hot-headed. A typical example of this was in the 125 Ulster in 1961, when, during the course of his battle for the lead with Degner's MZ and his team-mate Tom Phillis, displaying all the tenacity of a Samurai warrior, he appeared quite undeterred by an excursion up the bank at Leathamstown corner in his efforts to stay ahead of his rivals. Then, on the final lap at the hairpin, with Degner now in the lead; in a last ditch attempt, Takahashi literally barged his way past a startled Degner and beat him to the line to win his second grand prix. Unfortunately, it may have been his impetuosity that led to the first lap crash at Union Mills in the 125 TT, in which he sustained a fractured pelvis and head injuries, putting him out of action for the rest of 1962. Although he returned to GP racing in 1963, he never seemed to regain his previous form.

In addition to the RC145, Honda also fielded several pre-production versions of the CR93 that were ridden by various members of the team during 1962. Although similar to the RC145 version, with four valves per cylinder and a 180-degree crankshaft, the CR had a square bore and stroke of 43x43mm, its gear drive to the camshafts was taken up the left-hand side of the engine, and it featured wet-sump lubrication and a six-speed gearbox. A spine-type frame was used, with the engine gearbox unit forming a part of the frame as on the road-going models. Power output was quoted as 16.5ps at 11,500rpm. Production versions of the Honda CR93 began to appear at British circuits in 1963 and dominated the national 125cc class until the late 1960s. These superb little machines helped to launch the careers of World Championship riders such as Bill Ivy, Ralph Bryans and Kel Carruthers, as well as forging the careers of well-known riders such as Jim Curry, Rod Scivyer, Chris Vincent, Terry Grotefeld and Derek Chatterton, to name a few.

The expected challenge from the Suzuki team, which now included Ernst Degner, New Zealander Hugh Anderson, and Frank Perris, failed to materialize. Its single-cylinder, disc-valve, air-cooled (54x54mm) 123.67cc RT62 was producing 24ps at 11,000rpm, but had not yet reaped the benefit of Degner's 'expertise,' although Suzuki had already begun to experiment with MZ-style rearward-facing exhaust ports. With MZ able to contest only two GPs, it was, ironically, Dr Joe Ehrlich's British-built EMC/MZ clone that provided any sort of opposition. This was mainly due to the efforts of Mike Hailwood, who was lying second in the TT ahead of all the Japanese machines, until the last lap when the EMC ran a main bearing. Mike also finished third in the West German GP at Solitude, splitting the Honda team, while Mike's EMC team-mate Paddy Driver pipped him for third place in the Belgian GP, with EMC development rider Rex Avery in fifth. Built at the De Havilland aircraft factory, the EMC had been developed from a slave MZ engine that Dr Ehrlich had allegedly obtained from Walter Kaaden in exchange for a set of Norton 'roadholder' front forks.

The new 50cc class was also introduced in 1962, and attracted support from Honda, Suzuki, Kreidler from Germany, and Derbi from Spain, all of which were involved in the small capacity commuter machine market. It was Suzuki that established its superiority in this class with its single-cylinder disc-valve, air-cooled, eight-speed (40x39.5mm) 49.64cc RM62. Weighing only 59.8kg, and producing 10ps at 11,000rpm, it was on this machine that Ernst Degner won his first and only TT and World Championship. Against all expectations, it was Kreidler and not Honda who provided the strongest challenge to Suzuki. Kreidler employee Hans-Georg Anscheidt had two wins in Spain and Italy, while his team-mate, Dutchman Jan Huberts, won in France and East Germany. The Spanish Derbi factory showed great promise, when local ace Jose Busquets had a neck-and-neck race-long battle with Anscheidt's Kreidler in the Spanish GP, and was only just beaten to the flag. Despite a crash in 125cc race at the Ulster that made him miss two rounds, Degner's four wins out-scored points leader Anscheidt when the best six results were counted, to give Degner the title.

The Kreidler racer was based on the humble sports (40x39.7mm) 49.9cc Florette model, with twin disc-valves fed by two crankcase-mounted carburettors that resulted in a very narrow power band. To cope with this, a three-speed overdrive unit was mounted outboard of the standard four-speed gearbox, thereby providing 12 ratios. The overdrive unit being cable operated from the left-hand twist grip. Judging from their results, the mental agility required to operate this system during racing had obviously been mastered by the Kreidler riders. The engine was mounted horizontally in a chrome-moly tube frame, with swinging arm rear suspension and Earles-type front forks.

Although Honda was the favourite for the 50cc class, it was completely out-classed by Suzuki and Kreidler. Honda's single-cylinder, (40x39mm) 49cc, gear-driven double overhead cam, four-valve, four-stroke RC110 produced 9ps at 14,000rpm but was seriously outpaced from the start. During the season, though, and in response to urgent requests from the riders, it progressed from a six-speeder to an eight-, and finally a nine-speeder, and the power output increased to 10ps at 15,000rpm, in an attempt to keep pace with its rivals. In spite of this, though, Honda could finish only third in the Championship, largely due to the efforts of Luigi Taveri and Tommy Robb. The two of them finishing second and third respectively in the TT, and first and second in the Finnish GP. Prompted by this defeat, Honda produced a twin-cylinder (33x29.2mm) nine-speed RC112, with which Tommy Robb won the end-of-season inaugural non-Championship Japanese GP, beating Hugh Anderson on a Suzuki.

In the sidecar class, Max Deubel, with passenger Emil Horner, won his second consecutive Championship, taking three out of six wins with his ex-works BMW. Florian Camathias, back in action after his Modena crash in 1961, was runner-up, with his 1961 semi-kneeler BMW. He was passengered by Horst Burkhardt whose place was taken by Englishman Harry Winter later in the season. Until now the BMW brigade had failed to capitalise on the advantages of the 'kneeler' concept, first demonstrated by the late, great Eric Oliver back in 1954. Camathias had been experimenting with a multi-tubular, space frame outfit, which was still in the development stage. It was, therefore, Fritz Scheidegger who brought out the first of the really ultra-low, BMW kneeler outfits, built with the assistance of Rudi Kurth. With only a ten-inch front wheel, the outfit had a very low frontal area, but it suffered numerous teething problems, which were only ironed out late in the season. Despite a win in the Dutch TT, Scheidegger and Robinson could finish only third in the Championship. Chris Vincent and Eric Bliss had a surprise win in the Sidecar TT with their BSA outfit, after both Deubel and Camathias retired, and Colin Seeley and Wally Rawlings brought their immaculate Matchless G50 outfit into third place.

An interesting comparison of the performance of the different machines was provided at the Dutch TT at Assen, where riders had been timed over a section of the fastest straight. Mike Hailwood's 500 MV was predictably the fastest at 128mph, but surprisingly this figure was equalled by the 285cc RC171 Hondas of Redman and McIntyre. The next fastest 350 was Hailwood's MV at 125mph, and already down in speed compared to the Hondas. The quickest 250 was Jim Redman's Honda at 123mph. Tommy Robb's Honda and Ernst Degner's Suzuki were the fastest 125s at 112mph. In the 50cc category, with a speed of 88mph, Anscheidt's 50cc Kreidler proved to be equally as fast as Degner's Suzuki.

# 1963 Two-stroke challenge

**1963 SAW** the burgeoning Japanese two-stroke challenge intensify, with Yamaha returning to join Suzuki in the battle against the four-strokes. Honda's massive financial commitment during 1961 and 1962 had inevitably brought about cutbacks in its programme for 1963. Consequently, Honda lost its advantage in the 50cc and 125cc categories, and met with some renewed opposition in both the 250 and 350cc classes. In the 500cc class there was the prospect of some welcome opposition to Mike Hailwood and the MV from the Scuderia Duke team on the ex-works 1957 Gileras.

Geoff Duke had persuaded Gilera to release the 1957 works machines for his team, with Derek Minter and John Hartle as the riders. Sadly, however, what had been a praiseworthy effort never achieved its just rewards. The team was beset by mechanical unreliability, rider injuries, and personality clashes. The first setback occurred in May, when Minter and promising young rider Dave Downer were involved in the tragic crash at Brands Hatch that claimed the life of Downer while Derek himself received severe spinal injuries. Phil Read was drafted in as a replacement but didn't get along with Geoff Duke. The machines also suffered from a lack of backup from the factory, in the form of engine and chassis development. In the circumstances, Hartle's second place in the Senior TT at 103.67mph, with a lap at over 105mph until gearbox problems set in, was a particularly brave effort. Although Hartle and Read were first and second in the Dutch TT, after Hailwood's MV retired with a broken piston, during the rest of the season they were never a serious threat. Despite their best efforts, Hartle and Read were only third and fourth in the Championship. Derek Minter returned to the team for the Ulster GP, where he finished a brave third, followed by a second place in the East German GP. Mike Hailwood, however, was in scintillating form throughout the season, winning seven out of eight races, and setting many new race and lap records in the process. Runner-up for the second year running was Alan Shepherd, with podium finishes on his Tom Kirby G50 Matchless in Holland, Belgium, East Germany, and Finland. The Scuderia Duke 350 Gileras proved to be too fragile to provide any real opposition, and, although John Hartle finished second in the Junior TT, the machines were withdrawn soon after.

Quite unexpectedly, it was Tarquinio Provini on the Morini who posed the most serious challenge to Honda's 250cc class domination. His single-cylinder, ultra short-stroke, (72x61mm) double overhead cam machine reputedly produced 38bhp at 11,000rpm. Now with dry-sump lubrication, the loss of the under-engine oil sump had allowed the engine to be lowered in the frame, which, together with a very slim fairing and tailored riding position, gave the machine a very narrow frontal area. With twin-plug ignition, a seven-speed gearbox, and the extensive use of magnesium castings, it weighed only 238lb (107kg), which contributed to its estimated top speed of 140mph. Provini won the first round in Spain after a wheel-to-wheel battle with Redman during which the lead changed several times. Provini, however, was in his element on the twisty Montjuich Park circuit that suited his flamboyant riding style and eventually drew away from Redman. He then went on to prove that his Spanish win was no fluke with a convincing win on the fast Hockenheim circuit, setting new race and lap records. The French round had to be cancelled when dense fog descended on the Clermont Ferrand circuit. Jim Redman fought back with wins in the Isle of Man and the Dutch TT, but fell off in the 125cc race at Assen, breaking his collarbone, and consequently missed the Belgian GP. He was back in action at the Ulster, and in typically wet conditions he recorded his third win with Provini in second place. At the East German GP, on the first lap of the 250 race, a 'Kamikaze' out-braking manoeuvre by MZ rider Laslo Szabo, almost brought down the entire leading group, and led to some desperate avoiding action. As usual on their home circuit, the MZs were 'flying,' and Mike Hailwood and Alan Shepherd were a convincing first and second, while Redman could finish only third.

At Monza, Provini was provided with a teammate, newcomer Giacomo Agostini, who led for a whole lap before being passed by Provini and Redman, who then went at it 'hammer and tongs' for 14 laps, with the lead changing several times; Provini tucking himself almost out of sight in contrast to Redman's rather 'tall-in-the-saddle' style. Redman eventually dropped back and settled for second place. Provini won again in Argentina and, going into the final round in Japan, they were equal on points. Redman won the final round at Suzuka and took the title by just two points from Provini, who was off-colour and could finish only fourth.

Yamaha had returned after 18 months with the new and astonishingly fast RD56. Developed by Hiroshi Naito from the earlier RD48, the (56x50.7mm) 249.8cc machine reportedly produced 45ps at 11,000rpm, but was still an air-cooled, disc-valve twin-cylinder, with a seven-speed gearbox. In addition to petroil lubrication, a crankcase-mounted pump fed oil directly to the main bearings and big-ends. The machine's potential had been demonstrated at Daytona early in the year, when Fumio won the 250cc race and set a new absolute lap record of 131.2mph. The speed of the new machines surprised everyone in the Isle of Man, when Fumio Ito and Tony Godfrey led the Lightweight TT for a couple of laps. Unfortunately, Godfrey had to stop twice for plug changes, and, while trying to make-up time, crashed heavily at Milntown Cottage when the Yamaha seized. Although seriously injured, his life was saved by the prompt action of the new Shell/BP helicopter service that got him to a hospital without delay. Meanwhile, Ito was unable to stay ahead of the more experienced Redman and had to be content with second place.

The Belgian Grand Prix circuit at Spa Francorchamps had been modified over the years, resulting in it being granted the dubious honour of fastest GP circuit. The 8.7-mile (14.17km) circuit did indeed have more than its fair share of very fast and demanding curves. There was the exciting left-right sweep at Eau Rouge soon after the start, then came the fearful bumpy right-hand Burnenville curves, known as the 'Cocoa bends'. The next hazard was the very quick left-right kink at Masta, where the circuit originally dodged around a small cottage. The original hairpin in the village of Stavelot had been bypassed in the early fifties by a long sweeping banked right-hand curve, which led into the fastest part of the circuit, through the flat out curves at Blanchimont, leading to the only slow corner on the circuit, the hairpin at La Source.

It was on this circuit that the new RD56 Yamahas demonstrated their awesome potential, when Fumio Ito and his team-mate Yoshikazu Sunako simply left the opposition for dead. A clear fore-warning of the impending two-stroke challenge. Ito's winning record average speed of 115.49mph, and his lap record of 117.82mph, handsomely exceed the records set the previous year by Bob McIntyre on a Honda. Despite the fact that Ito's win pushed him up to third in the Championship table, the Yamaha team packed up and returned to Japan, to reappear at the final round at Suzuka with improved versions of the RD56 ridden by Fumio Ito and new signing for 1964 Phil Read, who finished second and third respectively.

MZ's new twin-cylinder 250 was now water cooled, and reputed to be producing 48bhp with increased reliability. Unfortunately, following Ernst Degner's defection in 1961, the team still faced severe travel restrictions and, due to underexposure in the GPs, MZ was unable to exploit the full potential of the new machine. However, Alan Shepherd demonstrated the speed of the new bike at the German GP at Hockenheim, before minor problems caused him to drop back. At its home East German GP at the Sachsenring, Mike Hailwood, having his annual outing on an MZ, and Alan Shepherd finished first and second, well ahead of Redman's Honda, with Mike setting the first over-100mph lap. The speed of the MZs was confirmed after the race by Jim Redman who frankly admitted that they were considerably faster than his Honda.

Suzuki took over the top of the 125cc class for the first time with its all 'western' team of Hugh Anderson, Frank Perris, Ernst Degner, and Austrian Bert Schneider. The new twin-cylinder, short-stroke (43x42.6mm) 123.7cc RT63, although still air-cooled, was producing 26ps at 12,000rpm, and featured MZ-style rearward facing exhaust ports with high level expansion chambers, an eight-speed gearbox, and a new duplex cradle frame. The engines featured crankcases split horizontally along the centre line of the crankshaft, and the two separate crankshaft assemblies each had a drive pinion that meshed with a common double-width gear on a jackshaft, which, in turn, transmitted the drive to the gearbox.

New Zealander Hugh Anderson, who had established his reputation in the late 1950s and early 1960s riding Tom Arter's 7R AJS and G50 Matchless, won the first of his 125cc Championships with a convincing six wins from nine rounds. In spite of having only the previous year's machines, Luigi Taveri and Jim Redman were to finish second and third in the Championship. Honda, however, had already taken steps to rectify this situation and, about mid-season, Redman flew back to Japan to test a new four-cylinder 125. The final version of this machine, called the 2RC146, appeared at the Japanese GP in November. MZ was once again out of the picture in the 125cc class, being able to attend only three GPs. MZ's new 125s were also water-cooled and had regained some of their lost performance. Hungarian rider Laslo Szabo rode one to a creditable third place in a lone appearance at the German GP at Hockenheim and, in the East German GP, Alan Shepherd was second, and Mike Duff, having a one-off MZ ride, was fifth. Shepherd was third and Laslo Szabo fourth in Finland.

Riding the 340cc Honda RC171, Jim Redman won the 350cc title again to score his second double 250/350 World Championship win, despite breaking his collarbone in the 125cc crash at the Dutch TT. In the Junior TT, which was run in rapidly deteriorating weather conditions, there was a real battle on the road between Jim Redman and Mike Hailwood (as was to be expected with them starting together at numbers 1 and 2). The two kept passing and re-passing one another, with Hailwood having to ride much harder to overcome the Honda's power advantage. Eventually, it all came to an end when Hailwood was forced to retire at the end of the fourth lap. Later in the season, Hailwood's slightly rejuvenated 350 MV, which sported a new massive front brake, posed a bit of a threat with a win in East Germany and again in Finland, where Redman had only one of the production twin-cylinder 305cc models. At the Sachsenring, Luigi Taveri rode a tremendous race on one of the CR77 305cc twin-cylinder Hondas to finish second to Mike Hailwood and ahead of team leader Redman. Together with his third place in the Dutch and the Ulster, Taveri consolidated his third place in the Championship. Honda eventually responded by bringing out a full-size (50x44.5mm) 349.3cc RC172, with an increased power output of 53ps, in time for Redman to win the Italian GP at Monza and secure his title. The 350cc RC171/172 proved to be one of Honda's most successful machines, giving Jim Redman 20 GP wins and three consecutive world titles.

### JIM REDMAN

Often referred to as 'Iron Man,' Jim Redman was initially a very under-rated rider, who admitted that he only rode as fast as it was necessary to win. Despite this, when the occasion demanded he could be a tough opponent, and rode some pretty tenacious races, particularly against Phil Read's Yamaha and Agostini's three-cylinder MV. He was also very strong mentally in his dealings with race organisers and team members, which sometimes caused some dissent. Born in Hampstead, London, circumstances had forced him to emigrate to Rhodesia (Zimbabwe) in 1952 where he started racing in 1954 and soon built up a reputation before coming to race in England and Europe in 1957. After three hard seasons of racing his Nortons in England and on the Continent, he had his first ride for Honda in the 1960 Dutch TT. Jim had come up through the school of hard knocks to achieve the position of Honda team leader, and understandably guarded his position quite jealously. His record as a rider, however, speaks for itself, with double 250/350cc TT wins three years running in 1963, 64 and 65, plus four consecutive 350cc World Championships from 1962 to 1965. In spite of his premature retirement from World Championship racing in 1966, Jim has continued to be involved with motorcycle racing and still rides in Historic events and demos.

Of particular technical interest were the new Honda twin-cylinder production racers. The 250cc CR72 and the 305cc CR77 were virtually identical except for cylinder dimensions – 54x54mm and 60x54mm respectively. The engines had gear train drive to the twin overhead camshafts, and four valves per cylinder. They had

180-degree crankshafts, wet-sump lubrication, six-speed gearboxes, and a dry clutch. The cylinder head was a one-piece casting, but the cylinder block was split vertically to allow the camshaft drive gears to be assembled, and the two halves were sealed with a simple rubber gasket. Spine-type frames similar to the roadster CB72/77 models were used, but all the works machines had additional frame bracing tubes. Some had bolted-on front downtubes, while others had a twin-tube arrangement behind the engine, supporting two gusset plates that carried the swinging arm pivot. Brakes and cycle parts were the same as on the four-cylinder models. The 'production' racers were distinguished from the 'pukka' works machines by a dark orange stripe along the side of the fairing, and they also had an unusual offbeat exhaust note, due to their 180-degree crankshafts and uneven firing intervals. Although no power output figures were available at the time, it's estimated that the 250 was producing about 42ps at 12,000rpm and the 305 at least 46ps at 11,000rpm.

Tommy Robb, who rode both versions during 1963, recalls that the twins were more tractable than the fours, although they did not handle as well, suffered from vibration, and were prone to gearbox problems. They were, however, very fast, much quicker than the average 500 Manx Norton or G50 Matchless. At Hockenheim, Tommy's 305 had no problem keeping up with Remo Venturi's Bianchi and, in the Junior TT, his Honda was timed at 134.0mph through the 'Highlander' speed trap, a good 2mph faster than Hailwood's 350 MV.

Frankie Stastny did his best for Jawa as usual, with a third in the Junior TT and a fourth in the Dutch TT, but his season was cut short by a crash in July at Piestany in Czechoslovakia in which he broke a leg. Although the earlier 250cc versions were no longer being used, since 1961 the reliable twin-cylinder 350cc Jawas had consistently finished in the wake of the Hondas and MVs. The double overhead cam engines with a bore and stroke of 59x63.6mm were producing a modest 49bhp at 10,600rpm, and employed a unique camshaft drive arrangement. A bevel-driven vertical shaft, located at the rear between the two cylinders, drove the inlet camshaft, while a second driveshaft placed horizontally across the top of the cylinder head, transmitted the drive from the centre of the inlet camshaft to the exhaust camshaft. During 1963, an experimental short-stroke version (62x57.9mm) was tried, but proved to be unreliable due to big-end failures caused by an increase in maximum rpm. Later, a 385cc version with square dimensions of 62x63.6mm was also raced.

1963 saw the return to GP racing of the Russian machines, and the team made unprecedented appearances at the Dutch TT and the Belgian GP. Sevostianov, Juri Randla, and Estonian Endel Kiisa rode 250 and 350cc machines similar to the 1962 versions, of which the 350 was more successful, gaining Sevostianov a fifth in East Germany and a fourth in Finland. A 352cc version was also ridden by Sevostianov to a sixth place in Finland. The machines were generally functional in appearance, perhaps a bit rough and ready by Western standards, but the riders were most certainly keen and enthusiastic. In fact, some of the hardened Continental Circus riders found the Russians' riding styles a bit uninhibited and their tactics rather aggressive.

The 50cc class was a Suzuki benefit, with Hugh Anderson winning his first Championship on the new RM63, an air-cooled, single-cylinder, disc-valve machine, now with a nine-speed gearbox and turning out 11ps at 13,000rpm. The engine also featured a third transfer port and a rearward-facing exhaust port. A scaled-down version of the new 125cc duplex cradle frame was used, and the complete machine weighed 135lb (61kg). Once again, it was Hans-Georg Anscheidt on the Kreidler who single-handedly took on the whole Suzuki team. With three wins to his credit Anscheidt was leading the Championship by three points from Hugh Anderson, until he crashed during practice for the Argentine GP and broke a collarbone. Strangely enough, although Honda had the twin-cylinder RC112 on which Tommy Robb had won the Japanese GP at the end of 1962, it decided not to contest the 50cc class in 1963. However an improved 50cc version called the RC113 was used by Luigi Taveri to win the final round in Japan in November.

Some significant events took place at the end-of-season Japanese GP, which had become a kind of prelude to the forthcoming season. Yamaha had signed Phil Read to lead its attack on the 250 World Championship in 1964, and he duly made his debut on the RD56 at Suzuka. The new 250cc Suzuki RZ63 square-four also made its first appearance, in what turned out to be a fairly disastrous and dramatic debut. During practice, Bert Schneider's RZ seized up and threw him off in front of Frank Perris who also crashed but was uninjured. Schneider, however, broke a collarbone putting him out of action. Three RZs started in the race, but on the first lap Degner slid off and, while trying to pick up his machine, passed out, just as the machine burst into flames and he became engulfed. Fortunately, Perris who had made a bad start arrived on the scene, saw his team-mate alight, threw down his own machine and dragged Degner clear, but he had already suffered severe burns, mainly around the head. Meanwhile, Hugh Anderson on the sole remaining RZ was forced to lay down his machine to avoid a fallen rider, although he remounted to finish ninth. It had not been a very auspicious start for the new square-four Suzuki.

Also at the Japanese GP, Honda had decided to renew its attack on the 50cc and 125cc classes in 1964, and brought out new machines. Jim Redman finished second in the 125cc race on one of the new RC146 four-cylinder machines. An improved version of the 50cc RC112 to be used in 1964 was also re-introduced as the RC113, which Luigi Taveri used to win the 50cc race from a whole gaggle of Suzukis led by Hugh Anderson.

In the BMW-dominated sidecar class, it was the usual three-cornered battle between Max Deubel/Emil Horner, Florian Camathias/Alfred Herzig, and Fritz Scheidegger/John Robinson. Throughout his career, Max Deubel had stuck to his 'sit up' outfit, which suited his smooth driving style, although for 1963 he had a new lightweight integral chassis built for him by Reynolds. Deubel and Horner won the first round in Spain, but at Hockenheim Camathias turned up with his new ultra low Helmut Fath-tuned FCS (Fath Camathias Special) on which he had a record breaking debut win. The BMW engine had been modified, and allegedly used many non-BMW components. The FCS name, however, led to some ill-feeling between Camathias and the BMW factory, which objected to its name not being used on the outfit; it was later renamed FCS/BMW.

At the TT, Max Deubel had a rare crash, in practice at Sarah's Cottage, in which Emil Horner was injured. With Barry Dungworth as substitute Deubel was nowhere in the running, but reasserted himself with a convincing win in the Dutch TT. Having won his first TT, and with two wins to his credit, Camathias was leading on points going into the final round in Belgium. On the fast Spa Francorchamps circuit, his FCS was really flying and he led the race with the title within his grasp, but due to his usual lack of restraint, his engine blew up. Scheidegger won and Deubel's second place was sufficient for him to clinch the title. Camathias had the consolation of second place in the Championship and Scheidegger was third.

During the TT races in the Isle of Man, the National Sprint Association set up the first of its 'speed traps' on the fast section past the 'Highlander' inn. The speeds recorded provide an interesting comparison between the performance of the various machines. The fastest was Mike Hailwood's 500 MV at 148.8mph, fractionally faster than John Hartle's Gilera at 148.3mph and Phil Read's Gilera at 147.7mph. Jim Redman's Honda was the fastest 350 at 142.6mph, but it was Tommy Rob's twin-cylinder Honda that was second fastest at 134.0mph, with Mike Hailwood's MV next at 132.7mph. Fastest 250s were the three Yamahas of Tony Godfrey, at an incredible 141.0mph, followed by Fumio Ito and Hiroshi Hasegawa. Suzuki topped the 125cc class with Frank Perris recording 118.7mph, followed by Degner, Schneider and Anderson. Suzuki was also fastest in the 50cc class, with Isao Morishita just under three figures with 94.9mph. Florian Camathias led the sidecars with his FCS/BMW at 128.3mph. Some of the classic British singles also recorded some impressive speeds. Roland Foll's Matchless recorded 134.0mph, and the fastest 500 Norton was Fred Stevens at 132.6mph.

*Tom Phillis on one of the production racer 125cc Hondas in the 1962 TT. (Elwyn Roberts Collection)*

*Moto Kitano on a 250cc Honda in the 1962 East German GP. (Elwyn Roberts Collection)*

*Derek Minter on the Hondis-entered Honda on which he won the 250cc Lightweight TT in 1962. (Elwyn Roberts Collection)*

*Winner of the 1962 125cc French GP, Kunimitsu Takahashi with Honda team-mates Jim Redman and Tommy Robb, who were second and third respectively.*

*Jim Redman (Honda) in the 250cc East German GP. (Elwyn Roberts Collection)*

*A grim looking Tommy Robb on a rather scruffy looking Honda four, circa 1962. (Courtesy Malcolm Carling)*

*Fumio Ito, who stunned the opposition in the 250cc Belgian GP in 1963 with a record-breaking win on the new RD48 Yamaha. (Courtesy Malcolm Carling)*

*Mike Hailwood (MV), winner of the 1963 500cc East German GP. (Elwyn Roberts Collection)*

*John Hartle, who finished second and lapped at over 105mph in the 1963 Senior TT on the 1957 Scuderia Duke Gilera. (Courtesy Malcolm Carling)*

*Luigi Taveri in the 1963 Dutch TT on the twin-cylinder Honda, on which he came third in the 350cc World Championship. (Courtesy Malcolm Carling)*

*Jim Redman frequently rode Hondas in the 125cc class. Here he is competing in the 1963 Lightweight TT. (Courtesy Malcolm Carling)*

*1963 125 World Champion Hugh Anderson on his Suzuki. (Courtesy Malcolm Carling)*

*Ernst Degner (Suzuki) in the 1963 125 Lightweight TT. (Courtesy Malcolm Carling)*

*Ernst Degner (125 Suzuki) leading team-mate Frank Perris in the 1963 Dutch TT. (Courtesy Malcolm Carling)*

*Remo Venturi on a 350cc Bianchi in the 1963 Dutch TT. (Courtesy Malcolm Carling)*

50cc Suzuki battle in the 1963 Dutch TT, with Hugh Anderson leading eventual winner Isao Morishita (6) and Michio Ichino (4). (Courtesy Malcolm Carling)

Hiroshi Hasegawa on a 250cc RD48 Yamaha in the 1963 Belgian GP. (Courtesy Malcolm Carling)

Yoshikazu Sunako on an RD48 Yamaha in the 1963 250 Lightweight TT. (Courtesy Malcolm Carling)

*Alan Shepherd, who was second in the 1963 500cc World Championship, on his Tom Kirby Matchless. (Courtesy Malcolm Carling)*

*Paddy Driver on his Tom Kirby Matchless in the 1963 Senior TT. He was third in the 1965 500cc Championship. (Courtesy Malcolm Carling)*

*The affable Tommy Robb in vivid action on his works Honda in the 1963 250 Lightweight TT. (Courtesy Malcolm Carling)*

*Popular Luigi Taveri in the 1963 Belgian GP. Despite his small stature, he was equally at home on a 250cc Honda four. (Courtesy Malcolm Carling)*

*Tarquinio Provini on the indecently fast single-cylinder 250cc Morini. He was third in the 1963 Belgian Grand Prix. (Courtesy Malcolm Carling)*

*Silvio Grassetti on a 250cc four-cylinder Benelli in the 1963 Belgian GP. (Courtesy Malcolm Carling)*

*Bert Schneider on a 125 Suzuki rounding the La Source hairpin in the 1963 Belgian GP. (Courtesy Karl-Gunter Peters)*

*Russian ace Nikolai Sevostianov on the twin-cylinder 350cc S360, in the 1963 Belgian GP. (Courtesy Malcolm Carling)*

*Phil Read finished third in the 1963 Senior TT on the Scuderia Duke Gilera. (Courtesy Malcolm Carling)*

*Chester Honda dealer Bill Smith was loaned a works 250 twin-cylinder Honda, on which he came third in the 1963 Lightweight TT. (Courtesy Malcolm Carling)*

*1963 World Champion Max Deubel and passenger Emil Horner, drifting their BMW outfit in the Belgian GP. (Courtesy Karl-Heinz Reiger)*

# 1964
# Redman & Read

**1964 WILL** be remembered for the titanic struggle for the 250cc World Championship between four-stroke champion Honda and its two-stroke challenger Yamaha. The two main protagonists in this contest, Jim Redman and Phil Read, engaged in a series of memorable wheel-to-wheel battles that lasted most of the season. By now, the level of competition in the 250cc class had made it the 'premier' class, over the lacklustre 350 and 500cc classes. Consequently, many race organisers resorted to running the 250cc race as the final event of the day.

Phil Read finally snatched the 250cc title away from Honda, riding an improved version of the RD56. The new machines, which were introduced at the TT, had new frames that allowed the engine to be mounted much lower, and also had the familiar wasp-waisted scarlet and white fairings. Read was supported by a new signing, Canadian Mike Duff, with erstwhile Honda teamster Tommy Robb providing additional support for the Isle of Man, Dutch TT, and Belgian GP. Jim Redman, on the other hand, had to fight a lone battle in defence of his title, with another uprated version of the four-cylinder Honda called the 2RC164.

The form book was upset at the early season Spanish GP, when Tarquinio Provini on a Benelli beat both Read and Redman. The Italian four-cylinder machine had a bore and stroke of 44x40.6mm, gear-driven double overhead cams, a seven-speed gearbox, and produced 45bhp at 14,500rpm. However, Provini was unable to sustain the challenge over the season. Alan Shepherd took advantage of a lifting of travel restrictions by MZ to embark on a full season. In a lone effort, and with just one machine, he won the US Grand Prix at Daytona, but only after a frantic telephone call to Walter Kaaden to cure a serious loss of performance during practice. In spite of a broken collarbone caused by a practice crash in the French GP, Alan was second in the TT and third in the Belgian GP, to take a well-earned third place in the Championship. On his usual MZ outing in the East German GP, Mike Hailwood was leading the 250cc race when he crashed, but set a new lap record at an incredible 102.06mph. The new 250 MZ was now producing 53bhp, and featured thermo-siphon water cooling, an eight-speed gearbox, and a new duplex cradle frame. On a couple of occasions one of these machines, bored out to 251cc, was provided for Alan Shepherd to ride in the 350cc class.

---

## ALAN SHEPHERD

Alan Shepherd, from Cumbria, started racing in 1954, and in 1956 finished third in the BSA Gold Star-dominated Junior Clubman's TT on his Inter Norton. This led to sponsorship from Bill Bancroft, with whom he won the 1958 Junior Manx Grand Prix on an AJS. During 1960 he rode the works development 7R AJS and G50 Matchless supplied through his sponsor Geoff Monty. At the Ulster GP on the 7R, he stayed in close pursuit of John Surtees on the MV, until the cam chain on the

AJS broke, but still set a new lap record. Stunned by the speed of the AJS, MV lodged a protest, but, when measured, the AJS was found to be within the capacity limit. It was this performance that attracted the attention of Walter Kaaden and eventually led to Alan riding for MZ in 1961. His virtually single-handed efforts during his three years with MZ had been particularly praiseworthy. More so because they often involved him making long journeys to the East German border to collect and return the machines before and after each GP. While riding the MZs, Alan also campaigned a Tom Kirby G50 Matchless, on which he was runner-up in the 500cc World Championships in 1962 and 1963. His efforts with the MZs were rewarded with the offer of a Honda contract at the end of 1964. Sadly, however, he never benefitted from it. During a test session at the Suzuka circuit in September 1963, while riding a 350 Honda four with an alleged handling problem, he crashed and suffered a fractured skull and severe concussion. Although he eventually recovered, he felt that his skill and judgement had been impaired and he decided to retire, at the age of only 27. Two grand prix wins hardly do justice to a racing career that, undoubtedly, would have been enhanced by his association with Honda.

---

Bad luck continued to dog the RZ64 Suzuki, with Frank Perris crashing during practice at Daytona and breaking a leg. The square-four power unit consisted of two (43x42.6mm) 123cc, twin-cylinder, water-cooled engines in tandem, and produced 50ps at 12,000rpm, with a choice of either five or six-speeds. Since the Japanese GP, new frames with larger diameter tubes had been built to cure flexing. The machines were phenomenally fast in a straight line, but were prone to sudden engine seizures, earning them the nickname (coined by Jack Ahearn) of 'Whispering Death'. Understandably, many of the team riders were wary of them, and Hugh Anderson eventually refused to ride one. Despite its potential, the RZ never posed a serious threat to Honda or Yamaha. Suzuki's best result was a third place in the French GP (Bert Schneider), but the machines were returned to Japan after the Belgian GP.

The epic Honda/Yamaha battles kicked off at the French GP at Clermont-Ferrand, where Redman and Read battled furiously; the lead changing several times until Redman's Honda went onto two cylinders and he was forced to retire, leaving Read to win comfortably. Their rivalry reached fever pitch in the Dutch TT at Assen, on the Van Drenthe circuit that had been built-in 1955 to replace the original prewar circuit. The new circuit, with its abrasive surface and a combination of fast, open curves and medium speed corners, was a real 'riders circuit'. In a race-long battle, during which they were frequently side-by-side while braking for the corners, Read led into the last corner, but Redman dived inside him and barged past, almost making contact with the Yamaha. As they accelerated toward the finishing line, with the Yamaha creeping up on the Honda, Redman realised that if he changed up a gear the slight loss of momentum would lose his advantage, so he held on with the Honda revving well over its recommended limit to win by less than a wheel.

The inherent dangers of such close racing was vividly demonstrated a week later at the Belgian GP. On the first lap, Read was leading Redman by mere inches on the approach to the very fast left-right kink at Masta, Redman saw a puff of smoke from the Yamaha's exhaust just as they peeled off into the left-hander. Realising that the Yamaha had seized, Redman swerved, missed the back of the Yamaha by inches, but went off the road at about 130mph, miraculously missing a telegraph pole and the side of a house, before fighting his Honda back onto the road. Mike Duff, who had been close behind on the other Yamaha, inherited the lead, and held on to the finish; winning his first grand prix after setting new race and lap records. Meanwhile, Redman, who had recovered from his involuntary off road excursion, thankfully settled for second place.

In the West German GP at Solitude, Read played a waiting game, shadowing Redman until the last lap before taking the lead to win. It was Mike Hailwood on the MZ who set the pace for the first two laps of the East German GP at the Sachsenring, with Read and Redman on his rear wheel. After setting a new lap record at over 102mph (164km/h), Mike dropped the MZ whilst exiting the town of Hohenstein-Ernsthal on the third lap, causing his pursuers to take avoiding action. Redman took advantage of the situation to slip into the lead. Once again Read sat behind the Honda before taking the lead with three laps to go. Redman, understandably, seemed reluctant to slipstream the Yamaha after the Belgian GP incident, but made a last desperate effort and drew alongside on the last corner. He couldn't match the acceleration of the Yamaha, however, and Read beat him to the line by a machine's length. In a wet race at the Ulster GP, Redman decided to play it safe and settled for second place behind Read's Yamaha.

The performance of the Yamahas had obviously stung Honda into action, and the company had been secretly developing a six-cylinder machine. In a desperate attempt to retain the 250cc Championship, Honda was forced to play its trump card, prematurely as it turned out, for the Italian GP at Monza. The 3RC164 (39x34.8mm) 249.43cc engine had been designed by Soichiro Irimajiri, who'd been involved in the design of the V12 Formula One GP car. It followed usual Honda practice, with central, gear-driven, double overhead cams, four valves per cylinder, wet-sump lubrication, and a seven-speed gearbox. Power output was 50ps at 18,000rpm, and the frame and cycle parts were the same as on the four-cylinder models. Disguised as a 350cc machine and concealed from prying eyes, the machine arrived at Monza while still in the development stage.

Predictably, Jim Redman took the lead from the start, with Read's Yamaha on his heels, but within a couple of laps the Honda six began to overheat, lost power, and was passed by Read. Redman struggled to stay in contact with Read, but was passed by Mike Duff's Yamaha as well on the last lap, and could only finish third. Several modifications were carried out to the Honda in time for the Japanese GP, where Redman won on an improved version called the RC165, while Read retired with mechanical problems. However, it was too little too late, and, despite having accumulated 58 points to Read's 50, when the six best results were counted the title went to Phil Read and Yamaha.

The four-stroke/two-stroke battle in the 50cc and 125cc classes continued unabated, with both Honda and Suzuki having mixed fortunes. Hugh Anderson won his second 50cc title with four wins from his nearest rivals, Ralph Bryans on a Honda and Hans-Georg Anscheidt on the incredible little Kreidler. The Suzuki RM64 was still an air-cooled, nine-speed, single-cylinder machine, but with a (41.5x36.8mm) shorter stroke engine, producing 12.5ps at 14,000rpm. Once again Honda had a disappointing start to the season in the 50cc class. The new twin-cylinder (33x29.2mm) 49.6cc RC114 now had four valves per cylinder, calliper rim front brakes, and produced 14ps at an incredible 20,000rpm, but all three machines retired in the Spanish GP. This had evidently not gone down too well with the Honda team management and, in the 125cc race, Tommy Robb and Kunimitsu Takahashi were rather ominously flagged off by the team manager. At the French GP poor Tommy Robb was told that his contract had been terminated and no reasons were given. Takahashi, too, was sent back to Japan. These harsh measures were probably a thinly veiled excuse for reducing the team and cutting costs. As a result, this left Honda newcomer Ralph Bryans on his own, battling it out against three Suzukis and Anscheidt's Kreidler.

Honda obviously got its act together eventually because Luigi Taveri, who had been riding for Kreidler, was brought back in to support Bryans, who won the three consecutive Dutch, Belgian and West German rounds, as well as the final round in Japan. At the Belgian GP, Ralph fought a lone battle throughout the race with Anscheidt's Kreidler, and the Suzukis of Anderson, Itoh and Morishita, in which the lead changed several times. As the bunch approached the La Source hairpin on the last lap, Anscheidt led from Bryans, who, cannily anticipating a problem, braked a bit earlier than his rivals. Anscheidt ran wide while Ralph nipped through on the inside and beat him to the flag. At Solitude in the West German GP on wet roads, Ralph's Irish road racing experience came into play, and he romped away to an easy win, setting new race and lap records. In Finland, Ralph lost a certain first place when his brakes failed, and Hugh Anderson inherited the lead and took the win. Although Ralph Bryans won the final round in Japan, Hugh Anderson had accumulated sufficient points earlier in the season to take the 50cc title. Anscheidt on the Kreidler once again proved to be a thorn in the side of the mighty Japanese teams, taking three second places in France, Belgium and Finland to finish third in the Championship.

The tables were turned in the 125cc class. Luigi Taveri won his second World Championship with five wins, riding the new four-cylinder (35x32mm) 124.9cc Honda 2RC146. This was virtually a scaled-down 250 with a seven-speed gearbox, weighed 87.5kg, and produced 24ps at 15,000rpm. These machines apparently had a very narrow power band, and were prone to carburation problems that made them difficult to ride. In spite of this, Taveri, Redman, and Bryans finished first, second and third in the TT, with Taveri winning by a mere three seconds in a last lap charge. Jim Redman had wins in the Dutch TT and the West German GP, which gave him second place in the Championship. At the Dutch TT he had to deputise for Luigi Taveri, who had been slightly injured in a practice crash, which led to his second close encounter of the day with Phil Read, this time on the new RA75 Yamaha.

It was the turn of the Suzuki team to have problems. The power of the 125cc RT64 had been increased to 30ps at 13,000rpm, probably at the expense of reliability, and the machines suffered from constant carburation problems that were only cured halfway through the season, when a change to Mikuni carburettors at the East German GP gave Hugh Anderson his first win of the season. He followed this with a brilliant win in the Ulster, when, despite almost sliding off at the hairpin, he fought his way up from sixth place into the lead to win, setting new race and lap records. Yamaha returned to the 125cc class for the first time since 1961, with the air-cooled, twin-cylinder (44x41mm) 124.7cc RA75; basically a scaled-down 250. It was introduced at the Dutch TT, where Phil Read demonstrated its potential with a second place, in his second encounter of the day with Jim Redman who won by a couple of seconds. These machines were used only once more, at the West German GP, when, in a wet race, Read slid off and had to retire, after which the machines were returned to Japan.

Down in Zschopau, MZ was having its own problems, and, in spite of building a completely new water-cooled 125, this proved to be no better than the 1963 version and was no match for the Japanese machines. One other machine worthy of mention was a very neat new 125cc twin-cylinder double overhead cam CZ, ridden by development rider Stanislaus Malina who finished fourth in the TT. The new machine that replaced the earlier single-cylinder model had a similar camshaft drive arrangement to the Jawa, with a vertical shaft driving the inlet camshaft, and a horizontal crossover shaft taking the drive from the inlet camshaft to the exhaust camshaft. It had a bore and stroke of 45x39.2mm, developed 24bhp at 15,600rpm, a six-speed gearbox, and a new duplex cradle frame. The 250cc CZ remained a single-cylinder, and Malina rode a bored-out 293cc version into third place at Monza.

Jim Redman coasted to his third consecutive 350cc World Championship, winning all eight rounds on the RC172 Honda. The 350 MV made just one appearance: at the Dutch TT, where Mike Hailwood finished second, after which the machine was withdrawn. A well-deserved third in the Championship was Mike Duff on his AJS, with a second in the Ulster and two third places in the TT and the East German. The now ageing 500 MV was still unchallenged, and Mike Hailwood cruised to yet another Championship title with seven wins. A feature of the 500cc class during 1964 was the closely-fought contest for top six places behind the MV; between Phil Read and Paddy Driver on Kirby G50s, Mike Duff on his Matchless, and Australian Jack Ahearn on a Norton. In the traditionally wet Ulster, and with Mike Hailwood a non-starter, Phil Read somewhat controversially changed from his Kirby Matchless to a Reg Dearden Norton to win from Ulster specialist Dick Creith on Joe Ryan's Norton, followed by Jack Ahearn, Rob Fitton, and Chris Conn on Nortons. Runner-up in the Championship, however, went to veteran Jack Ahearn, who had a win in the Finnish GP, second place in the West German GP, and third places in the Ulster and Italian GPs.

---

### JACK AHEARN

40-year-old Jack Ahearn from Sydney started his road racing career at Bathurst in 1946. Having established a reputation as one of Australia's top road racers, he was chosen to represent Australia at the TT in 1954, and later rode his Nortons on the Continent. Back in Europe in 1955, he was involved in the infamous Dutch TT riders' strike, for which, along with many others, he was unfairly suspended. As a result, he didn't return to Europe until 1958, whereupon he rode machines supplied to him by the AMC factory, including the prototype Matchless G50 which he raced a couple of times. Between 1959 and 1961, Jack raced successfully in Australia, before returning once again to Europe in 1962. Over the next four years, riding Nortons, he rode regularly in the TT and in the Continental Circus, where he was a consistent top six finisher in the GPs. In 1964, riding one of the notorious works square-four Suzukis, he crashed in the French GP, and again at Sarah's Cottage during TT practice. As a result of his experiences he coined the term 'Whispering Death' for these machines. A tough, no nonsense sort of person, Jack was much respected by his fellow 'privateers,' and his riding seemed to improve with age. The shark's mouth design on his fairings was, perhaps, an indication of his character.

---

The prospect of yet another Gilera/MV confrontation in the 500cc class never materialised. Following a sensational ride against Mike Hailwood at Daytona earlier in the year, 24-year-old Argentinian national champion Benedicto Calderella had been given one of the ex-Scuderia Duke Gileras for the World Championships. Due to the lack of backup from the factory, sundry mechanical problems, and injuries that caused him to miss several rounds, Calderella appeared at only three GPs. In the Dutch TT he tried too hard and almost fell off several times, before retiring with mechanical problems. In the Belgian GP he went out with mechanical problems, and at Monza, although he certainly tried very hard, he could not get to grips with Hailwood, and finished second with the consolation of a new lap record at 121.80mph (196.02km/h).

A most interesting development in the 350cc class was the new Russian four-cylinder S-364, or Vostok (literally East) that appeared for the first time at the East

German GP. It had been designed by Ing Sviatoslav Ivanitsky of the Central Construction and Experimental Bureau, and built at the Motorcycle Industry R&D Institute at Serpukhov. The new machine was a complete departure from the earlier twin-cylinder collaboration with the Czechs, and followed current trends as an in-line four-cylinder with double overhead camshafts driven by a central gear train. It had a bore and stroke of 49x46mm, giving it a capacity of 347cc, and the power output was quoted as 52bhp at 13,000rpm. The six-speed engine/gearbox unit was initially mounted in one of the earlier twin-cylinder-type frames, suitably modified, while later models had new 'featherbed'-type frames. Ridden by Nikolai Sevostianov and young Estonian Endel Kiisa, the Russian machines showed some promise in the early stages of the East German GP, running in third and fourth place before retiring with piston trouble. At the Finnish GP they appeared to be much improved, and, although Sevostianov retired, Kiisa finished third.

In the sidecar class, the prospect of Florian Camathias with a Gilera four outfit breaking Max Deubel's BMW domination was eagerly anticipated. It was seven years since a works Gilera sidecar outfit last appeared in the GPs, and Camathias had finally persuaded Gilera to lend him an engine and some technical support. The 1957 engine was tilted forward 30 degrees in the multi-tubular space frame, with integral sidecar chassis, pivoted fork front, and rear suspension, 16in wheels, and hydraulic brakes. A full kneeler riding position was adopted, with the fuel tank mounted in the sidecar floor, feeding a small header tank with a battery-operated fuel pump. The finished outfit looked superb, finished off with a traditional Gilera scarlet and white dustbin-type fairing.

In a fairy tale debut, Camathias won the Spanish GP with former passenger Roland Foll deputising for the stoic Alfred Herzig, who had been injured after one of his frequent involuntary ejections from the sidecar. Camathias may well have won the French GP as well, had he been able to control his impetuosity, but with a commanding lead he pressed on in inimitable fashion until the engine cried enough and blew up. The rest of the season was a catalogue of disasters, with the Gilera frequently failing to finish a race. One of its problems was apparently fuel starvation, plus the fact that the rather fragile engine could not withstand the full-blooded Camathias treatment.

Eventually, or perhaps inevitably, Max Deubel and Emil Horner won their fourth consecutive World Championship from Fritz Scheidegger and John Robinson, although both teams had two wins each. Camathias had lent his BMW/FCS to Colin Seeley and, with Wally Rawlings as passenger, he was second in the Isle of Man and had a superb win in the Dutch TT, beating Deubel, Scheidegger and all the other BMW contenders. Colin may well have finished as runner-up in the Championship had he not had to return the FCS to Camathias for the final round in Germany. Georg Auerbacher had converted his Rennsport BMW engine to a 'short-stroke' during the winter, with which he recorded a string of third places to finish fourth in the Championship.

Once again the speeds recorded during the TT races over the 'Highlander' section make interesting reading. Mike Hailwood's 500 MV was still the fastest at 144.6mph. Second fastest and fastest 350 was Jim Redman's Honda at 143.4mph. The 250 Yamahas seemed unable to match their previous year's performance, and were overtaken by the Suzuki square-four with Bert Schneider clocking 141.1mph, while Mike Duff's Yamaha was down to 135.3mph. The new 125cc four-cylinder Hondas had a slight edge on the Suzukis, with Redman fastest at 121.6mph and Frank Perris on a Suzuki at 120.8mph. The 50s had got into three figures for the first time; Anderson's Suzuki being the quickest at 103.2mph, followed by Anscheidt's Kreidler 102.0mph and Bryan's Honda 101.1mph. Not surprisingly, Florian Camathias' Gilera led the sidecars at 129.0mph, with Deubel leading the BMW brigade on 121.6mph. Some of the British 'singles' seemed to be going particularly well. Stuart Graham's Matchless was the fastest at 138.5mph, followed by the Nortons of Derek Minter, Jack Ahearn and Peter Darvill all at 136.9mph.

# 1965 Two-stroke consolidation

**BY THE** end of 1965, the two-strokes had established themselves as a force to be reckoned with. Yamaha consolidated its hold on the 250cc Championship, and Suzuki regained the 125cc title. Honda's run of success in the 350cc class was at last challenged with the introduction of the new three-cylinder MV, while in the 500cc class, the old four-cylinder MV remained unchallenged.

In the all-important 250cc class, Phil Read and Yamaha retained the World Championship, with seven wins on the RD56. The 1965 models had been improved, and were now fitted with a handlebar-mounted mixture lever, allowing the riders to enrich the main jet by several sizes, while allowing the slow running mixture to be run sufficiently lean and avoid plug fouling on slow corners; a problem that had plagued the machines in 1964. To underline Yamaha's success, Read's team-mate Canadian Mike Duff was second, and Read and Duff were joined by Bill Ivy as a supporting rider for the TT and the Dutch TT. Despite the success of the RD56, Yamaha decided to bring out the new RD05 V4 for the Italian GP at Monza, somewhat prematurely, and suffered a similar fate to the Honda six in 1964.

Phil Read took the advantage with his early season win in the US GP at Daytona, where Honda had decided not to enter. He followed this with a win in West Germany, from which Redman was absent due to his crash in the 350cc race at the Nürburgring. In the Spanish GP on the tortuous Montjuich Park circuit, Redman was still out of action, but Phil Read came under pressure from Tarquinio Provini on the four-cylinder Benelli, and the two fought it out for several laps until Provini slid off and retired. A well deserved second was Spanish ace Ramon Torras on a Bultaco, ahead of Mike Duff on the second Yamaha. Jim Redman was back in action at the French Grand Prix, on a much-improved version of the six-cylinder 250. He led comfortably until slowed by gearbox problems that eventually caused his retirement, while Phil Read notched up another win.

For the first time the French Grand Prix, won by Phil Read, was being run on the 4.06-mile (6.49km) undulating, tree-lined Les Essarts circuit near Rouen. Laid out on both sides of a valley, the circuit ran downhill through a series of left- and right-hand curves, to its lowest point at the Nouveau Monde hairpin. From here the circuit climbed the other side of the valley, through some tricky corners followed by a three-quarter-mile straight to the right-handed Virage du Gresil curve, which led on to the main Route National for half a mile to a right-handed cobbled hairpin. Finally, the track ran uphill through a very fast right curve on to the finishing straight.

At the TT, Phil Read set the first 250cc over-100mph lap from a standing start, only to retire on the second lap, leaving Redman to win. In the Dutch TT, Read scored another convincing win, with Redman second due to gear change problems. The Belgian GP saw a renewal of the previous year's battles that lasted the entire race, with the lead changing several times per lap. At the all important La Source hairpin on the last lap, hard man Redman refused to be intimidated and held his lead out of the corner to win by a few machines' lengths. In the East German GP it was Jim Redman's turn to score a convincing win by over two minutes from Read's Yamaha. In spite of his hard-fought wins in Belgium and East Germany, Redman had his work cut out. Honda had again cut back on its motorcycle racing programme and, after the Belgian GP, Jim had just one 250cc machine and only Nobby Clark to help him.

Jim was usually at his best when the odds were against him, but for once that slight modicum of luck that even the best rider needs had deserted him. In Czechoslovakia the Honda was seriously out-paced by Read and Duff's Yamahas, and Jim had to settle for third place. In the Ulster he slid off on a patch of oil on the last lap of the 350 race, and was a non-starter in the 250 race; Phil Read won again, consolidating his lead in the Championship. Phil Read had a DNF in Finland and Mike Duff's win on the Yamaha pushed the absent Redman down to third place in the Championship table. At the Italian Grand Prix Yamaha brought out one of the new V4 RD05s for Phil Read. The race was run in very wet conditions, and Provini on the Benelli four went into the lead and pulled away from the two Yamahas to take a well-deserved win. Read's RD05 began to suffer from teething problems, and he was forced to make several pit stops, eventually finishing well down in seventh place, but still retained his Championship lead.

At the beginning of October, it had been announced that Mike Hailwood would be riding a 250 Honda in the Japanese GP. This led to much speculation as to whether he had severed his connection with MV. It was fairly common knowledge that Mike was not very happy at MV, being confined to riding only the five hundred for most of the season. Mike duly won the 250 race in Japan, in which there were only eight starters and five finishers. After the race Mike, was openly critical of the handling of the Honda, and expressed his admiration for Jim Redman's efforts on such a machine. Jim Redman himself was a non-starter, having been stung in the eye by a bee, Phil Read slid off the V4 on the first lap, and Yoshimi Katayama crashed the only Suzuki square-four and broke a collarbone. Deputising for Mike Duff, Bill Ivy was third on a V4 prior to signing a Yamaha works contract for 1966.

### MIKE DUFF

Canadian Mike Duff, from Toronto, began racing in 1955. He arrived in Britain in 1960, where he soon established himself as an accomplished rider while riding for Tom Arter. His efforts were eventually rewarded when he joined the Yamaha team in 1964. While testing the new four-cylinder 250 Yamaha at Suzuka in October 1965, he had a catastrophic crash, coming into contact with the a metal guard rail surrounding the circuit. His injuries included a broken left thigh and a shattered pelvis, keeping him in hospital for several months. He returned to racing at the Dutch TT in 1966, finishing sixth in the 125cc race on one of the works twin-cylinder Yamahas. By now, however, with Bill Ivy firmly established as team-mate to Phil Read, Yamaha had little need for a third rider. A deal was eventually agreed in which Yamaha provided Mike with a 1965 RD56 for the rest of the GP season, on which he had a third in the East German GP, a fourth in Czechoslovakia, and a fifth in Belgium. His request for the loan of bikes for 1967 was turned down by Yamaha, so Mike reverted to the role of 'privateer' riding for Tom Arter once again. Eventually, the less glamorous role of private rider, coupled with the inevitable lack of success and prestige of a factory ride, prompted Mike to end his racing career. Many years later, in the 1980s, Mike went through a period of great emotional and psychological turmoil, that led to a gender change and he became Michelle Ann Duff. Displaying great courage, in 1998 Michelle re-entered the world of motorcycle racing at the Assen historic centennial race meeting, where she rode an RD56 and was reunited with many of her former racing friends, who welcomed her with no trace of prejudice.

---

Suzuki continued to persevere with newer versions of the 250cc square-four, re-numbered RZ65, which had undergone further frame modifications, an increase in power output to 56ps at 12,850rpm, and now came with a choice of either six- or seven-speed gearboxes. Hugh Anderson had refused to ride the machines, but they were ridden by Frank Perris, Australian Jack Ahearn, and newcomer Yoshimi Katayama. Frank Perris was a brave third in the TT, the highest place recorded by the square-four and Katayama came fourth in the Dutch TT and Belgian GP.

Although Jim Redman successfully defended his 350cc title with the much lower, lighter, Honda 2RC172, he was strongly challenged by rising star Giacomo

Agostini, on the new three-cylinder MV, which made its first appearance at the West German GP in April. The long-awaited three-cylinder (52x54mm) 344cc, with its crank throws set at 120 degrees, four valves per cylinder, and a seven-speed gearbox, was producing 62.5bhp at 13,500rpm. A completely new frame had been designed that made the new machine much lower and lighter than the older four-cylinder model.

The 4.8-mile (7.6km) Nürburgring South loop or 'Sudschleife,' previously used for National events, was being used for the first time as a grand prix venue, instead of the famous 14-mile (22km) Nordschleife. Situated roughly in the area covered by the present GP circuit, it had a reputation for being quite tricky. The usual start and finish straight common to both circuits was followed by an intimidating sharp left-hander under a concrete bridge that carried the main road past the 'Ring. Then came a long downhill section with left and right kinks through the pine forest towards the village of Mullenbach and the Mullenbach corner, a demanding right sweep in a dip with a climbing exit. From there the circuit climbed back through some tricky corners over a blind crest to rejoin the main circuit, which ran behind the pits to a right-hand hairpin and back on to the start and finish straight.

Agostini took the new MV3 to a debut win after a battle with Jim Redman's Honda that lasted most of the race. Redman led for several laps, with Agostini on his tail, until the MV went ahead with Agostini pulling away from the Honda. Riding on the limit Jim began to claw back his disadvantage and was closing up on the MV when he went off the road on one of the uphill corners, putting the Honda through a hedge and suffering cuts and bruises, an injured arm and mild concussion.

In the Junior TT, Mike Hailwood, on the new MV3, had the initial advantage and, having caught Redman on the road, the two of them stayed together, with Redman trying hard to shake off the MV. Unfortunately, Hailwood retired shortly after his pit stop at the end of the third lap, handing the lead to Redman. Meanwhile Phil Read on an over-bored 254cc RD56 had moved up to second spot. Redman, however, maintained his pace to win at a record average speed of 100.72mph. Read was second on the Yamaha, and Agostini, in his debut ride in the TT, was third on the other MV3.

On the scratchy Dutch TT circuit, Mike Hailwood, who excelled in such conditions, provided some serious opposition to Jim Redman. For several laps the two raced together, with Hailwood's MV3 taking the lead occasionally. Eventually, the superior speed of the Honda gave Redman a slight advantage, and he gradually pulled away to win, again setting new race and lap records. The 350cc race at the Sachsenring was run in a persistent drizzle under grey skies. Riding brilliantly on the tricky surface, with the MV slipping and sliding under him, Agostini went into the lead, which he gradually increased, while Redman played a waiting game. With three laps to go, the MV went out with a broken valve, handing the race to Redman. At the Czech GP in Brno, Jim Redman scored a convincing win, riding with his usual cool head and refusing to be intimidated by Agostini's attempts to get past. Eventually, Agostini overdid it and slid off, damaging the MV too badly to continue. During the early stages of the Ulster, Jim Redman was seriously challenged by Phil Read on a 254cc Yamaha, and the lead changed several times until the Yamaha went out with gearbox problems. During the wet closing stages of the race, and with a comfortable lead on the last lap, Redman slid off on a slippery patch of road at Leathamstown and broke a collarbone. The race was won by popular Czech veteran Frankie Stastny on the Jawa, with Redman's protégé Bruce Beale on a Honda second, and Stastny's team-mate Havel third.

With Redman out of action, Agostini had an easy win in Finland. Due to a serious and embarrassing organisational error by Honda, Jim Redman missed the crucial round at Monza. He had been told that a machine was not available, but, while he sat at home in Rhodesia, a 350 had, in fact, been flown out to Milan airport for him on the day practice commenced. Agostini duly won again at Monza and, going into the final round in Japan, he needed to win with Redman placed no higher than third to take the 350cc title. Fate, however, played a cruel trick and, while well in the lead, Agostini's MV3 went onto two cylinders, and he was passed by Redman and Mike Hailwood . Realising the situation, Mike went into the lead, to record his final win for MV, while Redman rode steadily to finish second and win his fourth consecutive 350cc Championship, with the unfortunate Agostini eventually finishing fifth. Interestingly, in third place was Honda test rider Isamu Kasuya on an experimental 250cc six-cylinder bored out to 255cc, probably a foretaste of things to come.

Hugh Anderson wrested back the 125cc Championship from Honda, with seven wins from 12 rounds, assisted by team-mates Ernst Degner, Frank Perris, and Yoshimi Katayama. Suzuki had added water cooling to the new RT65, and regained the reliability lost in 1964. The nine-speed models, now with Mikuni carbs, had a power output of 30ps at 14,000rpm. With Honda deciding not to attend the US GP at Daytona, Hugh Anderson took an immediate lead in the Championships, and followed it up with three more wins in West Germany, Spain, and France. In the Isle of Man and the Dutch TT, the Suzukis were outpaced by the new RA75 Yamahas, but Anderson reasserted himself towards the end of the season, with wins in Finland, Italy, and Japan, to clinch the Championship.

Luigi Taveri fought a losing battle against the two-strokes, using an updated version of the previous year's 4RC146. He tried very hard in the TT, catching up with the leader Phil Read on the Yamaha at Creg-ny-baa on the last lap, crossing the line first – with no sign of Read, who eventually appeared with the Yamaha running on one cylinder – to win by less than six seconds. The 125cc Hondas were suffering from serious carburation problems, and, due to disappointing results, were withdrawn and sent back to Japan after the Dutch TT. However, back in Japan, Honda was testing new five-cylinder machines that would be introduced at the end-of-season Japanese GP.

To add to Honda's problems, Yamaha had re-introduced its 125cc twin-cylinder. The new water-cooled RA75-A produced 28ps at 13,000rpm, and was allegedly a mobile test bed for the 250cc V4. Phil Read used it to win the 125 Lightweight TT, and was leading the Dutch TT until his bike went off-song, but his team-mate Mike Duff held off a challenge from the Suzukis of Katayama and Anderson to win. Despite their success, the Yamahas were withdrawn and returned to Japan after the Dutch TT.

There was some consolation for Honda; finally winning the 50cc Championship it had been trying to win since 1962. Its first win came in the West German GP, where Bryans and Taveri were first and second. Bryans was second to Anderson in Spain, but won convincingly in France, with Taveri second. In the TT, damp and blustery conditions greeted the 50cc riders. Mitsuo Itoh on a Suzuki led initially, but had to stop for a plug change, and Taveri took over the lead to win comfortably from Anderson's Suzuki. In the Dutch TT, Bryans had a start-to-finish win from Anderson and Taveri. There was drama on the last lap of the 50cc race in Belgium. Hugh Anderson's chain broke at the final La Source hairpin, but, by paddling as fast as he could, he crossed the line in second place, just ahead of Taveri. Bryans could only finish fifth, and tied for the lead in the Championship with Hugh Anderson on 32 points. At the final round in Japan, Bryans and Taveri on new RC115 twin-cylinder Hondas had a terrific scrap for the lead. Anderson made a tremendous effort and passed both of them, but Bryans re-took the lead. On the last lap, Anderson made a last desperate attempt but fell off in the process and Taveri just pipped Bryans on the line, but Ralph's second place assured him of the Championship, with Taveri second.

The twin-cylinder Honda RC115 had a new short-stroke (34x27.4mm) 49.7cc engine, with four valves per cylinder and a nine-speed gearbox. Power output was quoted as 13ps at 20,000rpm. To improve ground clearance the exhaust system was upswept, and a new, slimmer, light alloy fairing gave the machines a smaller frontal area. Suzuki had doubled up its single-cylinder to a water-cooled twin (32.5x30mm) 49.75cc RK65, with a 12-speed gearbox, producing 14.5ps at 16,000rpm and weighing 128lb (58.4kg). Although Hugh Anderson did his best, with several second places and just one win to his credit, he could finish only third.

Mike Hailwood won his fourth consecutive 500cc Championship on the four-cylinder MV, with eight wins out of ten rounds. His win in the wet and dry Senior TT was particularly noteworthy, with him falling off at Sarah's Cottage on the second lap – at the same spot where his new team-mate Agostini had already fallen. Hailwood picked up his battered MV, kicked the clip-ons back into position and re-started (strictly illegally against the direction of racing) and got it back to the pits where the handlebars were straightened out, then completed the race despite a broken screen and a flattened exhaust system. As usual, the two MVs were followed home at most of the GPs by the 'privateers' on Norton and Matchless. The most consistent being Paddy Driver, who had second places in the Ulster and Finland, and third places in the Dutch TT and East Germany, to take a well-earned third place in the Championship on his Tom Kirby G50. In the Ulster, Irishman and wet weather specialist Dick Creith took advantage of Mike Hailwood's absence and the atrocious weather conditions to win the 500cc race on Joe Ryan's Norton, followed by Paddy Driver, and Chris Conn on his Norton. This was the second successive Ulster win for a Norton, following Phil Read's win in 1964.

As far as the East European contenders were concerned, in the 350cc class it was still the twin-cylinder Jawas of Stastny and Havel consistently finishing behind the Japanese machines. Stastny won the Ulster after Jim Redman crashed out, and Havel had third places in the West German GP, the East German, and the Ulster. The

1965 Jawas were now producing 51bhp at 11,000rpm and had new duplex cradle frames. Riding the 251cc MZ in the 350cc class, Derek Woodman, who had taken Alan Shepherd's place, had two third places in East Germany and in the Ulster. The Russian-built 350cc four-cylinder Vostok also achieved its first podium place when Nikolai Sevostianov finished third in the Czech GP at Brno. MZ had now lifted its travel restrictions and, with Heinz Rosner re-instated as a team member, on the 250cc versions, Woodman and Rosner were able to achieve some podium places, Rosner recording two second places in Finland and the Italian GP, and Woodman was third in the East German. Due to the untimely death of the CZ development rider Stanislaus Malina in a road accident, the 125 and 250cc machines, sometimes incorrectly referred to as Jawas, were ridden by Frankie Stastny and Franta Bocek.

In the sidecar class, Fritz Scheidegger ended the long run of domination by German drivers since 1954. He finally persuaded BMW to provide some support, and, using one of the special short-stroke engines in his ultra-low outfit, he won the Championship with four wins, passengered as usual by John Robinson. Max Deubel and Emil Horner did their best with their conventional outfit, but unfortunately suffered some unreliability that blunted their effort. Third in the Championship was the ever consistent George Auerbacher with passenger Peter Rykers. Chris Vincent had purchased a BMW from Scheidegger and was an excellent second in the Dutch TT.

Sadly, Florian Camathias was still suffering the after-effects of a bad crash at the Avus in August the previous year, in which he suffered head injuries and passenger Herzig lost a leg. Back on the FCS outfit with Franz Ducret as passenger, he had just one win in the French GP at Rouen. His relatively unsuccessful season ended tragically when, during an International meeting at Brands Hatch in October, he crashed at Clearways and died instantly; sidecar racing losing one of its most colourful and spectacular exponents.

**FLORIAN CAMATHIAS**

From Montreux in Switzerland, 41-year-old Camathias was one of the great sidecar racing exponents of the Classic period. He had a fiery and somewhat impetuous driving style, which often led to disaster when victory was within his grasp, thereby considerably shortening what could have been a long list of successes. His name first appeared in the grand prix results at the Swiss GP at Bern in 1954, when he finished fifth on a BMW outfit. In his first TT in 1957 he finished third, and, in the Belgian GP at Spa, he was second, splitting the works BMWs of Schneider and Hillebrand; eventually promoting himself to third place in the World Championships. Having also ridden solos early in his racing career, in 1957 he raced an NSU Sportmax in the TT and the Classic GPs. By the early 1960s, he'd established himself amongst the top GP contenders, and, with his compatriot Fritz Scheidegger, he spearheaded the Swiss challenge to the German supremacy of Max Deubel and Helmut Fath. His career was also unfortunately punctuated by several bad crashes, from which he usually bounced back with undiminished vigour. Undoubtedly, his one and only TT win in 1963 and his seven GP wins are hardly a reflection of his talent as a sidecar driver. Although not officially confirmed, it is thought that his fatal crash at Brands Hatch on 10 October, was caused by steering failure due to a mechanical defect.

---

The annual 'Highlander' speed-trap at TT races in the Isle of Man revealed that, since 1964, speeds had risen only very slightly in some cases. Overall fastest was Jim Redman's 350 Honda at 147.5mph, which was at least 2mph faster than the 500 MVs of Hailwood and Agostini, which recorded 145mph. Jim Redman's Honda six was the fastest 250 at 144.7mph, followed by Woodman's MZ and the RD56 Yamahas of Duff and Read at 143mph. Agostini's new MV three recorded 142.9mph. The new RA75 Yamahas were fastest in the 125cc class with Read recording 125.9mph. Bryans topped the 50cc class on his Honda twin with 103.2mph.

Race-winner Jim Redman flat-out during his race-long battle with Phil Read's Yamaha in the 250cc Dutch TT in 1964. (Courtesy Malcolm Carling)

Phil Read has his RD56 Yamaha well cranked over in his pursuit of Jim Redman in the 1964 Dutch TT. (Courtesy Malcolm Carling)

*Above: Mike Hailwood (MV) on his way to winning the 500cc Dutch TT at Assen in 1964. (Courtesy Malcolm Carling)*

*Alan Shepherd was third in the 1964 250cc World Championship on the MZ. He's shown here in the Belgian GP where he finished third. (Courtesy Malcolm Carling)*

*One of the epic races of 1964, with Redman's 250 Honda mere feet in front of Read's Yamaha in the Dutch TT. (Courtesy Malcolm Carling)*

*A repeat of the 250cc battle in the 1964 Dutch TT, with Redman on a 125 Honda four leading Phil Read on the RA75 Yamaha. (Courtesy Malcolm Carling)*

*The two protagonists, Jim Redman and Phil Read, discussing race tactics (maybe!) in 1964. (Courtesy Malcolm Carling)*

*Phil Read and Tommy Robb with chief mechanic Sekui San at the weigh-in for the Dutch TT in 1964. (Courtesy Malcolm Carling)*

*Looks like a technical discussion between Alan Shepherd and Dr Walter Kaaden in 1964. (Courtesy Malcolm Carling)*

*Colin Seeley and Wally Rawlings (FCS BMW) at Quarter Bridge on their way to second place in the 1964 TT. (Courtesy Malcolm Carling)*

Florian Camathias and Roland Foll with the somewhat ill-fated Gilera outfit in the 1964 TT. (Courtesy Malcolm Carling)

Winner of the 1964 125 Lightweight TT, Luigi Taveri rounds Ramsey hairpin on his Honda four, followed by team-mate Ralph Bryans. (Courtesy Malcolm Carling)

*Ralph Bryans on his twin-cylinder 50cc Honda at Union Mills in the 1964 TT. (Courtesy Malcolm Carling)*

*Isao Morishita (50cc Suzuki) was third in the 1964 TT. (Courtesy Malcolm Carling)*

*Gustav Havel (Jawa) peels off into Creg-ny-Baa in the 1964 Junior TT. (Courtesy Malcolm Carling)*

*Jack Ahearn (Norton), second in the 500cc World Championship in 1964, at Parliament Square in the Senior TT. (Elwyn Roberts Collection)*

*CZ development rider Stanislaus Malina at Quarter Bridge in the 1964 125cc Lightweight TT. (Author collection)*

*German rider Walter Scheimann at Ramsey Hairpin on his CR93 Honda in the 1964 TT. (Courtesy Malcolm Carling)*

*Two Irish riders, two different styles. Ralph Bryans (125 Honda) leading Tommy Robb (Yamaha) in the 1964 Dutch TT. (Author collection)*

Czech veteran and Jawa stalwart Frantisek (Frankie) Stastny in the 1964 Dutch TT. (Courtesy Malcolm Carling)

*Jim Redman's 'protégé' Bruce Beale on a twin-cylinder Honda in the 1964 Dutch TT. (Courtesy Malcolm Carling)*

*Ralph Bryans on a 125cc four-cylinder Honda in the 1964 Dutch TT. (Courtesy Malcolm Carling)*

*Erstwhile Honda works rider Tommy Robb, now on a works Yamaha, in the 1964 Belgian GP. (Courtesy Malcolm Carling)*

*A rare shot of Mike Duff on Tom Arter's 'Porcupine' AJS in the 1964 Belgian GP. (Courtesy Malcolm Carling)*

*Argentinian Benedicto Caldarella made a brave but unsuccessful attempt on the 500cc World Championship on a Gilera in 1964. (Courtesy Malcolm Carling)*

*Ralph Bryans on one of the 125cc four-cylinder Hondas in the 1964 Ulster GP. (Courtesy Malcolm Carling)*

*1964 250 Ulster GP podium. Phil Read, with Jim Redman second and Ralph Bryans third. (Courtesy Malcolm Carling)*

Phil Read also rode a Tom Kirby Matchless in 1964, and was third in the 500cc World Championship. (Courtesy Malcolm Carling)

Regular Continental Circus exponent Jack Findlay on the McIntyre Matchless in the 1964 East German GP. (Elwyn Roberts collection)

Rex Avery did well to finish third in the 1964 Spanish GP on the 125cc De Havilland EMC. (Courtesy Malcolm Carling)

*Mike Duff was one of the riders who rode in four solo classes, seen here on his Matchless in 1964. (Courtesy Malcolm Carling)*

*Gustav Havel (350 Jawa) in the 1964 East German GP at the Sachsenring. (Courtesy Malcolm Carling)*

*Another shot of Ralph Bryans well tucked in on his 125cc Honda four in the 1964 Dutch TT. (Courtesy Malcolm Carling)*

Start of the 125cc Dutch TT 1965. (8) Read, Yamaha; (10) Woodman, MZ; (5) Degner, MZ; (1) Taveri, Honda; (9) Mike Duff, Yamaha. (Courtesy Malcolm Carling)

Giacomo Agostini on the new 350cc three-cylinder MV in the 1965 Dutch TT. (Courtesy Malcolm Carling)

'Old Elbows' Tarquinio Provini in inimitable style on the four-cylinder 250 Benelli in the 1965 French GP at Rouen. (Courtesy Karl-Heinz Reiger)

Mike Duff, winner of the 1965 125 Dutch TT, on his Yamaha. (Courtesy Malcolm Carling)

Renzo Passolini is obviously not superstitious. He was fourth in the 350cc Dutch TT in 1965 on his Aermacchi. (Courtesy Malcolm Carling)

1965 World Champion Fritz Scheidegger and John Robinson drifting their BMW outfit in the Dutch TT. (Courtesy Malcolm Carling)

*Swiss ace Luigi Taveri on the 125cc four-cylinder Honda in the 1964 TT. (Courtesy Luigi Taveri)*

*Pip Harris and Ray Campbell were third in the 1965 Belgian GP at Spa. (Courtesy Malcolm Carling)*

*Max Deubel and Emil Horner with their under-steering BMW, followed by the Scheidegger and Robinson (BMW); Dutch TT 1965. (Author collection)*

Frank Perris was a brave third in the 1965 250cc TT on the 'Whispering Death' square-four Suzuki. (Author collection)

Joe Dunphy, second in the 1965 Senior TT, sweeping into Union Mills on the Beart Norton. (Elwyn Roberts collection)

Derek Woodman justified his place in the MZ team by finishing third in the 125cc World Championship. (Courtesy Malcolm Carling)

Frankie Stastny, who had a surprise win in the 1965 Ulster GP, seen here on his 350 Jawa. (Courtesy Malcolm Carling)

Privateer battle between Derek Minter and John Cooper on Nortons in the 1965 Dutch TT. (Courtesy Malcolm Carling)

Jim Redman and Nobby Clark working on the Honda six in the paddock. (Courtesy Malcolm Carling)

Bruce Beale was fourth in the 1965 350 Championship on Jim Redman's ex-works twin-cylinder Honda. (Courtesy Malcolm Carling)

# 1966
# The four-strokes fight back

**TEMPORARILY, AT** least, the two-strokes took a step backward, while the four-strokes regained their lost advantage, winning four out of the five solo Championships. Honda's anticipated entry into the 500cc class followed the launch of the CB450, the company's first large-capacity production machine. It, therefore, seemed logical that Honda would want to capture the only remaining title it hadn't won so far. In response to this threat from Honda, MV finally pensioned off its ageing four-cylinder, and produced a brand new 500cc machine to defend its eight-year domination of the Championship. The 500cc class at last seemed to regain some of its lost prestige, with the promise of some fierce competition between Honda and MV.

There had been a great deal of speculation about the 500cc Honda. When it did appear, it was almost dull and conventional by the current standards. It followed the proven design of four cylinders across the frame, making it a scaled-up version of the smaller fours. The RC180 as it was called, had a bore and stroke of 57x48mm, giving it a capacity of 489.94cc, with the usual gear-driven twin overhead camshafts and four valves per cylinder. There was a return to wet-sump lubrication, with the usual finned sump under the engine, a six-speed gearbox, and magneto ignition. The semi-duplex cradle frame was similar to that used on the smaller models, with the addition of detachable front downtubes for extra rigidity. The exhaust system had been redesigned for better ground clearance, and the usual long, shallow taper megaphones were angled upwards slightly more than usual, terminating in sharply-angled reverse cones. Power output was quoted as 85ps at 12,000rpm, and the total weight was 337lb (153kg).

The new 500cc three-cylinder MV appeared for the first time at the Dutch TT, as a 350 bored out to 377cc, and later went through a series of updates during the year, being enlarged first to a 420cc, and then approximately (62x54mm) 490cc. In all other respects it resembled the 350cc version from which it was derived, with four valves per cylinder and 120-degree crankshaft, eventually producing 78bhp at 12,000rpm, and weighing only 118kg (260lb). Despite its obvious power disadvantage, the MV's lighter weight and better handling gave it the advantage over the Honda in most situations, making it the perfect grand prix machine. It did, however, have one Achilles heel that it inherited from the four-cylinder models, and that was its fragile valvegear that would not withstand over-revving by even as much as 100rpm without suffering valve failure.

Although Honda had signed Mike Hailwood ostensibly to lead the attack on the 500cc Championship, out of loyalty to Jim Redman, it gave him the choice of being either non-riding team manager or the main contender for the title. However, according to Redman his decision to bid for the 500cc title was purely a private arrangement between him and Mike Hailwood. The 500cc

Championship began at Hockenheim, where Redman took the new Honda to a relatively easy debut win over Agostini, still on one of the older 'fours'. Due to the FIM ruling limiting riders to a maximum of 500 kilometres per day, Hailwood was a non-starter. There was eager anticipation at the Dutch TT, with Agostini on the new MV 3 ready to take on the Hondas of Redman and Hailwood. Redman had the best Honda, while Hailwood was on a makeshift second-string machine, part 350 and part 500. Redman and Agostini led away from the start, while Mike had to make a second attempt to start his bike, but soon got up to third place. The speed of the new MV surprised Jim Redman when Agostini passed him quite easily down one of the straights. Mike Hailwood, however, was in a tigerish mood, and breaking the lap record he caught and passed both Redman and Agostini. Then the gearbox on Mike's Honda began to play up; he missed a gear changing down for a corner, found a false neutral and went off the road into a shallow ditch from which he emerged unscathed, but Jim had been forced into taking avoiding action, losing precious seconds. Riding on the limit, which Jim was quite capable of when the occasion demanded, he clawed himself back to within two seconds of the MV. A sudden shower of rain that had soaked a part of the circuit made the conditions very tricky. It was then the turn of the MV gearbox to play up, allowing Redman to squeeze past, and, during the last five laps, the pair passed and re-passed each other several times. As they started the last lap, Jim had a slender lead that he held to the finish to win by just over two seconds.

There was drama at the Belgian GP. Under a heavily-darkened sky rain began to fall as the race started. Mike, on another 'makeshift' 500, led from Agostini who was back on one of the old four-cylinder MVs, both of them well ahead of Redman. Then came disaster: by now a full scale thunderstorm was in progress, and on the second lap Redman's Honda aquaplaned away from him on the approach to the Burnenville bends and Jim crashed, breaking an arm. Several other riders also fell off on the waterlogged circuit. Despite the conditions Mike had built up a lead of 30 seconds over Agostini, but it was not to be Honda's day. Hailwood suddenly pulled into the pits with a recurrence of the gearbox problems, and had to watch helplessly as Agostini splashed round to an easy win. A furious scrap for second place between Stuart Graham and Gyula Marsovsky on Matchless G50s and Jack Ahearn an a Norton, was eventually won by Graham after a gallant ride.

Agostini now led the Championship, Redman was likely to miss at least the next three rounds, and Hailwood had not yet scored a single point. To add to Honda's problems, the FIM maximum mileage rule often prevented Hailwood from riding in the 250, 350 and 500cc classes. A plan to promote either Ralph Bryans or Luigi Taveri into one of the bigger classes was abandoned, and Stuart Graham was brought in to support Hailwood in the 250cc class. This still left Mike Hailwood with a mountain to climb to win the 500cc Championship, defend the 350cc Championship, and win back the 250cc Championship from Yamaha. In the Moto GP era, when riders confine themselves to just one class, it would be interesting to speculate on how today's riders would cope with having to ride in three long races of 20 laps or more on the same day, on the circuits and under the conditions that existed in the 1960s.

Stuart Graham, from Crewe in Cheshire, was the son of former 500cc World Champion Les Graham. He started racing in 1961 on a 125cc Honda Benly, progressing to a Bill Webster-sponsored Aermacchi. In 1963, Stuart began riding for Liverpool-based sponsor Jim Ball, on Jim Bowen-prepared 7R AJS and G50 Matchless. He had been doing fairly well in his first year as a professional GP rider, with a fourth place in West Germany and a fifth in the Dutch TT on the G50. He had obviously inherited his late father's wet weather riding skills when he won the three-cornered scrap with Marsovsky and Ahearn to finish second in the rain-lashed Belgian GP. It was obviously this performance that led to his temporary inclusion in the Honda team. Despite being thrown in at the deep end on the unfamiliar Honda six, he was fourth in his debut ride in East Germany, and did his best to back-up Mike Hailwood with a second place in another wet race in Finland, and was second again in the Isle of Man. In spite of this he was not retained by Honda for 1967.

The Hailwood/Agostini confrontation commenced at the next round in East Germany. At the height of their battle the Honda broke a crankshaft while Agostini, now well in the lead on a 420cc version, inexplicably continued at undiminished speed, until he made a rare mistake and crashed at over 120mph, wrecking the MV and escaping with just severe bruising. The surprise winner was Czech veteran Frankie Stastny, riding a 442cc version of the twin-cylinder Jawa. In another wet race in Czechoslovakia Hailwood won, with Agostini probably still feeling the effects of his crash at the Sachsenring, settling for a safe second. The positions were reversed in yet another wet race in Finland, when Mike Hailwood was forced to take to the slip road on a corner, letting Agostini through to take the win. By now it seemed very unlikely that Jim Redman would race again in 1966, and, at the Ulster GP, after a couple of practice laps, he announced his retirement. Mike Hailwood won in the Ulster quite comfortably, setting new race and lap records, with Agostini finishing second.

In the TT, postponed until September because of the seaman's strike in June, Gilera made one more attempt to win the Senior TT, and a machine had been prepared for Derek Minter. During practising, after some initial handling problems had been sorted out, the Gilera appeared to be going well. Unfortunately, during the final practice session, Derek Minter, out on a quick lap, arrived at Brandish corner to find out too late that the road was wet after a sudden shower and crashed, injuring an arm, which put him out of the race. In the Senior TT, Mike Hailwood was in determined mood and lapped at over 105mph from a standing start, but Agostini was equally determined to maintain his 12 point lead and matched Hailwood, also with a 105mph lap. Mike maintained his forceful pace and increased his lead to 55 seconds by the end of the fourth lap. As rain began to fall in the Ramsey area, Agostini eased off, deciding to settle for a safe second place, while Mike increased his lead to win by nearly two minutes.

Going into the last round at Monza, Agostini had 34 points to Hailwood's 30, which meant that Mike had to win to take the title. However, even before the race started Honda was in trouble. First, Mike's practice bike blew up and then his race bike did the same. He started the race on an untried bike cobbled together from two machines. The two contenders fought it out for seven laps, until the Honda blew up and Agostini raced on to win the first of his many 500cc titles, while Honda had the consolation of winning the Constructors' title. Privateer Jack Findlay was third in the Championship, with several podium finishes on his Matchless.

Mike Hailwood retained Honda's unbroken run of 350cc Championships, winning six of the ten rounds on the new RC173. This final four-cylinder version had been updated using the same frame as the 500, with the detachable front downtubes, and a box section swinging arm. It also had the new exhaust system, similar to the 500, in which the megaphones were now more upswept and terminated in sharply-angled reverse cones. The power output had also been increased to 70ps at 14,000rpm. Giacomo Agostini was runner-up in the Championship on the three-cylinder MV, with three wins to Hailwood's six. Mike, however, was at the top of his form, and was able to assert his superiority with relatively comfortable wins. Agostini won in East Germany after the usually reliable 350 Honda suffered an engine failure, and won again in the Isle of Man after Hailwood retired on the first lap of the Junior TT. Agostini won the penultimate round at Monza, where Mike, who had already clinched the title, was a non-starter, having decided to concentrate on the 500 race.

For the TT, Benelli had produced a four-cylinder 350 with four valves per cylinder, but unfortunately Provini had a massive crash on it during practice near Alpine Cottage, on the very fast approach to Ballaugh bridge, and suffered serious injuries that led to his retirement from racing. At first it was thought that Provini had been 'blinded' by the September sun, but examination of the Benelli revealed a broken frame, which may or may not have been caused by the accident. Amongst the rest of the contenders, the new 350 Aermacchi was also starting to show its pace, and Renzo Passolini achieved a couple of podium places, including a second at Monza on one of the works machines, finishing third in the Championship table. The evergreen Frankie Stastny and his team-mate Gustav Havel were, as always, consistent finishers in the top six on their twin-cylinder Jawas, and were rewarded with second and third places respectively, in the East German GP at the Sachsenring.

Riding an improved version of the six-cylinder 250, called the RC166, Mike Hailwood won back the 250cc title for Honda with a convincing ten wins from 12 rounds. The new RC166 that was still developing 60ps, had undergone various modifications to strengthen the frame and improve the roadholding. Twin oil coolers had been fitted into the sides of the fairing to cure overheating, and a detachable panel, which joined the two sides of the fairing below the engine, formed an air scoop directing cool air to the sump. Phil Read was runner-up in the Championship on the eight-speed, disc-valve, water-cooled (44x42.5mm) 249cc RD05 V4 Yamaha, reputed to be producing 70ps at 14,000rpm. Although it had an obvious power advantage, the V4 proved to be somewhat unwieldy, compared to the 1965 RD56, and Read and Ivy had difficulty in exploiting its full potential. On Phil Read's recommendation, Bill Ivy had been drafted into the Yamaha team to replace Mike Duff, who had been seriously injured in the aforementioned crash on an RD05 during testing at the Suzuka circuit before the Japanese GP in 1965.

At the first three rounds of the 250cc Championship, Mike Hailwood was virtually unchallenged, with only his team-mate Jim Redman for company. At the Dutch TT, in a wet race, Hailwood romped away to an easy win. Phil Read found the V4 tricky to handle in the prevailing conditions, but was able to keep his Yamaha ahead of Redman to finish second. A surprise entry was former racer Bob Anderson, making a brief return to two wheels, riding a spare V4 Yamaha on which he finished fifth. In Belgium, on the fast Francorchamps circuit that favoured the faster Yamaha, Hailwood and Read raced alongside each other for about seven laps, with the lead changing several times. Although Mike usually had the advantage at the La Source hairpin, Phil used the tremendous acceleration of the Yamaha to retake the lead down to Eau Rouge and up the hill. Then Phil started to experience some bad slides and, on one occasion, nearly took Mike out with him on a fast curve. Eventually, Mike pulled out a slight lead, after Phil was baulked at Eau Rouge by a lapped rider, and drew away to win at a record average speed of 122.33mph, while Phil Read set a new lap record of 124.08mph.

At the Czech GP, Mike Hailwood had to take over Stuart Graham's machine after his own had blown up in practice. The race started in the rain, and, taking advantage of a misfire on the Honda, Phil Read pulled out a slight lead, but Mike was soon back in his slipstream where he stayed until the last lap before scratching past to snatch a last minute victory. Phil Read was a non-starter in Finland after the V4s had been withdrawn, and Stuart Graham finished second to Mike, with Frankie Stastny third on one of the CZs. The Ulster GP round was a complete debacle. Mike Hailwood was a non-starter due to the maximum mileage rule, and Phil Read led the race for a while until one by one the 'works' machines began to drop out. First to go was Rosner's MZ, followed by Graham's Honda and Mike Duff's Yamaha twin, then it was Read's Yamaha. Fred Stevens, having his first ride on an MZ, now led the race, until he too retired. The race was eventually won by New Zealander Ginger Molloy on a 'works' Bultaco, with the Bultacos of Marsovsky and Kevin Cass second and third.

Prospects for the Lightweight TT looked good, with the Honda sixes of Hailwood and Graham opposed by the V4 Yamahas of Read and Ivy. Phil Read took the lead on the road, but Mike Hailwood, who started 40 seconds later, caught him on the mountain descent. The two flashed past the start together, with Read still in front, but at Ginger Hall on the second lap, Read's Yamaha expired with a broken crankshaft. Interest now centred on the battle for second place between Stuart Graham and Bill Ivy, who kept swapping places until Ivy's Yamaha went off-song. Graham was now second when he made his pit stop, but had trouble re-starting the Honda and pushed it all the way to St Ninians crossroads before it fired. Ivy was next into the pits, and lost a lot of time while the Yamaha mechanics looked at the engine and changed some plugs. Graham was now second and, at the end of the next lap, Ivy pulled into the pits again and retired with a broken carburettor mounting. Meanwhile, Mike Hailwood was going like a train and obviously enjoying himself. The two Honda sixes reeled off the last two laps, with Hailwood setting a new race record of 101.79mph, which exceeded Redman's 1965 lap record, and a new lap record of 104.29mph.

Despite Phil Read's valiant effort in the Belgian GP and again in the Czech GP, the V4 Yamaha had failed to win a single race, and the machines were withdrawn from the penultimate round at Monza. Hailwood and Graham had the race to themselves, apart from a brief challenge by Mike Duff on an RD56 Yamaha. Duff dropped back with plug trouble, and Graham retired with gearbox problems. The season came to an unsatisfactory end when the Japanese GP was transferred to the Fisco circuit. Honda withdrew its entries in protest, leaving the Yamahas of Hasegawa, Read and Motohashi to fill the first three places. At the end of the season Mike Hailwood had set an all-time record, winning a total of 19 GPs in three separate classes.

Heinz Rosner and Derek Woodman were able to achieve the occasional podium finish on the 250cc MZs whenever the Japanese machines faltered, while Rosner also rode a 251cc version in the 350cc class, on which he was second in Finland and third in Czechoslovakia. Derek Woodman fell victim to the atrocious wet conditions in the 500cc Belgian GP and crashed his G50 Metisse, breaking a femur. Fred Stevens took his place on the 250 MZ in the Ulster and, at one stage, was leading the race until his engine failed two laps from the finish. The Spanish Bultaco factory scored its first grand prix win when New Zealander Ginger Molloy won the 250 Ulster on one of the works single-cylinder TSS models – the Honda, Yamaha and MZ teams all retired with various mechanical problems. Gyula Marsovsky and Kevin Cass, also on Bultacos, were second and third. Tommy Robb also on a bored-out works 250 Bultaco, exploited his wet weather ability to finish third in the 350 Ulster.

Popular Luigi Taveri fittingly won his third and last World Championship in his final year of grand prix racing, winning back the 125cc Championship for Honda with five wins. The new five-cylinder (35.5x25.14mm) 124.42cc RC149 produced 34ps at 20,500rpm. Since its introduction at the Japanese GP in 1964, all-up weight had been reduced from 109.5kg (241lb) to 85kg (187lb), twin oil coolers had been fitted, and the fifth exhaust pipe now ended on the right-hand side, with its megaphone mounted under the rider's leg. Although undoubtedly very fast, the RC149 was inclined to be very temperamental, suffering from carburation problems that, on several occasions, seriously affected their performance. For a change, Yamaha and not Suzuki was one of the main contenders in the 125cc class, with its RA75-A, water-cooled, disc-valve twin, on which the power output had been increased to 30ps to become the RA97.

Bill Ivy won the first round in Spain for Yamaha. Taveri and Bryans had serious misfiring problems with their Hondas and were only able to finish second and third due to the retirements suffered by the other teams. On the fast Hockenheim circuit, Taveri and Bryans easily outpaced the Yamahas and Suzukis to finish first and second. In the Dutch TT, Ivy and Read on the Yamahas established themselves at the front, though hotly pursued by Taveri, who had an anxious moment when he hit a patch of oil and was forced to take to the grass verge. Despite Read's efforts to hold him up, Taveri eventually passed him and set off after Ivy, but just failed to catch him before the finish. The Swiss rider was in a determined mood at the East German round, and fought his way into the lead, passing the Yamahas of Ivy and Read. Meanwhile, Suzuki rider Yoshimi Katayama, riding brilliantly, engaged Ivy in a battle for second place. Taveri extended his lead with a new lap record to win comfortably, with Katayama a well-deserved second. At Brno in Czechoslovakia, Taveri and Bryans were first and second after a brief challenge by Hugh Anderson on the Suzuki, who dropped back after a stop for a plug change.

There was a dramatic finish to the 125cc race in Finland. Phil Read led from the start, but Taveri worked his way up from fourth and, setting a new lap record, he closed right up on Read as they went into the final corner on the last lap. Using every ounce of acceleration from his five-cylinder Honda, Taveri drew alongside Read's Yamaha and both riders crossed the line together. The timekeepers were unable to separate them, but the FIM jury declared Read the winner. The incident sparked off a controversy, that questioned the validity of a jury decision in such situations and calling for a more accurate photo-finish system. The died-in-the-wool FIM, of course, did nothing about it.

Yamaha had brought two of the new water-cooled 125cc V4s to the Ulster for Read and Ivy. Bill arrived battered and bruised after crashing Tom Kirby's G50 in the Hutchinson 100, but was ordered not to ride by Mr Hasegawa the team manager. Phil Read tried the V4 in practice, but reverted to the twin-cylinder model for the race, with Tommy Robb deputising for Ivy on the second machine. In the race, Phil Read led away from the start, but Luigi Taveri had his sights set on the Championship and passed Read on the second lap. Ralph Bryans, on the other Honda, finally overcame the usual carburation problems and, setting a new lap record, he caught and passed Read to take second place.

At the TT, Bill Ivy was still suffering the aftereffects of his Hutchinson 100 crash, but rode brilliantly to win his first TT and set a new lap record of 98.55mph, despite a couple of minor off-road excursions, including a brush with the stone wall at the Gooseneck that punched a hole in his screen. Phil Read was second, with Hugh Anderson on the first Suzuki in third. The Hondas were more temperamental than usual, putting Taveri and Bryans out of contention, although Mike Hailwood, having a rare 125cc ride, kept going to finish sixth, followed by Bryans and Taveri well down on time.

---

### LUIGI TAVERI

Luigi Taveri, from Samstagern in Switzerland, has had a distinguished racing career that started in 1949. He established his reputation at first riding Velocettes, AJS and Nortons, that included a spell as passenger to sidecar driver Hans Haldeman, before having his first ride for MV at the end of 1954. Over the next three years he proved his worth as a lightweight jockey riding for MV in the 125 and 250cc classes. After leaving MV, he rode for Ducati and MZ, before rejoining MV briefly in 1960. Honda was quick to recognise his talent and, in 1961, he became a full-time Honda team rider in the 125 and 250cc classes. In 1962, he won his first TT on the 125cc Honda, and went on to win his first World Championship with six 125cc GP wins. His 125 Honda was outpaced by the Suzukis in 1963, but Luigi continued to provide good support in the 50cc and 250cc classes as well. Also in 1963, riding one of the 350cc twin-cylinder Hondas, he had several podium places to finish a very worthy third in the 350cc Championship. On the new four-cylinder Honda in 1964, he won back the 125cc Championship, and also won his third TT. In his final grand prix year in 1966, riding the new five-cylinder Honda, he won back his 125cc crown, after which he announced his retirement from grand prix racing.

Very popular with riders and spectators alike, Luigi often showed that, despite his small stature, he was equally at home on larger-capacity machines. With several ex-works machines at his disposal, he continued to race in non-Championship events in 1967, before finally retiring. He did, however, continue to appear regularly in Historic events on his Hondas for several more years.

---

For once Suzuki was unable to match the pace of its rivals in the 125cc class. Despite having a very strong team that included Frank Perris, Ernst Degner, Yoshimi Katayama and newcomer Hans-Georg Anscheidt, the twin-cylinder RT66, which was now producing 32ps, had a relatively unsuccessful year. The only highlights were Katayama's second place in the East German and Hugh Anderson's third place in the TT in an unaccustomed fifth place in the Championship.

A newcomer to the 125cc class was a twin-cylinder, disc-valve, water-cooled, nine-speed Kawasaki. It was ridden by the promising young Japanese rider Toshio Fujii, who had sensationally won the Melano Trophy at the Hutchinson 100 in 1965 on a 50cc works Suzuki. Working alone, with just one machine and no factory back-up, he struggled through most of the season to overcome various mechanical problems. He was befriended by well-known sponsor Peter Chapman, who arranged to have a new frame built for him by Ian Telfer. Further problems during TT practice caused him to miss most of the sessions and, while trying desperately to make up for lost time, he crashed at Cruickshank's corner and received fatal injuries. His efforts had not been in vain, though, because Kawasaki later produced the successful KA-1 based on the machine used by Fujii in 1966. Another newcomer to the 50cc class was the Japanese tyre manufacturer Bridgestone, with a twin-cylinder, disc-valve model turning out 14ps at 16,000rpm. Its regular rider Isao Morishita, a former Suzuki works rider, finished sixth in the Dutch TT, and later in the season the machines were also ridden by Tommy Robb and Jack Findlay.

Having joined Suzuki, Hans-Georg Anscheidt's virtuosity in the 50cc class was at last rewarded with his first World Championship. The power output of his title-winning twin-cylinder, water-cooled, 14-speed RK66 had been increased to 16.5ps at 17,000rpm. With only six rounds in the Championship, Anscheidt's two wins in West Germany and Italy, plus two second places put him just one point ahead of his Honda rivals on aggregate at the end of the season. His win at Monza was particularly impressive, when, after a bad start, he charged through the field and passed the two leading Hondas to win, upping the lap record by an incredible 11mph. Honda's withdrawal from the Japanese GP at Fisco cost it dear, and Anscheidt's win put him two points ahead of Bryans to take the Championship.

The Honda RC116 that first appeared at the Japanese GP in 1965 had undergone further changes. It was now an ultra short-stroke (35.5x25.14mm) 49.77cc with a ten-speed gearbox, and power output had been stepped up to 15ps at 21,000rpm. It also featured a new high-level exhaust system and a new, slimmer, fairing. With only one win to his credit, Ralph Bryans was unable to retain his title, although he did win his first and only TT with a start-to-finish win and a new lap record. Luigi Taveri won the first round in Spain from a fast closing Anscheidt. The two Hondas were really flying at the Dutch TT, and Taveri and Bryans engaged in a private battle at the front of the field, with Taveri eventually taking the win. However, Bryans managed to snatch the runner-up spot in the Championship by just one point from his team-mate Luigi Taveri, when the best four results were counted.

Fritz Scheidegger and John Robinson won the Sidecar Championship convincingly, on their ultra-low kneeler outfit, winning all five rounds. Their win, however, was not confirmed until the end of the year, when Scheidegger appealed against his disqualification after winning the sidecar TT. It was alleged that he had used an unauthorised fuel, when, in fact, he had filled his tank from a public filling station on the way to the start, having already declared that he would not be using the fuel supplied by the ACU. His appeal was upheld and he was reinstated as the winner of the sidecar TT, getting back the eight points that put him two points ahead of Deubel. Max Deubel, with a string of second places, could only finish second in the Championship. At the end of the year he retired to run a restaurant business in his home town of Wiehl. Colin Seeley and Wally Rawlings were third in the Championship with their BMW outfit, on the strength of their second place in the French GP at Clermont Ferrand. Since his accident at the Nürburgring in 1961, Helmut Fath had been quietly working on the design and development of his own four-cylinder engine with which to make his comeback. The URS, named after Fath's home town of Ursenbach, made its debut at the West German GP, but suffered various problems during the season that frequently caused its retirement.

## FRITZ SCHEIDEGGER

Tall, bespectacled, and looking more like an academic than a motorcycle racer, 36-year-old Fritz Scheidegger was a motor engineer and garage proprietor in his home town of Courtelay in Switzerland. He started racing BSA machines in 1953, on which he won both the solo and sidecar Swiss Championships. He then acquired a BMW outfit with which he made his grand prix debut in 1957, and won his first grand prix at Clermont Ferrand in 1959 with passenger Horst Burkhardt. He finally won his first World title in 1965, and retained it in 1966 with regular passenger John Robinson. Fritz was one of the great innovators, helping to revolutionise the future design of racing sidecar outfits with his very low slung 'kneeler' outfits. He had a reputation for doing most of his preparation in the paddock just prior to a race, and his outfits often looked scruffy and unfinished, with much evidence of recent welding and fabrication. Tragically, it may well have been such last-minute preparation that led to the mechanical failure that caused his fatal accident at Mallory Park in March 1967, when his brakes failed on the approach to Shaw's hairpin.

Once again we are indebted to the NSA 'Highlander' speed trap in the Isle of Man, for some indication of the top speeds of some of the machines. The 150mph barrier was finally broken, with Hailwood's 500 Honda and Agostini's 420 MV both recording 151.3mph. Fastest 350 was Agostini's MV3 at 142.9mph, which proved to be slower than the 250 RD05 Yamaha of Bill Ivy, which recorded 149.1mph, making it the third fastest machine. Hailwood's Honda six recorded 145.2mph. Ralph Bryan's five-cylinder Honda topped the 125cc class with 128.1mph, only marginally faster than Ivy's Yamaha, which clocked 127.2mph. Bryans also topped the 50cc class with his Honda at 103.5mph, followed by Degner's Suzuki, which recorded 102mph. Amongst some of the other works machines, Rosner's 250 MZ recorded 132.4mph, Pagani's 350 Aermacchi 125.4mph, and Stastny's 440cc Jawa 140.1mph. Peter Williams' Arter Matchless and Selwyn Griffiths' Ray Cowles Matchless both went through the trap at 129.9mph.

# 1967 Hailwood & Agostini

**THIS WAS** the last year of the battle of the giants, at the end of which things started to gradually go downhill as another ten-year cycle drew to a close. Technical development had reached a peak in both the four- and two-stroke fields, while the cost of financing this development and demonstrating it on the tracks was beginning to take its toll. The Honda versus MV confrontation in the 350cc and 500cc classes was renewed, as was the Honda versus Yamaha battle in the 250cc class. The 50cc and 125cc classes were now almost exclusively two-stroke dominated.

Giacomo Agostini retained his 500cc title, and MV also won the Constructor's Championship. Clearly, the 490cc three-cylinder, which eventually became (approximately 62x55mm) 497cc, remained basically unchanged from the previous year, and was by far the more suitable tool for the job. In spite of giving away around 5hp to the Honda, Agostini was able to exploit its better roadholding and power-to-weight ratio to stay in contention with the Honda throughout the season. Without wishing to detract in any way from Agostini's performance, his task was made that much easier by the frequent DNFs suffered by Hailwood. Despite Mike's valiant efforts, mechanical problems, particularly with the gearbox, and handling problems combined to make his task of wresting the 500cc title away from Agostini almost impossible.

The Honda RC181 had been enlarged to 499cc by increasing the bore from 57mm to 57.56mm, with the benefit of a slight increase in power output. Other modifications were the use of magnesium engine castings, twin fairing-mounted oil coolers as on the six-cylinder 250, and a much neater and lighter exhaust system, with shorter megaphones without the pronounced reverse cones. Ceriani-type front forks carried a front wheel with a massive 248mm double-sided front brake. The wheel spindle mounting incorporated an eccentric adjustment to allow minor alterations to the steering geometry. It was the frame, however, that lacked any significant change in design. The steering head area had been heavily triangulated, although the detachable front downtubes were abandoned. During the course of the season, strengthening gussets and triangulation were added at various points on the frame in a vain attempt to cure the problem; but such piecemeal efforts failed to achieve any significant improvement in the handling. In fact, Mike referred to it as the bike he most hated to ride. In desperation, he got permission from Honda for Colin Lyster to design a new frame, which he tried out in practice at the West German GP, but Honda later changed its mind and vetoed the project.

The Hailwood/Agostini encounter kicked off at the West German GP. It was an inauspicious start for Hailwood, who retired when in the lead, handing the race to Agostini who took a crucial lead in the Championship. Next came the Senior TT, which produced one of the most dramatic and epic battles in the history of the TT races. A brief account of the race would, therefore, seem appropriate.

Agostini led for the first four laps and pulled out a lead of 12.6 seconds. Hailwood, meanwhile, was struggling with a Honda that could be seen snaking and weaving alarmingly as he pushed it beyond the limit in his efforts to stay in contention. In addition, he was having problems with a loose twist grip, that a stop at the pits failed to cure. However, by a superhuman effort, on the fifth lap he led the MV by a mere one second at Ramsey. With the tactical advantage of being second on the road, Agostini responded to signals at Ramsey to retake the lead at the Bungalow by 2.5 seconds, but a couple of miles later the MV broke its rear chain. Bitterly disappointed and in tears, Agostini free-wheeled back to the start. Unaware of the drama, Hailwood started his last lap and, when he stopped out on the circuit to fix the loose twist grip, a spectator informed him that Agostini was out and he was able to cruise round safely to win. As a result of Agostini's retirement, Peter Williams on the Arter Matchless inherited second place with two laps at over 101mph. Steve Spencer on the Lancefield Norton was third and also lapped at over 100mph. Mike Hailwood later admitted that he would not have won if Agostini had kept going. During the course of his fifth lap, Mike set a new lap record of 108.77mph, which stood until 1975 when it was broken by Mick Grant on a 750cc Kawasaki.

Mike Hailwood excelled on riders' circuits, such as Assen, where he demonstrated his supreme ability to win the 500cc race after another hard fought battle with Agostini. In the Belgian GP on the fast Spa Francorchamps circuit, which favoured the much faster Honda, Agostini shocked the Honda camp with a convincing win over Hailwood and a new lap record at 128.58mph (206.92km/h). At the East German GP, Agostini won while Hailwood retired with more gearbox problems. In Czechoslovakia, Hailwood at last recorded another win to reduce the Championship deficit to six points, while Agostini took a tactical second place. The weather for the Finnish GP was pretty awful, making the narrow, bumpy Imatra circuit very tricky. Agostini led from the start, followed by John Hartle on Ray Cowles' Matchless. Mike Hailwood made a bad start and had just got up to third place when the Honda aquaplaned away from him on a corner and demolished itself against one of the many trees lining the circuit, while Mike slid after it narrowly missing the trees himself. John Hartle was a gallant second to Agostini, with his second runner-up place in the series.

The Ulster GP turned out to be a damp squib, after Agostini retired on the first lap with clutch trouble, leaving Hailwood to win easily. John Hartle was second again on the Matchless, just ahead of Jack Findlay on his McIntyre Matchless and John Blanchard, giving the Fath/Seeley four-cylinder URS it's grand prix debut. The final dramatic moments in Honda's ill fated attempt to win the 500cc Riders Championship, were played out under untypically grey skies at Monza in Italy. Agostini led the Championship with 44 points to Hailwood's 38. Hailwood had to win to take the Championship, even if Agostini finished second. Unfortunately for Hailwood, though, with a comfortable lead and only four laps to go, the Honda gearbox problem re-occurred, Agostini took the lead and went on to win with Mike second. Understandably bitterly disappointed at being thwarted for the second year running, at the finish Hailwood abandoned his Honda against the pit wall and walked away in disgust, while the Honda team mechanics looked visibly upset. It was with some reluctance that Mike eventually took his place on the podium. The gloomy wintry conditions for the final round at Mosport Park in Canada probably reflected Mike Hailwood's mood. With Agostini needing to finish no higher than sixth, Hailwood's only chance lay in a hollow victory through Agostini's retirement; something that he would have hated. Inevitably, Mike won, and Agostini took another tactical second place to clinch the Championship. Although they both had 46 points each when the best six results were counted, Agostini was declared the winner with three second places to Hailwood's two.

Further down the Championship table, John Hartle's remarkable performance on his Ray Cowles-sponsored Matchless, with three second places in the East German, Finnish and Ulster GPs, gave him a well-deserved third place in the Championship. Another notable rider was Peter Williams – fourth in the Championship on the Arter Matchless – who was second in the West German GP and the Senior TT, and third in the Dutch TT. One of two new machines to appear among the top six at the GPs was the twin-cylinder, Bill Hannah-sponsored Paton of Fred Stevens, who was third in the Belgian GP. The other machine was the first solo version of Helmut Fath's URS in a Colin Seeley-built frame, on which John Blanchard finished fourth in the Ulster GP.

Mike Hailwood's 350cc Championship win was achieved relatively easily. His new six-cylinder Honda proving to be more than a match for Agostini's three-cylinder MV, winning six out of eight rounds. The RC174 Honda was not, as has often been described, simply a bored-out 250. In fact, it had a completely different bore and stroke, 41x37.5mm, giving it a capacity fractionally over 297cc. In all other respects, including a seven-speed gearbox, it was almost identical to the smaller 250. Its power output of 65ps at 17,000rpm was less than the previous year's four-cylinder version, but being smaller and lighter 118kg (260lb) gave it a distinct advantage over its rivals, in spite of giving away

50cc. This machine became a favourite of Hailwood's, and with it he lapped some circuits quicker than most 500cc machines. In fact, his Junior TT lap record of 107.73mph, was only just over 1mph slower than his Senior lap record on the 500cc Honda.

Agostini was runner-up in the 350cc Championship with a string of second places on the three-cylinder MV. His only win was in the Ulster, when Mike, who had already clinched the Championship, stood down to concentrate on the 500cc race. Deputizing for Hailwood, Ralph Bryans, using his circuit knowledge to good advantage, pushed Agostini very hard until a miss-fire on the Honda forced him to drop back and finish second. In the Italian GP, Ralph walked away to a record-breaking win, leaving Agostini and Renzo Passolini on the four-cylinder Benelli, trailing in his wake until they both blew up their engines trying to keep up. His second place in the final round in Japan earned him third place in the Championship.

## RALPH BRYANS

Belfast-born Ralph Bryans started racing in 1959 at the age of 17. He forged his career on the Irish road circuits, riding for such people as the legendary Joe Ryan. After a particularly noteworthy performance in the 1963 Ulster GP, he was offered a Honda contract for 1964, to ride in the 50cc class of the World Championships. He narrowly failed in his bid, although he and winner Hugh Anderson both won four GPs each. He eventually won the title in 1965, and during the '65 and '66 seasons he provided solid support for his team-mate Luigi Taveri in the 125cc class. In 1967, Ralph had the onerous task of being the sole supporting rider to Mike Hailwood in the 250 and 350cc classes. However, he rose to the challenge admirably, with what were undoubtedly the two best rides of his career, winning the 250cc West German GP from Phil Read and Bill Ivy, and in the Italian GP at Monza he won the 350 race and put up a courageous fight in the 250cc race in which he consistently out-rode the Yamahas of Read and Ivy, only losing out on sheer straight-line speed in the final dash for the line by mere fractions of a second.

---

Renzo Passolini had taken Provini's place on the four-cylinder Benelli, now painted in the company's traditional silver and green colours. The (51x42mm) 343cc 16-valve engine produced 64bhp at 13,800rpm, which Provini put to good use with a couple of fine third places behind Hailwood and Agostini, particularly at the Dutch TT where he strongly challenged Agostini for second place. For MZ, Heinz Rosner and Derek Woodman scored several podium places on the over-bored 250s, including a second place by Rosner in Czechoslovakia.

Despite the immense pressure on him, Mike Hailwood retained the 250cc Championship for Honda. It was no easy task, and the final outcome was not even decided after the final round. The power output of the RC166 Honda had been increased slightly to 63ps, and apart from some minor frame modifications it was basically the same as the previous year's model. The Honda lacked some of its previous reliability, probably stemming from over-development of the six-cylinder engine. Ironically, the 1966 version of the RC166 ridden by Ralph Bryans, proved to be initially more successful than the 1967 model. In fact, halfway through the season, Bryans held second place in the Championship with 33 points, while Hailwood was down in fourth place with 26.

Mike had a puncture in the Spanish GP and an unspecified engine problem in the West German that gave Phil Read the initial advantage, but Ralph Bryans kept the Honda flag flying with a second place in Spain and a win at in West Germany. In fact, Ralph was lucky to win at Hockenheim. He took the lead after Phil Read stopped for a plug change, but Phil then began a relentless charge through the field. Urged on by Mike Hailwood from the pits, Ralph Bryans pressed on as hard as he could, eventually winning by just over four seconds from the rapidly-closing Phil Read. Mike Hailwood scored his first win of the season at the TT, when he responded to an early challenge by Phil Read to eventually win comfortably. At the Sachsenring Hailwood and Read engaged in another battle royal, with Hailwood making up on the twisty sections what he was losing out to the Read's faster Yamaha on the long straights, until the Honda blew up with a broken valve. At this stage Hailwood had only 26 points to Read's 34. The Yamahas were really flying at Brno in Czechoslovakia, where Read and Ivy just streaked away to win easily from Hailwood and Bryans. Despite his earlier crash in the 500cc race in Finland, Mike was determined to make amends, and, after passing Read's Yamaha on the first lap and riding in determined fashion on the soaking wet roads, he pulled away to win comfortably. Phil Read eventually retired with waterlogged ignition and Bill Ivy inherited second spot.

For once the Ulster GP was enjoying good weather, and, from the start of the 250 race, the two Hondas and the two Yamahas immediately engaged in battle. In determined mood Read led at the end of the first lap, but as they came down to the hairpin for the second time, Read left his braking too late, locked his front wheel and went down in front of Hailwood, who had to ride around man and machine, narrowly missing the straw bales. Phil Read tried to re-start but the Yamaha was un-rideable. Bill Ivy took up the chase of Hailwood's Honda, to which Mike replied by setting a new lap record. Ralph Bryans moved up into second place when Ivy's Yamaha slowed, and the race finished in that order. Mike Hailwood's win gave him a two point lead with 46 points to Read's 44 from a possible maximum of 56, and with three more rounds to go the title could go either way. At Monza the two Yamahas were once again dominant, with the two Hondas trying desperately to keep in touch until Hailwood's Honda blew up. Ralph Bryans took up the chase and, with probably the most brilliant ride of his career, put up a courageous fight against the Yamahas of Read and Ivy, consistently out-riding them on the corners to take the lead several times, only to lose out on sheer speed in the final dash for the finish by mere fractions of a second.

After the penultimate round of the 250cc Championship in Canada, won by Mike Hailwood, Phil Read had 56 points and Mike had 54, but taking their seven best results into account they both tied with 50 points each. The final round in Japan was expected to be the tie-breaker, but both Hailwood and Read failed to finish and an incredible situation arose. If the best eight results were counted Read was the winner with 56 points to Hailwood's 54, but on the basis of wins, the title should have gone to Hailwood who had five wins to Read's four. A public controversy raged for a while until the FIM Autumn congress. When the rules that had originally been drafted in French were translated, Mike Hailwood was officially declared 250cc World Champion.

The 1967 250cc RD05A Yamaha was producing 70ps at 15,000rpm, but both Honda and Yamaha suffered from mechanical problems throughout the season, which ruled out a repeat of the Hailwood/Read battles of 1966. This was reflected in the fact that the two rivals finished together in the same race only four times in the 13-round series. While Yamaha had its share of mechanical failures, its main problem was trying to harness the power of the V4 into a rideable chassis. In spite of a weight reduction and various frame modifications, including provision for rake adjustment on the steering head, the machines proved difficult to handle, particularly on bumpy circuits. The addition of lead weights to the front of the machine to improve weight distribution did little to improve matters, making life difficult for Phil Read and Bill Ivy.

Yamaha took over the 125cc class from Suzuki, and Bill Ivy and Phil Read dominated the Championship, finishing first and second at most rounds, with Ivy winning eight out of 12 races to take the title. Although it had tested the mini V4 RA31 in 1966, Yamaha had decided to stick with the proven twin-cylinder, water-cooled, eight-speed RA97 that was now turning out 35ps at 15,000rpm. Hugh Anderson had retired from racing, and former Honda teamster Stuart Graham joined Hans-Georg Anscheidt and Yoshimi Katayama in the Suzuki team, riding the twin-cylinder, water-cooled RT67, which now had ten speeds and was turning out 35ps at 14,000rpm. Stuart Graham fought gamely to take several second places, and won the very wet Finnish GP, a testimony to his wet weather ability no doubt inherited from his father, the late Les Graham, winner of the 1949 500cc World Championship and a well-known wet weather exponent. Yoshimi Katayama's win in the West German GP was the only other Suzuki success. Kawasaki had entrusted its KA1, an eight-speed, disc-valve, water-cooled twin to Dave Simmonds, who demonstrated its potential with a third place in Finland and some other places in the top six.

Suzuki completely dominated the 50cc class, with Hans-Georg Anscheidt winning his second consecutive Championship, with Katayama and Graham second and third. The updated Suzuki RK67 twin-cylinder, water-cooled, 14-speeder was turning out 17.5ps at 17,300rpm. Stuart Graham won his first and only TT, and Katayama had two wins in the French GP and the Dutch TT. The Suzukis were usually chased home by the Spanish Derbis of Australian Barry Smith and future Spanish 50cc Champion Angel Nieto, who recorded his first GP podium finish placing second in the Dutch TT.

In the sidecar class, a new German Champion emerged to take Max Deubel's place. Former solo cum sidecar racer Klaus Enders had made his GP debut in 1966 with a fourth place in the Belgian GP on his Dieter Busch-prepared sleek, low BMW outfit. In 1967, with passenger Ralf Engelhard, he won his first GP at Hockenheim, and went on to win the Championship with four more wins. Sadly, reigning World Champion Fritz Scheidegger was missing from the lists, having lost his life in the previously mentioned crash at Mallory Park early in May. Enders' closest rivals were George Auerbacher, who had two wins in the Spanish and Italian rounds, and Siegfried 'Siggi' Schauzu, who won in the Isle of Man, both using works engines. British pair Tony Wakefield and passenger Graham Milton were fourth in the Championship on their BMW outfit, with a couple of podium places in West Germany and France. Helmut Fath's new URS outfit re-appeared and showed considerable promise, but once again the engine suffered some serious problems and it rarely finished a race.

*TT winner Mike Hailwood on the glorious-sounding 250cc six-cylinder Honda at Quarter Bridge in the 1966 TT. (Author collection)*

*A brand new Honda six was flown out for Stuart Graham who was second in the 1966 250 Lightweight TT. (Author collection)*

*Mike Hailwood cranks the RC180 500cc Honda four around Quarter Bridge en route to winning the 1966 Senior TT. (Author collection)*

*Ralph Bryans at Quarter Bridge on the RC149 five-cylinder Honda in the 1966 125 TT. (Author collection)*

*1966 125cc World Champion Luigi Taveri on the five-cylinder Honda in the Spanish GP. (Courtesy Luigi Taveri)*

*1966 World Champion Fritz Scheidegger and John Robinson at Ramsey Hairpin in the TT. (Author collection)*

*Ulster GP 1966. 125cc winner Luigi Taveri with Ralph Bryans (second) and Phil Read (third). (Author collection)*

Derek Woodman was second in the 1966 Spanish GP on the 250cc MZ. (Courtesy Malcolm Carling)

Fred Stevens deputising for the injured Derek Woodman, on a 250 MZ in 1966. (Courtesy Malcolm Carling)

Renzo Passolini on a 350 works Aermacchi in the 1966 East German GP. (Elwyn Roberts collection)

500cc German GP at Hockenheim in 1967, with Mike Hailwood (Honda) already ahead of his rivals, including Williams, Fitton, Agostini and Stevens. (Courtesy Malcolm Carling)

Swiss/Hungarian Gyula Marsovsky rounds Creg-ny-Baa on his Matchless in the 1967 Senior TT. (Author collection)

John Hartle, a remarkable third in the 1967 World Championships, on Ray Cowles' Matchless. (Elwyn Roberts collection)

1967 Sidecar World Champions Klaus Enders and passenger Ralf Engelhardt (BMW) in the German GP at Hockenheim. (Courtesy Karl-Heinz Reiger)

# 1968
# Read & Ivy

**THE YEAR** began amidst 'alarums and excursions'. At the 1967 Autumn Congress the FIM decided that, as from the end of 1968, 50cc machines would be restricted to one cylinder, 125 and 250cc machines to two cylinders, and 350cc and 500cc machines to four cylinders. All classes would be restricted to no more than six-speed gearboxes. This was in response to the FIM's view that the proliferation of increasingly complex and expensive-to-develop machines was totally unrelated to ordinary motorcycles. As a result, further shockwaves hit grand prix racing. Early in the year, Honda announced that it was withdrawing from World Championship motorcycle racing.

Suzuki, too, had decided to withdraw in view of the impending FIM restrictions, although it did make the 1967 machines available to Hans-Georg Anscheidt. Only Yamaha decided to continue racing up to the end of 1968 with its current machines, while most of the other manufacturers in the 350 and 500cc classes remained relatively unaffected by the new regulations. Once again it seemed that the World Championships were about to experience another ten year decline, having come back, full circle to a similar situation to 1958, with the two premier classes reverting to a one-make domination by MV.

One of the major rider casualties of this situation was Mike Hailwood, who had decided to accept a Honda deal to continue racing the 1967 works machines on a private basis, provided they weren't ridden in any World Championship events. Giacomo Agostini duly reigned supreme in the 350 and 500cc classes on the three-cylinder MVs, and, in a remarkable display of consistency and reliability, he won every single round in both classes; a total of 17 GPs, including the Junior and Senior TTs.

John Hartle had been due to ride MVs in the TT, but crashed the works Triumph in the preceding Production race and had to sit out the Junior TT. He started in the Senior TT on the MV, but crashed again at Cronk-ny-Mona, and suffered injuries that put him out of action for some time.

Following Agostini home was the usual array of Nortons and Matchless, with the odd Linto thrown in. Most successful was Jack Findlay on his McIntyre Matchless with a string of second places in Spain, Holland, Belgium, Czechoslovakia and Finland, to claim second place in the Championship. Third in the title standings was Swiss Hungarian Gyula Marsovsky on his Matchless, while Rob Fitton's second place in the Ulster earned him fourth place ahead of Alberto Pagani's Linto.

Benelli had also reintroduced its 491cc four-cylinder, which was now a (54x54mm) 494cc, at the Italian GP in September, where two models had been prepared for Mike Hailwood and Passolini. Hailwood had originally arranged a one-off ride on the MVs, but fell out with Count Agusta on being ordered to let Agostini win both races. In the very wet race, Hailwood slid off and retired, while Passolini rode a steady race to finish second.

### JACK FINDLAY

Thirty-three-year-old Australian Jack Findlay, from Mooroopna in Victoria, started racing in Australia in 1955, and came to Europe in 1958 as a relative unknown, but soon became one of the professional Continental Circus riders. From the early 1960s he was based in France and rode under a French licence. In 1963, he acquired the ex-Bob McIntyre Matchless G50 special, which he renamed the 'McIntyre Matchless,' and on it over the next few years, he became one of the more successful 'privateers' in the Classic GPs. He had a bad year in 1967, during which he was injured in two separate crashes, but still managed two podium places, in the East German GP and the Ulster GP. His luck changed in 1968 when he had second places in the Spanish, Dutch, Belgian, Czechoslovakian and Finnish rounds, to finish second in the Championship. During 1969, Jack was the subject of a film by French director Jérôme Laperrousaz, called *Continental Circus*, which followed his exploits during the grand prix season. Ironically, and in marked contrast to 1968, the 1969 season proved to be fairly disastrous for Jack who suffered several crashes. The excellent film, however, faithfully captured the highs and the lows, the drama and the tragedy of grand prix racing.

With Honda and Suzuki out of the picture, the 125 and 250cc Championships were dominated by the V4 Yamahas ridden by Phil Read and Bill Ivy. The 125cc water-cooled, disc-valve V4 RA31A finally made its grand prix appearance, and was claimed to be producing 44ps at 18,000rpm, while the previous year's RD05A remained basically unchanged. Problems within the team arose when Yamaha decreed that Ivy was to win both classes, but later relented to let Read win the 125cc and Ivy the 250. This led to some serious rivalry between the two riders that eventually escalated into a bitter personal feud. At one stage the FIM stepped in amidst allegations of team orders by Yamaha, while the media had a field day publicizing the feud. The on-track rivalry also produced some fierce battles between the two riders, during which at times they were in danger of taking each other out.

At first things mostly went according to plan until the first signs of dissent began at the TT. Bill Ivy won the 250cc race, in response to alleged 'mind games' played by Phil Read before the start. Then came the 125cc race, when a determined Bill Ivy hurled the little V4 Yamaha round the TT course to take the lead after setting a new lap record at an incredible 100.32mph. He then stopped on the last lap to cheekily ask some spectators who was winning, before continuing at a slower pace to let Read win as per team orders. Incidentally Ivy's lap was the first over 100mph by a 125cc machine and remained unbroken until 1989. At the Dutch TT they raced together for the full 17 laps of the 250 race with Ivy inching ahead to take the win on the line. In the 125 race Ivy retired and Read won. There was no 125cc race in Belgium where Read won the 250 race and Ivy retired. At the East German GP team orders prevailed; Read won the 125 and Ivy the 250.

The rivalry between the two riders finally exploded out into the open at the Czech GP. By now it seemed fairly certain that Yamaha would pull out of racing at the end of the year. Read therefore felt he had nothing to lose and with the 250cc title still attainable he decided to go for it. After winning the 125 race and clinching the Championship, just before the start of the 250 race, Read informed Ivy of his intention to win against team orders. Read led from the start and ignoring slow down signals from his pit he raced on to win and Ivy was second. A furious row erupted after the race in which Ivy accused Read of not keeping to the agreement. This happened in full view of the press, who heard it all and predictably gave the situation maximum publicity. The matter also came to the attention of the FIM who threatened to take action if it could be proved that at any time previously or in the future, the riders had deliberately fixed the race between themselves.

With three more rounds left in the 250 World Championships, Ivy had 38 points and Read 36, with the six best results to be counted. Read won in Finland after Ivy fell off in the very wet race. In the Ulster, Ivy won and Read retired with a holed radiator. At the crucial final round in Italy the pair fought it out at close quarters for three laps until Ivy tried to pass Read at the 'Parabolica' curve, took to the grass and almost fell off. His machine then went off-song, and Read won. An unusual situation then arose. Both riders had a maximum score of 52 points, reduced to 46 points when the six best results were counted, they also had an equal number of wins and second places. The FIM then decided to add their race times from the four events in which they finished together, the title being awarded to the rider with the fastest time. With a time of 2m 05.3s faster, Phil Read was finally declared 250cc World Champion. As anticipated, early in the new year Yamaha announced that it was withdrawing from racing, and Read and Ivy were told their services would not be required.

The situation in the 250 and 350cc classes in 1968 was now far more open, with many previously out-paced machines emerging from the shadows cast by the MV and Honda domination. Although he was never seriously challenged, Agostini's nearest rival was, once again, Renzo Passolini on the 350cc Benelli four, who was second in the Championship with second places in West Germany, the TT, and the Italian GP. The gear-driven double overhead cam, 16-valve Benelli had a bore and stroke of 52x40.6mm, and was turning out 64bhp at 13,800rpm. Third in the 350cc Championship was Kel Carruthers on his private Aermacchi with a loaned works engine. He was second in the Ulster Grand Prix and third in East Germany. MZ and Bultaco, too, began to enjoy some success in the 350cc class. Riding a 251 and later a 300cc MZ, Heinz Rosner had two second places in East Germany and Czechoslovakia to finish fourth in the Championship. Bultaco had produced a 350cc version of the TSS for works rider Ginger Molloy, who had a second place in the Dutch TT and was fifth in the Championship. The 350 Aermacchi was proving a popular alternative to the older Nortons and Ajays amongst the 'Privateers,' the highest placed British machine being Billie Nelson's Norton in tenth place. The new V4 two-stroke Jawa made a promising debut, ridden to third place in the Czech GP at Brno by the evergreen Frankie Stastny.

Heinz Rosner went one better to finish third in the 250cc Championship on the MZ. The water-cooled engine now had one-piece cylinder heads and barrels, and the power had been increased to 54bhp at 11,500rpm, with no loss of reliability – Rosner was consistently in the first three during the season, including second places in the Spanish, Belgian, Finnish, and Ulster GPs. Dr Kaaden had experimented with a three-cylinder 125cc in 1967, but this was abandoned due to the new regulations. The 1968 125cc MZs were, therefore, basically unchanged, and, once again, Rosner and Gunter Bartusch achieved podium places behind the Yamahas of Read and Ivy, in the absence of Suzuki and Honda.

A sign of things to come in the 250cc class was the appearance of Rod Gould with his production Yamaha TD1C engine mounted in a Bultaco frame – on which he was fourth in the Championship with third places in Belgium, Finland and Ireland. The Spanish Bultacos were also able to achieve some promising results with the 250cc water-cooled TSS, on which works rider Ginger Molloy was second in the West German and third in the Spanish event. On the 125cc version he was also second in Spain and second in the Dutch TT. A newcomer to the 250cc class was the single-cylinder, air-cooled, two-stroke Spanish Ossa ridden by Santiago Herrero. The 249cc disc-valve engine developed by Eduardo Giro had a bore and stroke of 70x65mm, transistorised ignition, 42mm Dell'Orto carb, a six-speed gearbox driving through a dry clutch, and was developing around 40bhp at 11,000rpm. Lubrication was by fuel/oil mixture with an auxiliary feed direct to the big-end and main bearings. The huge finned engine unit was attached to a welded box-section aluminium monocoque frame that carried both fuel and oil.

With the exception of Hans-Georg Anscheidt who won his second World Championship on an ex-works Suzuki, the 50cc class was dominated by the Dutch and Spanish machines. Paul Lodewijkx was second on a Jamathi, and Australian Barry Smith won the TT and was third in the Championship on a Derbi. Future 50cc multiple World Champion Angel Nieto was fourth on a Derbi, but his Championship effort was blunted by a crash at Barregarrow in the Isle of Man, and he never rode there again.

### SIDECARS

In the sidecar class, Helmut Fath's painstaking five-year development of his four-cylinder URS finally paid off, and, after recording his first grand prix win since his accident in 1961, on the very same Nürburgring south circuit. Passengered by Wolfgang Kalauch, he went on to take the title, the first by a rider/constructor, with two more wins in Finland and West Germany. The URS engine was a double overhead cam, inline four-cylinder, with a bore and stroke of 60x44mm giving it a capacity of 498cc. Power output of the fuel-injected engine was estimated at well in excess of 70bhp at 13,000rpm. Second in the Championship was popular Georg Auerbacher with Hermann Hahn in the chair, and third was Siggi Schauzu with Horst Schneider.

---

### HELMUT FATH

Helmut Fath was a brilliant engineer, as well as a tenacious sidecar driver. He started racing in 1950 with a BMW outfit, making his grand prix debut in 1958 when he finished third in the Championship. Finding his standard Rennsport outfit uncompetitive against the works machines of Walter Schneider, during the winter of 1959/60 he converted his engine to a short-stroke unit fitted with his own fuel-injection system. He won his first and only TT in 1960 and went on to take the World title with four GP wins. In 1961 he won the first GP in Spain, but was involved in a tragic crash at a national meeting on the Nürburgring south circuit, in which he was seriously injured, and his passenger Alfred

Wohlgemuth was killed. He was absent from the racing scene over the next five years, during which he designed and built the four-cylinder URS engine, named after the first three letters of his home town of Ursenbach, in the Black Forest region of Germany. His first race with the URS outfit was at Hockenheim in 1966, but over the next two years the URS was plagued with teething problems and unreliability. It all came together in 1968 when he won the opening round of the Championship at the same Nürburgring south circuit, and went on to take the World title with two more wins, with new passenger Wolfgang Kalauch. In 1969, he looked set to retain his title with three wins, but disaster struck when he crashed at a minor meeting in Finland, badly breaking a leg, and had to miss the final round.

Fath retired from racing, and his engines and equipment were taken over by Friedl Munch and raced by Horst Owesle, who won the sidecar Championship in 1971 on what was basically a Fath URS. In the meantime, Fath had turned 'tuner,' and prepared the 250 Yamaha on which Phil Read won the World Championship in 1971. He also designed and built a new 500cc water-cooled, flat-four, disc-valve two-stroke. In 1974, the new flat-four appeared in solo form with Billie Nelson as development rider. Unfortunately, Billie Nelson was killed at Optija in Yugoslavia, and the flat-four engine was later used in the ARO sidecar outfits raced by Siggi Schauzu and Helmut Schilling in 1976 and Werner Schwartzel in 1977. In 1979, Fath finally gave up the struggle of trying to be a successful private manufacturer, and died in 1993 after a short illness.

---

Surprisingly, Klaus Enders and Ralf Engelhardt had a poor year and could only finish sixth in the Championship with their works BMW. In the TT, while well in the lead, Enders' engine failed on the last lap, allowing Siggi Schauzu to score his first TT win. Early leader in the Sidecar Championship had been the relative newcomer, German (BMW) driver Johann Attenberger, with second place in the TT and a split-second win over Enders in the Dutch TT. In the Belgian GP at Spa, after early leaders Fath, Enders and Schauzu had all retired with mechanical problems, Attenberger and Georg Auerbacher found themselves battling for the lead. Exiting the very fast right-handed Burnenville bends on the last lap, Attenberger, who was leading, lost control, probably after clipping the kerb, causing the outfit and its occupants to literally fly off the road at high speed. Attenberger and passenger Josef Schillinger were flung out and killed instantly, while Auerbacher who had witnessed the incident from close quarters, crossed the finishing line in tears. It had been a sad end to a promising career.

# 1969
# The end of an era

**ONCE AGAIN** the World Championships seemed to have come full circle to where they had been at the end of 1957. Prospects did not seem too good following the withdrawal of the Japanese 'big three,' with their exotic, technically-complex machines. The 350 and 500cc classes had reverted to a one-make domination by MV, while the 50, 125 and 250cc classes were now open to a greater variety of mainly Continental makes.

Agostini duly took his second 350/500 double World Championship on the three-cylinder MVs, winning 18 grands prix in the process. The only serious but all too brief challenge to Agostini's MVs came from the new 350cc Jawa, ridden by Bill Ivy. The type 673, water-cooled, disc-valve two-stroke was a 90-degree V4 (50x44mm) 345.6cc, producing 52bhp at 13,000rpm, and was still very much in the experimental stage. It also had a reputation for seizing and had already inflicted injury on several riders, including Frankie Stastny. Jawa was, therefore, without a regular rider.

At the end of 1968, Bill Ivy had decided to quit motorcycle racing and later bought an ex-works Brabham with the intention of racing in Formula Two in 1969. However, after a visit to the Jawa factory early in the year, he signed up to ride the new V4 Jawa, with the intention of mixing his motorcycle racing with Formula Two. In his first ride on the Jawa in the Spanish GP he retired with a seized engine, but in the West German GP at Hockenheim he finished a good second, with team-mate Frankie Stastny third. It was at the Dutch TT that Bill really challenged Agostini, taking an early lead, only to have one cylinder cut out, causing him to drop back to second. Suddenly, the faulty cylinder chimed in, Bill fought his way back to the front and even began to pull away from the MV. With the race almost won, the Jawa went back onto three cylinders, Agostini regained the lead and went on to win. It had been a typically heroic ride by Bill, which had driven the massive crowd wild with excitement.

Two weeks later on July the 12th, tragedy struck at the Sachsenring in the former East Germany. On his first practice lap on a rather treacherous damp circuit, while taking a fast left-hand curve, the Jawa seized, throwing Bill off into an unprotected wall. In spite of the machine's fearsome reputation, Silvio Grassetti took over the Jawa for the rest of the season and achieved some commendable results, including a second place in the Italian GP at Imola, and recording the Jawa's one and only GP win, at Opatija in Yugoslavia.

### BILL IVY

27-year-old Bill Ivy, or 'Little Bill' as he was affectionately known, was well loved and admired for his indomitable spirit and his cheerful, fun loving, and sometimes cocky personality. He started racing on a 50cc Itom in 1959, progressing to a 125cc and eventually to 350 and 500 and 650cc machines. Despite his small stature, Bill was exceptionally strong and quite fearless. He once floored an overzealous Belgian policeman who had tried to evict him from the pit area at the Spa Francorchamps circuit. His 'giant killing' acts in the early 1960s on Tom Kirby's 7R and G50, against such established stars as Derek Minter and John Cooper, had endeared him to race fans in the UK. His decision to quit motorcycle racing and race Formula Two cars in 1969 was mainly prompted by the aftermath of the feud with Phil Read. In his Formula Two races he had displayed exceptional talent that was recognised by many motor racing experts and drivers. In spite of having to mix both car and motorcycle racing, he approached his rides on the Jawa with his usual full-blooded commitment. Following his death, the stunned disbelief by thousands of racing enthusiasts all over the world was testimony to his popularity. The actual cause of his accident remains a mystery, despite many theories and witness accounts. The most plausible explanation being that Bill had taken his left hand off the handlebar to adjust his helmet strap that had worked loose, just at the precise moment when the engine seized. Being unable to reach the clutch lever in time, the rear wheel locked and the machine went down throwing Bill off. His helmet came off and he suffered serious head and chest injuries to which he succumbed in hospital.

---

The absence of any serious oriental opposition to MV in the 500cc class did throw the spotlight on some new machines that moved in to fill the other podium places. The most successful of these being the Linto that first appeared in 1968 when it was ridden in the GPs by Alberto Pagani, who finished second in the East German GP. Designed by Lino Tonti who had been responsible for the twin-cylinder Bianchi, the heart of the twin-cylinder Linto was a specially-designed crankshaft-cum-crankcase assembly with geared primary drive and a six-speed gearbox. The rest of the engine consisted of two 250cc Aermacchi cylinder heads, barrels, con rods and pistons, giving the machine a capacity of 497cc. Like the Aermacchi, the engine was mounted horizontally, with the cylinders facing forwards. The 1969 machines were reputed to be producing 64bhp at 10,000rpm, and a total of 15 are thought to have been built.

Regular Continental Circus exponent Swiss Hungarian Gyula Marsovsky had changed his faithful G50 Matchless for a Linto, on which he was second in the 500cc Championship, with a second place in the Czech GP, plus some consistent top six places, but crashed late in the season while riding in the Freiburg Hillclimb and was seriously injured. Another Linto, ridden by works development rider Alberto Pagani, won the Italian GP in the absence of Agostini. Some of the other Linto riders were Jack Findlay, Johnny Dodds, Steve Ellis, Keith Turner, and Walter Scheimann. For most of its other riders, however, the Linto proved to be a disappointment, and though undoubtedly fast, with a maximum speed of 160mph (256km/h) plus, it suffered from chronic unreliability caused by primary drive gear failure, broken pistons, ignition problems, and frame breakages.

Another Italian contender for the runner-up spot behind the MV was the twin-cylinder Paton, which achieved more consistent results than the Linto due to its better reliability. Designed and built by ex-Mondial race shop chief Giuseppe Pattoni, the first twin-cylinder Paton had made its appearance as a 250 in 1963, followed by a 350cc version in 1966. Sponsored by Liverpool-based car dealer Bill Hannah, 350 and 500cc Patons were ridden in the World Championships in 1967 by Fred Stevens. Billie Nelson took over from Fred Stevens in 1968, and, in 1969, he finished fourth in the World Championships, with second places in the French, East German and Finnish GPs. The 1969 500cc Paton followed Pattoni's original concept as a gear-driven, double overhead cam parallel twin, with cylinder dimensions of (73.5x57mm) giving it a capacity of just under 484cc. It had the trademark 180-degree crankshaft, wet-sump lubrication, a six-speed gearbox, and produced around 65bhp.

Helmut Fath's solo URS also made a brief reappearance in the World Championships in 1969. The 500cc four-cylinder engine was mounted in a Rickman Metisse frame and ridden by veteran Karl Hoppe, who, in his only GP ride for the year, finished second in the West German at Hockenheim. Aermacchi also entered the 500cc class, with a (80x80mm) 402cc machine, ridden by Gilberto Milani who finished second in the Italian GP at Imola, splitting the Linto's of Pagani and Dodds.

One other interesting new machine in the 350cc class was the V4 CZ 860GP that appeared at the Czech GP in Brno. Designed by Frantisek Pudil, the four-stroke, 90-degree V4 had a bore and stroke of (50x44mm), gear-driven overhead camshafts, and four valves per cylinder. The dry-sump engine had an eight-speed gearbox, dry clutch, 28mm Dell'Orto carburettors, and produced 53bhp at 16,000rpm. The unusual frame had duplex top tubes, from which a semi-cradle arrangement extended halfway down on each side, to which the engine was attached, acting as part of the frame. The engine was mounted in line with the rear cylinders, inclined backwards at 10 degrees. Ceriani forks and double-sided brakes were used. The bike was ridden by development rider Bohumil Stasa, who was sixth in Czechoslovakia and fourth in Yugoslavia.

Some of the British machines also did rather well in the 500cc class, with a return to some podium finishes behind the lone MV of Agostini. Alan Barnett was second in the Senior TT on Tom Kirby's Matchless Metisse, and Peter Williams was second in the Dutch TT on the Arter Matchless. In the Belgian GP, with Agostini well out in front on his own, interest centred on the battle for the runner-up spot between Percy Tait on the works Triumph Daytona and Alan Barnett on the Kirby Metisse; Tait winning after Barnett's bike went off-song during the final stages. Promising young Irishman Brian Steenson was a well-earned second in the Ulster on his G50 Seeley, and in the end of season Yugoslav GP, Godfrey Nash scored the last ever grand prix win by a Manx Norton, which, together with a third place in the Finnish GP, hoisted him up to third place in the Championship.

Back in 1962, Yamaha had started producing the TD series of 250cc 'production' racers as a Clubman's machine for private riders. This had been gradually improved and updated over the years. In 1969, the company introduced the vastly improved 250cc TD2, as well as a new 350cc TR2, both suitable for grand prix competition. Both models had twin-cylinder, air-cooled, piston-ported engines, with five-speed gearboxes, mounted in RD56-type frames. The (56x50mm) 247cc TD2 produced 44ps at 10,500rpm, and the (61x59.6mm) 348cc TR2, 54ps at 9500rpm. With the V4s now retired, and four-cylinder machines outlawed from 1970 by the new regulations, the new twin-cylinder Yamahas were set to take over the 250 and 350cc classes. Even the previously successful 350 Aermacchis found themselves outclassed by the TR2 Yamahas, despite some good early season results by Kel Carruthers on a works short-stroke 350.

For 1969, Rod Gould and Swedish rider Kent Andersson had the new 250cc TD2 Yamahas. Kent Andersson gave the TD2 its first grand prix win in the German GP at Hockenheim, and, with another win in the Finnish GP, and several podium places, he went on to finish second in the World Championships. Rod Gould also had several podium finishes, including second places in France, Belgium and Czechoslovakia. Phil Read, who rode a works 250 Benelli in the TT, did not do a full GP season but scored a double 250/350 to win the Italian GP at Imola in September, on his private TD2 and TR2 Yamahas. The new 350cc TR2 Yamaha also proved to be popular with several riders, including Rod Gould, Jack Findlay, Walter Scheimann, and Italian Giuseppe Vicenzi all switching to two-stroke power. Runner-up in the 350cc Championship was Silvio Grassetti, who started the season with a TR2 Yamaha before bravely switching to the temperamental V4 Jawa, on which he was second in the Italian GP at Imola, and gave the V4 Jawa its first and only grand prix win at Opatija in Yugoslavia. Giuseppe Vicenzi scored a couple of podium places on his Yamaha to finish third in the Championship.

However, it was the 250cc Ossa of Santiago Herrero that posed the biggest threat to the new Yamahas. The single-cylinder, disc-valve machine, that now had Ceriani forks and four leading-shoe Ceriani front brake, weighed only 220lb (99.6kg) and produced 42bhp. Herrero won the first round at Jarama in Spain, and again at Le Mans in France. In only his second TT, he finished third to lead the Championship by three points from Kent Andersson. In Belgium, he had a race-long battle with Rod Gould's Yamaha, on the ultra-fast Spa Francorchamps circuit that favoured the faster Yamaha, to win by mere fractions of a second. In Finland, he tangled with a backmarker and crashed, but remounted to finish sixth. Then disaster struck in the Ulster GP, when he crashed at Wheeler's corner and broke his left arm. With his arm still in plaster he finished a brave fifth in the penultimate round at Imola.

Going into the last round in Yugoslavia, Herrero's arm was still in plaster when he arrived at Opatija, and he led the Championship by one point from Kel Carruthers on the Benelli and Kent Andersson on the Yamaha in joint second place. Benelli had recruited Gilberto Parlotti to help Carruthers, and the two of them were able to exert pressure on the game Spanish rider. Herrero led initially, and was obviously trying very hard to stay in front, but was caught out by the damp track and crashed, handing the race and the Championship to Carruthers.

Blond haired Spaniard Santiago 'Santi' Herrero must surely be regarded as the first of the Spanish superstars, forerunner of Jorge Lorenzo and Danni Pedrosa who would emerge a couple of decades later to dominate Moto GP. If not for his tragic death in 1970 at the age of 27, and given competitive machines, he may well have established Spanish talent in the premier classes much earlier. Born in Madrid in 1943, he started racing in 1963 on a 50cc Derbi, and was soon snapped up by the Spanish Lube factory. On the 125cc Lube he began winning National events, and finished second in the Spanish Championships in 1965. In 1966 he was engaged by Eduardo Giro to ride the 250 Ossa in the National Championships, which he won. In his GP debut on the Ossa in the 1968 Spanish GP, he led the V4 Yamahas of Ivy and Read for several laps before retiring with mechanical problems.

Regarded by many as a very stylish rider, Herrero had developed his neat, tucked-in style from his 50cc racing days. His single-handed effort against the Yamahas in 1969 must be regarded as one of the most outstanding performances in GP racing. His battle against the Yamahas was resumed in 1970, with the little Ossa now developing nearly 50bhp. In trying to offset the Yamahas' speed advantage in the French GP, he tried too hard and crashed. Picking up his battered machine, he set off in pursuit of the leaders and, in a super-human effort, fought his way back up to second place behind Rod Gould, but had to be content with second place.

He won in Yugoslavia, with Andersson and Gould second and third, to take the lead in the Championship by two points going into the TT. Here, however, the odds were stacked even further against him, in a field made up almost entirely of Yamahas. Lying only fifth in the early stages of the race, and pushing hard, he had to take to the slip road at Braddan Bridge and dropped the Ossa, breaking the screen. Starting the last lap, he'd fought his way up to third place as he approached the fast but tricky double left-hander at the 13th milestone before Kirkmichael. The Ossa hit a patch of wet tar that caused a wobble and a slide from which Herrero was unable to recover and he crashed heavily. Stan Woods who was not far behind also crashed trying to avoid man and machine. Herrero was airlifted to hospital, but had sustained serious head and internal injuries to which he succumbed two days later. The brave Spanish rider in the red and white crash helmet with the white shamrock would be seen no more. Neither would the incredible single-cylinder Ossa, as the company withdrew from racing following Herrero's death.

Perhaps sensing that this was its best opportunity, Benelli had decided to give the 250cc Championship its best shot, and succeeded. For 1969 it produced two versions of the four-cylinder, one had a new 16-valve cylinder head, said to be turning out 64bhp at 14,400rpm. The four-valve version proved to be just as fast, and both models had an eight-speed gearbox. When Renzo Passolini dropped out due to injuries, Australian Kel Carruthers and Phil Read were taken on for the Lightweight TT, which Carruthers won. With Passolini still out of action, Benelli retained Carruthers, who had podium finishes in Holland and Belgium, won the Ulster, and finished second in the penultimate round at Imola, which put him one point behind Championship leader Herrero. Carruthers eventually won the final round in Yugoslavia to win the Championship. This proved to be the last 250cc World Championship to be won by a four-stroke for the foreseeable future.

The 125cc Championship was won by Dave Simmonds on the works development Kawasaki, which he had campaigned since 1967. The eight-speed (43x42.6mm) twin-cylinder, disc-valve KA-1 was producing 30ps at 15,000rpm. This was not, however, a factory-backed effort in the accepted sense, and, during the season, Dave had to overcome numerous mechanical problems by himself, with a very limited supply of spares. In spite of the presence of some formidable opposition, including Dieter Braun on an ex-works RT67 Suzuki, Dave amazingly won eight of the 11 rounds to take one of the most well-deserved Championship wins, in what had been essentially a single-handed effort.

Quiet, polite and well spoken, Dave was a qualified electrical engineer who started racing on a 50cc Itom in 1960. Over the next few years he raced 50 and 125cc Tohatsu and 250cc CR72 and 305cc CR77 Hondas with considerable success on British circuits, winning the ACU British 250cc Championship in 1965. In the late 1960s he turned professional grand prix racer and later married Julie Boddice, daughter of Bill Boddice of the well-known sidecar racing dynasty. Sadly, at the age of 32, he lost his life in a tragic accident in October 1972, when in a typical act of friendship he tried to put out a fire in Jack Findlay's caravan in the paddock at the Rungis circuit hear Paris.

Following the departure of the complex twin-cylinder Japanese machines outlawed by the new FIM regulations, the 50cc class became dominated by European makes. The Dutch seemed to have a penchant for the 50cc class, and seemed to have an uncanny ability to extract remarkable performance from tiny two-stroke, single-cylinder engines. They also produced several talented 50cc World Championship riders, such as Aalt Toersen, Paul Lodewijkx, and Jan DeVries.

Foremost among the Dutch machines were the former German Kreidlers, now run by the Dutch concessionaire Van Veen, who gradually developed the superb, diminutive, water-cooled, disc-valve machines, which were eventually turning out about 17bhp. The engines were mounted in lightweight semi-duplex frames, with Ceriani-type forks, and small, Fontana, double-sided, two leading-shoe brakes. The Spanish, too, were not far behind the Dutch when it came to producing quick 50cc racing machines, and over the next decade the 50cc class was dominated by the Dutch Van Veen Kreidlers and the Spanish Derbi.

Diminutive Spanish rider Angel Nieto, whose name was to become synonymous with 50cc grand prix racing over the next decade, won the 1969 Championship on the Spanish water-cooled, disc-valve Derbi, after a season-long battle with Dutchman Aalt Toersen on a Kreidler. The two riders ended the season on equal points and, despite the fact that Toersen had won three races to Nieto's two, the title went to the Spaniard on a technicality.

## SIDECARS

With Klaus Enders back on form, the Sidecar Championship developed into a battle between him and Helmut Fath with the URS. Enders/Engelhardt won the first round at Hockenheim, Fath/Kalauch won in France, Enders finally won his first TT, and Fath finished third behind Siggi Schauzu. Fath won in Holland, and Enders failed to score any points. In Belgium, Fath scored a convincing win over Enders to take the lead in the Championship. The unfortunate Fath suffered another DNF in Finland while leading the race, and Enders won to take a two point lead in the Championship. Then, disaster struck; while riding in a minor meeting near Helsinki, Fath crashed and broke a leg, as did his passenger Billie Nelson. With Fath out of action, Enders won the Ulster GP comfortably to clinch the Championship, while Fath had to be content with the runner-up spot.

*Bill Ivy on a 125cc V4 Yamaha in the 1968 Czech GP at Brno. (Courtesy Franz Besendorfer)*

*Giacomo Agostini (MV), winner of the 500cc German GP Nürburgring South in 1968. (Courtesy Franz Besendorfer)*

Hans-Georg Anscheidt on an ex-works 125cc Suzuki in the 1968 German GP. (Courtesy Franz Besendorfer)

Helmut Fath made a brilliant comeback to win the 1968 World Championship. Seen here with Wolfgang Kalauch in the German GP. (Courtesy Franz Besendorfer)

George Auerbacher and passenger Helmut Hahn with their BMW in the 1968 German GP. (Courtesy Franz Besendorfer)

Arsenius Butscher and passenger Josef Huber with their BMW in 1968. (Courtesy Karl-Gunter Peters)

*Kel Carruthers on a Drixton Aermacchi in the 1968 German GP. (Courtesy Franz Besendorfer)*

*Frank Perris on a TR250 Suzuki in the 1968 Lightweight TT. (Courtesy Franz Besendorfer)*

A typical 1960s road circuit at Brno in Czechoslovakia, with Phil Read leading Heinz Rosner and Bill Ivy in 1968. (Courtesy Franz Besendorfer)

Start of the 500cc GP at Monza in 1968, with Agostini (MV) alongside Hailwood and Passolini on the Benellis. (Courtesy Franz Besendorfer)

Angelo Bergamonti on a Hannah Paton in the 1968 500cc Spanish GP. (Courtesy Franz Besendorfer)

Heinz Rosner (MZ) at the Gooseneck, in the 1968 Junior TT. (Author collection)

*Bill Ivy on the ill-fated 350cc V4 Jawa in the 1969 German GP at Hockenheim. (Courtesy Franz Besendorfer)*

*1969 125cc World Champion Dave Simmonds on the Kawasaki. (Courtesy Franz Besendorfer)*

Giacomo Agostini (MV) at Quarter Bridge in the 1969 Junior TT. (Author collection)

Winner of the 1969 250 Lightweight TT, Kel Carruthers (Benelli), at Parliament Square, Ramsey. (Elwyn Roberts collection)

1969 Sidecar TT winners Klaus Enders (BMW) and Ralf Endelhardt exiting Governor's Bridge. (Courtesy Franz Besendorfer)

Spanish 50cc ace Angel Nieto (Derbi) won his first World Championship in 1969. (Courtesy Franz Besendorfer)

Georg Aubacher and passenger Herman Hahn (BMW) in the 1969 TT. (Courtesy Franz Besendorfer)

*Helmut Fath and passenger Wolfgang Kalauch with the URS in the 1969 TT. (Courtesy Franz Besendorfer)*

*Phil Read on a 250 works Benelli in the 1969 Lightweight TT. (Courtesy Franz Besendorfer)*

*Rod Gould leading on one of the new TD2 Yamahas that would eventually dominate the 250cc class. (Courtesy Franz Besendorfer)*

*1969 350 German GP. Bohumil Stasa (CZ) leads Ginger Molloy (Bultaco), Gilberto Milani (Aermacchi), Karel Bojer (CZ), and Dave Simmonds (Kawasaki). (Courtesy Franz Besendorfer)*

*Billie Nelson on the 500cc Hannah Paton in the 1969 German GP. (Courtesy Franz Besendorfer)*

*Karl Hoppe (Fath URS) and Jack Findlay (Linto) were second and third in the 1969 German GP. (Courtesy Franz Besendorfer)*

*Dieter Braun on an ex-works 125 Suzuki in the 1969 Dutch TT. (Courtesy Franz Besendorfer)*

*The main 50cc Protagonists in 1969. L-R Rudi Kunz (Kreidler), Angel Nieto (Derbi), Paul Lodewijkx (Jamathi), Jan DeVries (Kreidler) and Barry Smith (Derbi). (Courtesy Franz Besendorfer)*

*Spanish hero Santiago Herrero on his 250 Ossa. Circa 1969. (Courtesy Franz Besendorfer)*

*Czech Bohumil Stasa (350 V4 CZ) in the 1969 German GP at Hockenheim. (Courtesy Franz Besendorfer)*

*Santiago Herrero also rode a 50cc Derbi in 1969. (Courtesy Franz Besendorfer)*

*Russians Nikolai Sevostiano (2) and Endel Kiisa with the 500cc four-cylinder at the Sachsenring in 1969. (Courtesy Karl-Heinz Reiger)*

*Alan Barnett (Kirby Metisse) finished second in the 1969 Senior TT. (Elwyn Roberts collection)*

*Kel Carruthers (Benelli) and Dave Simmonds (Kawasaki) start the 1969 250cc TT. (Courtesy Franz Besendorfer)*

# Epilogue

**AS THE** 1960s came to a close, the withdrawal of the technically complex machines brought to an end one of the most unique and exciting periods in the history of motorcycle grand prix racing. The entire nature of World Championship grand prix racing was set to change significantly over the coming decades. The rapid growth of two-stroke technology would see the evolution of new machines in all categories, and the eventual demise of the four-strokes. Although MV Augusta held out for a few more years, mainly in the 500cc class, it too eventually succumbed to the two-strokes, with the introduction of the YZR500 Yamaha in 1973. The steady development of the increasingly popular Yamaha twin-cylinder TD2 and TR2 production racers unfortunately led to what can only be described as 'one-make racing' in the 250 and 350cc classes, which became almost 100 per cent Yamaha. In 1976, Giacomo Agostini recorded the last grand prix win by a four-stroke for decades to come, when he won the 350cc Dutch TT on an MV. It would take another 25 years and a major change in the FIM regulations before four-stroke machines finally made a successful return to grand prix racing in 2002.

The mainly American-led safety lobby eventually saw the demise of many of the old traditional circuits, with the move towards newer, safer, purpose-built circuits. The arrival of the American riders in grand prix racing in the late 1970s, with their much more professional approach, helped to raise the standard of grand prix racing. The relaxation of advertising constraints opened the door to lucrative sponsorship deals. Riders also began to receive previously undreamed of retaining fees, and the cost of racing rose astronomically. The vast sums of money being invested inevitably led to excesses. However, the status of motorcycle grand prix in general reached new highs in keeping with the times, to eventually become Moto GP as we know it today.

**Chris Pereira**

# Grand Prix results 1960-1969

*Winning speed and best lap speed provided for each event*

## 1960 125CC

| TT Races Isle of Man June 13 | | Dutch TT Assen June 25 | | Belgian GP Spa Francorchamps July 3 | |
|---|---|---|---|---|---|
| 1 C Ubbiali (MV)<br>2 G Hocking (MV)<br>3 L Taveri (MV)<br>4 J Hempleman (MZ)<br>5 RHF Anderson (MZ)<br>6 N Taniguchi (Honda)<br>Record lap – C Ubbiali (MV) | 85.60mph<br>(137.75km/h)<br><br><br><br><br>86.13mph<br>(138.61km/h) | 1 C Ubbiali (MV)<br>2 G Hocking (MV)<br>3 A Gandossi (MZ)<br>4 J Redman (Honda)<br>5 E Degner (MZ<br>6 G Suzuki (Honda)<br>Fastest lap – C Ubbiali (MV) | 76.30mph<br>(122.79km/h)<br><br><br><br><br>78.34mph<br>(126.65km/h) | 1 E Degner (MZ)<br>2 J Hempleman (MZ)<br>3 C Ubbiali (MV)<br>4 B Spaggiari (MV)<br>5 G Hocking (MV)<br>6 M Hailwood (Ducati)<br>Fastest lap – Hempleman & Spaggiari | 100.32mph<br>(161.54km/h<br><br><br><br><br>101.97mph<br>(164.11km/h) |
| **Ulster GP Dundrod August 6** | | **Italian GP Monza September 11** | | | |
| 1 C Ubbiali (MV)<br>2 G Hocking (MV)<br>3 E Degner (MZ)<br>4 B Spaggiari (MV)<br>5 L Taveri (MV)<br>6 J Hempleman (MZ)<br>Record lap – E Degner (MZ) | 83.38mph<br>(134.18km/h)<br>Record<br><br><br><br>85.67mph<br>(137.88km/h) | 1 C Ubbiali (MV)<br>2 B Spaggiari (MV)<br>3 E Degner (MZ)<br>4 J Redman (Honda)<br>5 G Hocking (MV)<br>6 K Takahashi (Honda)<br>Fastest lap – B Spaggiari (MV) | 97.76mph<br>(155.82km/h)<br><br><br><br><br>99.48mph<br>(160.09km/h) | | |

## 1960 250CC

| TT Races Isle of Man June 13 | | Dutch TT Assen June 25 | | Belgian GP Spa Francorchamps July 3 | |
|---|---|---|---|---|---|
| 1 G Hocking (MV)<br>2 C Ubbiali (MV)<br>3 T Provini (Morini)<br>4 RN Brown (Honda)<br>5 M Kitano (Honda)<br>6 N Taniguchi (Honda)<br>Record lap – C Ubbiali | 93.64mph<br>(150.69km/h)<br><br><br><br><br>95.51mph<br>(153.69km/h) | 1 C Ubbiali (MV)<br>2 G Hocking (MV)<br>3 L Taveri (MV)<br>4 J Hempleman (MZ)<br>5 M Hailwood (Mondial)<br>6 E Degner (MZ)<br>Record lap – T Provini (Morini) | 82.90mph<br>(133.42km/h)<br>Record<br><br><br><br>85.53mph<br>(137.63km/h) | 1 C Ubbiali (MV)<br>2 G Hocking (MV)<br>3 L Taveri (MV)<br>4 M Hailwood (Ducati)<br>5 A Pagani (Aermacchi)<br>6 G Beer (Adler)<br>Record lap – C Ubbiali (MV) | 113.53mph<br>(182.71km/h)<br>Record<br><br><br><br>115.19mph<br>(185.39km/h) |
| **German GP Solitude July 24** | | **Ulster GP Dundrod August 6** | | **Italian GP Monza September 11** | |
| 1 G Hocking (MV)<br>2 C Ubbiali (MV)<br>3 K Tanaka (Honda)<br>4 RH Dale (MZ)<br>5 L Taveri (MV)<br>6 K Takahashi (Honda)<br>Record lap – G Hocking (MV) | 90.54mph<br>(147.70km/h)<br>Record<br><br><br><br>94.58mph<br>(152.34km/h) | 1 C Ubbiali (MV)<br>2 T Phillis (Honda)<br>3 J Redman (Honda)<br>4 M Hailwood (Ducati)<br>5 K Takahashi (Honda)<br>6 L Taveri (Honda)<br>Record lap – C Ubbiali (MV) | 90.83mph<br>(146.17km/h)<br>Record<br><br><br><br>93.61mph<br>(150.65km/h) | 1 C Ubbiali (MV)<br>2 J Redman (Honda)<br>3 E Degner (MZ)<br>4 K Takahashi (Honda)<br>5 G Milani (Honda)<br>6 Y Sato (Honda)<br>Fastest lap – C Ubbiali (MV) | 109.05mph<br>(175.50km/h)<br><br><br><br><br>110.79mph<br>(178.29km/h) |

## 1960 350CC

| French GP Clermont-Ferrand May 2second | | TT Taces Isle of Man June 17 | | Dutch TT Assen June 25 | |
|---|---|---|---|---|---|
| 1 G Hocking (MV)<br>2 F Stastny (Jawa)<br>3 J Surtees (MV)<br>4 RN Brown (Norton)<br>5 P Driver (Norton)<br>6 F Perris (Norton)<br>Record lap – J Surtees (MV) | 70.68mph<br>(113.82km/h)<br><br><br><br><br>75.44mph<br>(121.48km/h) | 1 J Hartle (MV)<br>2 J Surtees (MV)<br>3 R McIntyre (AJS)<br>4 D Minter (Norton)<br>5 R Rensen (Norton)<br>6 RHF Anderson (Norton)<br>Record lap – J Surtees (MV) | 96.70mph<br>(155.62km/h)<br>Record<br><br><br><br>99.20mph<br>(159.64km/h) | 1 J Surtees (MV)<br>2 G Hocking (MV)<br>3 RHF Anderson (Norton)<br>4 RN Brown (Norton)<br>5 P Driver (Norton)<br>6 J Hempleman (Norton)<br>Record lap – J Surtees (MV) | 83.50mph<br>(134.52km/h)<br>Record<br><br><br><br>85.06mph<br>(136.82km/h) |
| **Ulster GP Dundrod August 6** | | **Italian GP Monza September 11** | | | |
| 1 J Surtees (MV)<br>2 J Hartle (Norton)<br>3 H Anderson (Norton)<br>4 RHF Anderson (Norton)<br>5 RH Dale (Norton)<br>6 P Driver (Norton)<br>Record lap – A Shepherd (AJS) | 93.39mph<br>(150.29km/h)<br>Record<br><br><br><br>95.42mph<br>(153.56km/h) | 1 G Hocking (MV)<br>2 F Stastny (Jawa)<br>3 J Hartle (Norton)<br>4 RH Dale (Norton)<br>5 RHF Anderson (Norton)<br>6 H Anderson (AJS)<br>Fastest lap – G Hocking (MV) | 109.73mph<br>(176.58km/h)<br><br><br><br><br>111.69mph<br>(179.69km/h) | | |

## 1960 500CC

| French GP Clermont-Ferrand May 22 | | TT Races Isle of Man June 17 | | Dutch TT Assen June 25 | |
|---|---|---|---|---|---|
| 1 J Surtees (MV)<br>2 R Venturi (MV)<br>3 RN Brown (Norton)<br>4 P Driver (Norton)<br>5 L Richter (Norton)<br>6 F Ito (BMW)<br>Record lap – J Surtees (MV) | 75.52mph<br>(121.60km/h)<br><br><br><br><br>76.73mph<br>(123.54km/h) | 1 J Surtees (MV)<br>2 J Hartle (MV)<br>3 M Hailwood (Norton)<br>4 T Phillis (Norton)<br>5 RH Dale (Norton)<br>6 RN Brown (Norton)<br>Record lap – J Surtees (MV) | 102.44mph<br>(164.856km/h<br><br><br><br><br>104.08mph<br>(168.56km/h) | 1 R Venturi (MV)<br>2 RN Brown (Norton)<br>3 E Mendogni (MV)<br>4 P Driver (Norton)<br>5 M Hailwood (Norton)<br>6 RH Dale (Norton)<br>Fastest lap – R Venturi (MV) | 83.67mph<br>(134.65km/h)<br><br><br><br><br>86.43mph<br>(139.09km/h) |
| **Belgian GP Spa Francorchamps July 3** | | **German GP Solitude July 24** | | **Ulster GP Dundrod August 6** | |
| 1 J Surtees (MV)<br>2 R Venturi (MV)<br>3 RN Brown (Norton)<br>4 M Hailwood (Norton)<br>5 J Redman (Norton)<br>6 E Mendogni (MV)<br>Record lap – J Surtees (MV) | 120.53mph<br>(193.92km/h)<br><br><br><br><br>122.67mph<br>(197.45km/h) | 1 J Surtees (MV)<br>2 R Venturi (MV)<br>3 E Mendogni (MV)<br>4 RH Dale (Norton)<br>5 J Hempleman (Norton)<br>6 R Glaeser (Norton)<br>Fastest lap – J Surtees (MV) | 92.77mph<br>(149.39km/h)<br><br><br><br><br>94.21mph<br>(151.59km/h) | 1 J Hartle (Norton)<br>2 J Surtees (MV)<br>3 A Shepherd (Matchless)<br>4 R Rensen (Norton)<br>5 J Redman (Norton)<br>6 T Phillis (Norton)<br>Record lap – J Surtees (MV) | 93.37mph<br>(150.26km/h)<br><br><br><br><br>99.32mph<br>(159.84km/h) |
| **Italian GP Monza September 11** | | | | | |
| 1 J Surtees (MV)<br>2 E Mendogni (MV)<br>3 M Hailwood (Norton)<br>4 P Driver (Norton)<br>5 J Hartle (Norton)<br>6 J Redman (Norton)<br>Fastest lap – J Surtees (MV) | 115.02mph<br>(185.10km/h)<br><br><br><br><br>118.33mph<br>(190.43km/h) | | | | |

## 1960 SIDECARS

| Fren GP Clermont-Ferrand May 22 | | TT Races Isle of Man June 15 | | Dutch TT Assen June 25 | |
|---|---|---|---|---|---|
| 1 H Fath/A Wohlgemuth (BMW)<br>2 F Scheidegger/H Burckhardt (BMW)<br>3 F Camathias/J Chisnell (BMW)<br>4 .Deubel/E Horner (BMW)<br>5 E Strub/H Cecco<br>6 J Rogliardo/M Godillot (BMW)<br>Record lap – H Fath (BMW) | 66.51mph<br>(107.66km/h)<br>Record<br><br><br><br>67.44mph<br>(108.64km/h) | 1 H Fath/A Wohlgemuth (BMW)<br>2 P Harris/R Campbell (BMW)<br>3 C Freeman/B Nelson (Norton)<br>4 L Wells/W Cook (Norton)<br>5 F Camathias/R Foll (BMW)<br>6 A Ritter/M Blauth (BMW)<br>Record lap – H Fath (BMW) | 84.10mph<br>(135.30km/h)<br>Record<br><br><br><br>85.82mph<br>(138.06km/h) | 1 P Harris/R Campbell (BMW)<br>2 H Fath/A Wohlgemuth (BMW)<br>3 F Scheidegger/H Burkhardt (BMW)<br>4 E Strub/H/Cecco (BMW)<br>5 B Boddice/E Godfrey (BSA)<br>6 M Deubel/H Hohler (BMW)<br>Record lap – F Camathias/R Foll (BMW) | 75.26mph<br>(121.11km/h)<br>Record<br><br><br><br>77.39mph<br>(124.45km/h) |
| **Belgian GP Spa Francorchamps July 3** | | **German GP Solitude July 24** | | | |
| 1 H Fath/A Wohlgemuth (BMW)<br>2 F Scheidegger/H Burkhardt (BMW)<br>3 E Strub/H Cecco (BMW)<br>4 J Beeton/E Bulgin (BMW)<br>5 A Ritter/H Hohler (BMW)<br>6 J Rogliardo/M Godillot (BMW)<br>Fastest lap – F Camathias/R Foll (BMW) | 100.02mph<br>(161.32(km/h)<br><br><br><br><br>101.41mph<br>(163.57km/h) | 1 H Fath/A Wohlgemuth (BMW)<br>2 F Camathias/G Rufenacht (BMW)<br>3 F Scheidegger/H Burkhardt (BMW)<br>4 M Deubel/H Hohler (BMW)<br>5 O Kolle/D/Hess (BMW)<br>6 A Ritter/E Horner (BMW)<br>Fastest lap –.Fath/A Wohlgemuth (BMW) | 80.18mph<br>(129.32km/h)<br><br><br><br><br>82.03mph<br>(132.30km/h) | | |

## 1961 125CC

| Spanish GP Montjuich Park April 23 | | German GP Hockenheim May 14 | | French GP Clermont-Ferrand May 21 | |
|---|---|---|---|---|---|
| 1 T Phillis (Honda) | 107.32km/h | 1 E Degner (MZ) | 158.43km/h | 1 T Phillis (Honda) | 112.82km/h |
| 2 E Degner (MZ) | (66.69mph) | 2 A Shepherd (MZ) | (98.44mph) | 2 E Degner (MZ) | Record |
| 3 J Redman (Honda) | | 3 W Brehme (MZ) | | 3 J Redman (Honda) | (70.11mph) |
| 4 M Hailwood (EMC) | | 4 H Fischer (MZ) | | 4 M Hailwood (EMC) | |
| 5 J Grace (Bultaco) | | 5 L Taveri (Honda) | | 5 L Taveri (Honda) | |
| 6 R Quintanilla (Bultaco) | | 6 K Takahashi (Honda) | | 6 K Takahashi (Honda) | |
| Fastest lap – M Hailwood (EMC) | 108.92km/h | Fastest lap – E Degner (MZ) | 160.59km/h | Record lap – Phillis/Degner | 114.24km/h |
| | (68.18mph) | | (99.89mph) | | (70.99mph) |
| TT Races Isle of Man June 12 | | Dutch TT Assen June 24 | | Belgian GP Spa Francorchamps July 2 | |
| 1 M Hailwood (Honda) | 141.99km/h | 1 T Phillis (Honda) | 127.08km/h | 1 L Taveri (Honda) | 161.09km/h |
| 2 L Taveri (Honda) | (88.23mph) | 2 J Redman (Honda) | Record | 2 T Phillis (Honda) | (100.09mph) |
| 3 T Phillis (Honda) | | 3 A Shepherd (MZ) | (78.87mph) | 3 J Redman (Honda) | |
| 4 J Redman (Honda) | | 4 P Read (EMC) | | 4 E Degner (MZ) | |
| 5 S Shimazaki (Honda) | | 5 W Musiol (MZ) | | 5 A Shepherd (MZ) | |
| 6 R Rensen (Bultaco) | | 6 R Avery (EMC) | | 6 W Brehme (MZ) | |
| Record lap – L Taveri (Honda) | 142.34km/h | Record lap – T Phillis (Honda) | 129.68km/h | Record lap – T Phillis (Honda) | 162.17km/h |
| | (88.45mph) | | (80.57mph) | | (100.83mph) |
| East German GP Sachsenring July 30 | | Ulster GP Dundrod August 12 | | Italian GP Monza September 3 | |
| 1 E Degner (MZ) | 141.43km/h | 1 K Takahashi (Honda) | 140.83km/h | 1 E Degner (MZ) | 158.95km/h |
| 2 T Phillis (Honda) | (87.88mph) | 2 E Degner (MZ) | Record | 2 T Tanaka (Honda) | Record |
| 3 K Takahashi (Honda) | | 3 T Phillis (Honda) | (87.51mph) | 3 L Taveri (Honda) | (98.77mph) |
| 4 L Szabo (MZ) | | 4 J Redman (Honda) | | 4 T Phillis (Honda) | |
| 5 W Brehme (MZ) | | 5 M Hailwood (Honda) | | 5 J Redman (Honda) | |
| 6 J Redman (Honda) | | 6 L Taveri (Honda) | | 6 R Avery (EMC) | |
| Record lap – K Takahashi (Honda) | 143.97km/h | Record lap – T Phillis (Honda) | 143.11km/h | Record lap – T Phillis (Honda) | 161.85km/h |
| | (89.46mph) | | (88.93mph) | | (100.56mph) |
| Swedish GP Kristianstad September 17 | | Argentine GP Buenos Aires October 15 | | | |
| 1 L Taveri (Honda) | 138.01km/h | 1 T Phillis (Honda) | 114.27km/h | | |
| 2 K Takahashi (Honda) | (83.48mph) | 2 J Redman (Honda) | (71.00mph) | | |
| 3 J Redman (Honda) | | 3 K Takahashi (Honda) | | | |
| 4 W Musiol (MZ) | | 4 S Shimazaki (Honda) | | | |
| 5 O Svensson (Ducati) | | 5 N Taniguchi (Honda) | | | |
| 6 T Phillis (Honda) | | 6 H Pochetino (BultacoO | | | |
| Record lap – L Taveri (Honda) | 138.75km/h | Fastest lap – T Phillis (Honda) | N/A | | |
| | (86.22mph) | | | | |

## 1961 250CC

| Spanish GP Montjuich Park April 23 | | German GP Hockenheim May 14 | | French GP Clermont-Ferrand May 21 | |
|---|---|---|---|---|---|
| 1 G Hocking (MV) | 113.02km/h | 1 K Takahashi (Honda) | 186.41km/h | 1 T Phillis (Honda) | 120.81km/h |
| 2 T Phillis (Honda) | (70.23mph) | 2 J Redman (Honda) | (115.89mph) | 2 M Hailwood (Honda) | Record |
| 3 S Grassetti (Benelli) | | 3 T Provini (Morini) | | 3 K Takahashi (Honda) | (75.07mph) |
| 4 J Redman (Honda) | | 4 E Degner (MZ) | | 4 T Provini (Morini) | |
| 5 H Fischer (MZ) | | 5 A Shepherd (MZ) | | 5 S Grassetti (Benelli) | |
| 6 D Shorey (NSU) | | 6 H Fischer (MZ) | | 6 J Redman (Honda) | |
| Fastest lap – G Hocking (MV) | 115.13km/h | Record lap – K Takahashi (Honda) | 189.56km/h | Record lap – G. Hocking (MV) | 123.66km/h |
| | (71.58mph) | | (117.79mph) | | (76.84mph) |
| TT Races Isle of Man June 12 | | Dutch TT Assen June 24 | | Belgian GP Spa Francorchamps July 2 | |
| 1 M Hailwood (Honda) | 158.33kh/h | 1 M Hailwood (Honda) | 138.88km/h | 1 J Redman (Honda) | 185.03km/h |
| 2 T Phillis (Honda) | (98.38mph) | 2 R McIntyre (Honda) | Record | 2 T Phillis (Honda) | Record |
| 3 J Redman (Honda) | | 3 J Redman (Honda) | (86.30mph) | 3 M Hailwood (Honda) | (114.96mph) |
| 4 K Takahashi (Honda) | | 4 S Grassetti (Benelli) | | 4 S Shimazaki (Honda) | |
| 5 N Taniguchi (Honda) | | 5 F Stastny (Jawa) | | 5 F Ito (Yamaha) | |
| 6 F Ito (Yamaha) | | 6 F Ito (Yamaha) | | 6 Y Sunako (Yamaha) | |
| Record lap – R McIntyre (Honda) | 160.25km/h | Record lap – M Hailwood (Honda) | 141.23km/h | Record lap – J Redman (Honda) | 187.05km/h |
| | (99.58mph) | | (87.75mph) | | (116.29mph) |
| East German GP Sachsenring July 30 | | Ulster GP Dundrod August 12 | | Italian GP Monza September 3 | |
| 1 M Hailwood (Honda) | 157.12km/h | 1 R McIntyre (Honda) | 153.68km/h | 1 J Redman (Honda) | 180.94km/h |
| 2 J Redman (Honda) | Record | 2 M Hailwood (Honda) | Record | 2 M Hailwood (Honda) | (112.43mph) |
| 3 K Takahashi (Honda) | (97.63mph) | 3 J Redman (Honda) | (95.44mph) | 3 T Phillis (Honda) | |
| 4 T Phillis (Honda) | | 4 T Phillis (Honda) | | 4 T Provini (Morini) | |
| 5 A Shepherd (MZ) | | 5 A Shepherd (MZ) | | 5 F Stastny (Jawa) | |
| 6 W Musiol (MZ) | | 6 K Takahashi (Honda) | | 6 S Grassetti (Benelli) | |
| Record lap – M Hailwood (Honda) | 159.14km/h | Record lap – R McIntyre (Honda) | 156.00km/h | Record lap – M Hailwood (Honda) | 183.67km/h |
| | (98.90mph) | | (96.94mph) | | (114.12mph) |

| Swedish GP Kristianstad September 17 | | Argentine GP Buenos Aires October 15 | | | |
|---|---|---|---|---|---|
| 1 M Hailwood (Honda) | 152.26km/h | 1 T Phillis (Honda) | 126.88km/h | | |
| 2 L Taveri (Honda) | (94.34mph) | 2 K Takahashi (Honda) | (78.84mph) | | |
| 3 K Takahashi (Honda) | | 3 J Redman (Honda) | | | |
| 4 J Redman (Honda) | | 4 F Ito (Yamaha) | | | |
| 5 F Stastny (Jawa) | | | | | |
| 6 T Phillis (Honda) | | Only 4 finishers | | | |
| Record lap – J Redman (Honda) | 155.73km/h | | | | |
| | (96.77mph) | | | | |

## 1961 350CC

| German GP Hockenheim May 14 | | TT Races Isle of Man June 16 | | Dutch TT Assen June 24 | |
|---|---|---|---|---|---|
| 1 F Stastny (Jawa) | 112.17mph | 1 P Read (Norton) | 95.10mph | 1 G Hocking (MV) | 85.66mph |
| 2 G Havel (Jawa) | (180.92km/h) | 2 G Hocking (MV) | (153.04km/h) | 2 R McIntyre (Bianchi) | (138.16km/h) |
| 3 R Thalhammer (Norton) | | 3 R Rensen (Norton) | | 3 F Stastny (Jawa) | |
| 4 R Rensen (Norton) | | 4 D Minter (Norton) | | 4 E Brambilla (Bianchi) | |
| 5 H Pesl (Norton) | | 5 F Stastny (Jawa) | | 5 P Read (Norton) | |
| 6 F Perris (Norton) | | 6 R Ingram (Norton) | | 6 F Perris (Norton) | |
| Fastest lap – F Stastny (Jawa) | 113.73mph | Fastest lap – G Hocking (MV) | 99.80mph | Record lap – G Hocking (MV) | 87.28mph |
| | (183.43km/h) | | (160.61km/h) | | (140.79km/h) |
| East German GP Sachsenring July 30 | | Ulster GP Dundrod August 12 | | Italian GP Monza September 3 | |
| 1 G Hocking (MV) | 96.20mph | 1 G Hocking (MV) | 94.17mph | 1 G Hocking (MV) | 112.58mph |
| 2 F Stastny (Jawa) | (155.17km/h) | 2 A King (Bianchi) | (149.49km/h) | 2 M Hailwood (MV) | (181.59km/h) |
| 3 R McIntyre (Bianchi) | | 3 F Stastny (jawa) | | 3 G Havel (Jawa) | |
| 4 G Havel (Jawa) | | 4 P Read (Norton) | | 4 A Shepherd (Bianchi) | |
| 5 E Brambilla (Bianchi) | | 5 A Shepherd (AJS) | | 5 S Grassetti (Benelli) | |
| 6 B Schneider (Norton) | | 6 M Duff (AJS) | | 6 H Anderson (Norton) | |
| Record lap – G Hocking (MV) | 97,58mph | Fastest lap – G Hocking (MV) | 95.33mph | Record lap – G Hocking (MV) | 114.28mph |
| | (157.39km/h) | | (153.77km/h) | | (184.33km/h) |
| Swedish GP Kristianstad September 17 | | | | | |
| 1 F Stastny (jawa) | 93.97mph | | | | |
| 2 G Havel (Jawa) | (151.58km/h) | | | | |
| 3 T Robb (AJS) | | | | | |
| 4 R Thalhammer (Norton) | | | | | |
| 5 R Langston (AJS) | | | | | |
| 6 M Duff (AJS) | | | | | |
| Fastest lap – G Hocking (MV) | 95.11mph | | | | |
| | (153.40km/h) | | | | |

## 1961 500CC

| German GP Hockenheim May 14 | | French GP Clermont-Ferrand May 21 | | TT Races Isle of Man | |
|---|---|---|---|---|---|
| 1 G Hocking (MV) | 120.26mph | 1 G Hocking (MV) | 74.56mph | 1 M Hailwood (Norton) | 100.60mph |
| 2 F Perris (Norton) | (193.55km/h) | 2 M Hailwood (Norton) | (119.99km/h) | 2 R McIntyre (Norton) | (161.90km/h) |
| 3 H-G. Jaeger (BMW) | | 3 A Paba (Norton) | | 3 T Phillis (Norton) | |
| 4 M Hailwood (Norton) | | 4 G Marsovsky (Norton) | | 4 A King (Norton) | |
| 5 E Hiller (BMW) | | 5 F Messerli (Matchless) | | 5 R Langston (Matchless) | |
| 6 L John (BMW) | | 6 R Foll (Matchless) | | 6 T Godfrey (Norton) | |
| Fastest lap – G Hocking (MV) | 124.58mph | Fastest lap – G Hocking (MV) | 76.21mph | Fastest lap – G Hocking (MV) | |
| | (200.94km/h) | | (122.92km/h) | | 102.39mph |
| | | | | | (165.15km/h) |
| Dutch TT Assen June 24 | | Belgian GP Spa Francorchamps July 2 | | German GP Sachsenring July 30 | |
| 1 G Hocking (MV) | 87.53mph | 1 G Hocking (MV) | 119.63mph | 1 G Hocking (MV) | 99.70mph |
| 2 M Hailwood (Norton) | (140.87km/h) | 2 M Hailwood (Norton) | (192.64km/h) | 2 M Hailwood (Norton) | (160.82km/h) |
| 3 R McIntyre (Norton) | Record | 3 R McIntyre (Norton) | | 3 B Schneider (Norton) | |
| 4 P Read (Norton) | | 4 M Duff (Matchless) | | 4 D Farnsworth (Norton) | |
| 5 F Perris (Norton) | | 5 R Langston (Matchless) | | 5 J Findlay (Norton) | |
| 6 R Miles (Norton) | | 6 P Driver (Norton) | | 6 A Resko (Norton) | |
| Record lap – G Hocking | 88.73mph | Record lap – G Hocking (MV) | 123.47mph | Record lap – G Hocking (MV) | 101.18mph |
| | (143.12km/h) | | (198.83km/h) | | (163.20km/h) |
| Ulster GP Dundrod August 12 | | Italian GP Monza September 3 | | Swedish GP Kristianstad September 17 | |
| 1 G Hocking (MV) | 90.49mph | 1 M Hailwood (MV) | 116.50mph | 1 G Hocking (MV) | 97.49mph |
| 2 M Hailwood (Norton) | (144.78km/h) | 2 A King (Norton) | (187.49km/h) | 2 M Hailwood (MV) | (156.90km/h) |
| 3 A King (Norton) | | 3 P Driver (Norton) | | 3 F Perris (Norton) | |
| 4 R Langston (Matchless) | | 4 A Pagani (Norton) | | 4 B Schneider (Norton) | |
| 5 D,Chatterton (Norton) | | 5 B Schneider (Norton) | | 5 M Duff (Matchless) | |
| 6 T Thorp (Norton) | | 6 J Findlay (Norton) | | 6 P Pawson (Norton) | |
| Fastest lap – G Hocking (MV) | 98.37mph | Record lap – G Hocking (MV) | 118.50mph | Record lap – G Hocking | 102.52mph |
| | (157.39km/h) | | (191.14km/h) | | (165.37km/h) |

| Argentine GP Buenos Aires October 10 | | | | | |
|---|---|---|---|---|---|
| 1 J Kissling (Matchless)<br>2 J-C Salatino (Norton)<br>3 F Perris (Norton)<br>4 S Perkins (Norton)<br>5 E Salatino (Norton)<br>6 G Costa (Norton)<br>Fastest lap – J-C Salatino (Norton) | 76.53mph<br>(123.63km/h)<br><br><br><br><br>n/a | | | | |

## 1961 SIDECARS

| Spanish GP Montjuich Park April 23 | | German GP Hockenheim May 14 | | French GP Clermont-Ferrand May 21 | |
|---|---|---|---|---|---|
| 1 H Fath/A Wohlgemuth (BMW)<br>2 F Scheidegger/H/Burkhardt (BMW)<br>3 E Strub/R Foll (BMW)<br>4 A Butscher/E Butscher (BMW)<br>5 H Luthringshauser/H Vester (BMW)<br>6 J Rogliardo/M Godillot BMW)<br>Fastest lap – H Fath (BMW) | 66.30mph<br>(106.95km/h)<br><br><br><br><br>66.99mph<br>(108.06km/h) | 1 M Deubel/E Horner (BMW)<br>2 F Scheidegger/H Burkhardt (BMW)<br>3 O Kolle/D Hess (BMW)<br>4 A Rohsiepe/L Bottcher (BMW)<br>5 A Butscher/E Butscher (BMW)<br>6 L Neussner/F Reitmaier (BMW)<br>Fastest lap – M Deubel (BMW) | 103.94mph<br>(167.66km/h)<br><br><br><br><br>105.64mph<br>(170.39km/h) | 1 F Scheidegger/H Burkhardt (BMW)<br>2 M Deubel/E Horner (BMW)<br>3 E Strub/R Foll (BMW)<br>4 A Butscher/E Butscher (BMW)<br>5 O Kolle/D Hess (BMW)<br>6 A Rohsiepe/L Bottcher<br>Fastest lap – F Scheidegger (BMW) | 66.12mph<br>(106.66km/h)<br><br><br><br><br>67.23mph<br>(108.44km/h) |
| **TT Races Isle of Man June 12** | | **Dutch TT Assen June 24** | | **Belgian GP Spa Francorchamps July 2** | |
| 1 M Deubel/E Horner (BMW)<br>2 F Scheidegger/H Burkhardt (BMW)<br>3 P Harris/R Campbell (BMW)<br>4 A Rohsiepe/L Bottcher (BMW)<br>5 C Freeman/B Nelson (Norton)<br>6 C Seeley/W Rawlings (Matchless)<br>Record lap – M Deubel (BMW) | 87.45mph<br>(141.05km/h)<br>Record<br><br><br><br>87.71mph<br>(141.57km/h) | 1 M Deubel/E Horner (BMW)<br>2 E Strub/K Huber (BMW)<br>3 J Beeton/E Bulgin (BMW)<br>4 A Rohsiepe/L Bottcher (BMW)<br>5 H Curchod/A Beyeler (BMW)<br>6 A Butscher/E Butscher (BMW)<br>Record lap – M Deubel (BMW) | 76.42mph<br>(123.26km/h)<br>Record<br><br><br><br>77.95mph<br>(125.73km/h) | 1 F Scheidegger/H/Burkhardt (BMW)<br>2 M Deubel/E Horner (BMW)<br>3 P Harris/R Campbell (BMW)<br>4 O Kolle/D Hess (BMW)<br>5 C Vincent/E Bliss (BSA)<br>6 A Rohsiepe/L Bottcher (BMW)<br>Record lap – F Scheidegger (BMW) | 104.41mph<br>(168.40km/h)<br>Record<br><br><br><br>105.43mph<br>(170.06km/h) |

## 1962 50CC

| Spanish GP Montjuich Park May 6 | | French GP Clermont-Ferrand May 13 | | TT Races Isle of Man June 4 | |
|---|---|---|---|---|---|
| 1 H-G Anscheidt (Kreidler)<br>2 J Busquets (Derbi)<br>3 L Taveri (Honda)<br>4 W Gedlich (Kreidler)<br>5 T Robb (Honda)<br>6 K Takahashi (Honda)<br>Record lap – H-G. Anscheidt (Kreidler) | 60.55mph<br>(97.45km/h)<br><br><br><br><br>62.43mph<br>(100.54km/h) | 1 J Huberts (Kreidler)<br>2 K Takahashi (Honda)<br>3 L Taveri (Honda)<br>4 T Robb (Honda)<br>5 S Suzuki (Suzuki)<br>6 M Itoh (Suzuki)<br>Fastest lap – J. Huberts (Kreidler) | 60.15mph<br>(96.79km/h)<br><br><br><br><br>62.48mph<br>(100.55km/h) | 1 E Degner (Suzuki)<br>2 L Taveri (Honda)<br>3 T Robb (Honda)<br>4 H-G Anscheidt (Kreidler)<br>5 M Itoh (Suzuki)<br>6 M Ichino (Suzuki)<br>Fastest lap – E Degner (Suzuki) | 75.12mph<br>(120.89km/h)<br><br><br><br><br>75.52mph<br>(121.53k/hh) |
| **Dutch TT Assen June 30** | | **Belgian GP Spa Francorchamps July 8** | | **German GP Solitude July 15** | |
| 1 E Degner (Suzuki)<br>2 J Huberts (Kreidler)<br>3 H-G Anscheidt (Kreidler)<br>4 S Suzuki (Suzuki)<br>5 M Itoh (Suzuki)<br>6 W Gedlich (Kreidler)<br>Fastest lap – J Huberts (Kreidler) | 69.76mph<br>(112.27km/h)<br><br><br><br><br>71.16mph<br>(114.05km/h) | 1 E Degner (Suzuki)<br>2 H-G Anscheidt (Kreidler)<br>3 L Taveri (Honda)<br>4 S Suzuki (Suzuki)<br>5 W Gedlich (Kreidler)<br>6 M Ichino (Suzuki)<br>Fastest lap – E Degner (Suzuki) | 85.69mph<br>(137.33km/h)<br><br><br><br><br>85.84mph<br>(138.24km/h) | 1 E Degner (Suzuki)<br>2 H-G Anscheidt (Kreidler)<br>3 M Itoh (Suzuki)<br>4 L Taveri (Honda)<br>5 S Suzuki (Suzuki)<br>6 M Ichino (Suzuki)<br>Fastest lap – E Degner (Suzuki) | 74.52mph<br>(120.20km/h)<br><br><br><br><br>75.88mph<br>(122.21km/h) |
| **East German GP Sachsenring August 19** | | **Italian GP Monza September 9** | | **Finnish GP Tampere September 23** | |
| 1 J Huberts (Kreidler)<br>2 M Itoh (Suzuki)<br>3 H Anderson (Suzuki)<br>4 L Taveri (Honda)<br>5 T Robb (Honda)<br>6 D Shorey (Kreidler)<br>Fastest lap – J Huberts (Kreidler) | 75.34mph<br>(121.25km/h)<br><br><br><br><br>76.18mph<br>(122.68km/h) | 1 H-G Anscheidt (Kreidler)<br>2 M Itoh (Suzuki)<br>3 J Huberts (Kreidler)<br>4 H Anderson (Suzuki)<br>5 I. Morishita (Suzuki)<br>6 L Taveri (Honda)<br>Fastest lap – H-G Anscheidt (Kreidler) | 83.64mph<br>(121.25km/h)<br><br><br><br><br>85.30mph<br>(137.62km/h) | 1 L Taveri (Honda)<br>2 T Robb (Honda)<br>3 H-G Anscheidt (Kreidler)<br>4 E Degner (Suzuki)<br>5 T Tanaka (Honda)<br>6 H Anderson (Suzuki)<br>Fastest lap – L Taveri (Honda) | 59.71mph<br>(96.13km/h)<br><br><br><br><br>60.96mph<br>(98.08km/h) |
| **Argentine GP Buenos Aires October 14** | | | | | |
| 1 H Anderson (Suzuki)<br>2 E Degner (Suzuki)<br>3 H-G Anscheidt (Kreidler)<br>4 M Itoh (Suzuki)<br>5 J Huberts (Kreidler)<br>6 G Beer (Kreidler) | 65.79<br>(105.88km/h) | | | | |

## 1962 125CC

| Spanish GP Montjuich Park May 6 | | French GP Clermont-Ferrand May 13 | | TT Races Isle of Man June 6 | |
|---|---|---|---|---|---|
| 1 K Takahashi (Honda)<br>2 J Redman (Honda)<br>3 L Taveri (Honda)<br>4 M Hailwood (EMC)<br>5 R Avery (EMC)<br>6 F Villa (Mondial)<br>Record lap – L Taveri (Honda) | 67.98mph<br>(109.68km/h)<br><br><br><br><br>69.79mph<br>(112.31km/h) | 1 K Takahashi (Honda)<br>2 J Redman (Honda)<br>3 T Robb (Honda)<br>4 L Taveri (Honda)<br>5 E Degner (Suzuki)<br>6 J. Kissling (Bultaco)<br>Record lap – K Takahashi (Honda) | 67.29mph<br>(108.27km/h)<br><br><br><br><br>71.28mph<br>(114.70km/h) | 1 L Taveri (Honda)<br>2 T Robb (Honda)<br>3 T Phillis (Honda)<br>4 D Minter (Honda)<br>5 J Redman (Honda)<br>6 R Avery (EMC)<br>Record lap – L Taveri (Honda) | 84.88mph<br>(144.64km/h)<br><br><br><br><br>90.13mph<br>(145.95km/h) |
| **Belgian GP Spa Francorchamps July 8** | | **German GP Solitude** | | **Ulster GP Dundrod) August 11** | |
| 1 L Taveri (Honda)<br>2 J Redman (Honda)<br>3 P Driver (EMC)<br>4 M Hailwood (EMC)<br>5 R Avery (EMC)<br>6 G Vicenzi (Ducati)<br>Record lap – L Taveri (Honda) | 102.00mph<br>(164.53km/h)<br><br><br><br><br>103.11mph<br>(166.32km/h) | 1 L Taveri (Honda)<br>2 T Robb (Honda)<br>3 M Hailwood (EMC)<br>4 R McIntyre (Honda)<br>5 J Grace (Bultaco)<br>6 H Anderson (Suzuki)<br>Fastest lap – L Taveri (Honda) | 84.20mph<br>(135.59km/h)<br><br><br><br><br>85.51mph<br>(137.61km/h) | 1 L Taveri (Honda)<br>2 T Robb (Honda)<br>3 J Redman (Honda)<br>4 T Tanaka (Honda)<br>5 H Anderson (Suzuki)<br>6 P Driver (EMC)<br>Record lap – T Robb (Honda) | 83.30mph<br>(134.05km/h)<br><br><br><br><br>84.70mph<br>(136.31km/h) |
| **East German GP Sachsenring August 19** | | **Italian GP Monza September 9** | | **Finnish GP Tampere September 23** | |
| 1 L Taveri (Honda)<br>2 J Redman (Honda)<br>3 H Fischer (MZ)<br>4 T Robb (Honda)<br>5 K Enderline (MZ)<br>6 W Musiol (MZ)<br>Record lap – L Taveri (Honda) | 88.83mph<br>(142.96km/h)<br><br><br><br><br>90.19mph<br>(145.24km/h) | 1 T Tanaka (Honda)<br>2 L Taveri (Honda)<br>3 T Robb (Honda)<br>4 J Redman (Honda)<br>5 A Pagani (Honda)<br>6.P Driver (EMC)<br>Fastest lap – L Taveri (Honda) | 97.11mph<br>(156.29km/h)<br><br><br><br><br>99.02mph<br>(159.35km/h) | 1 .J Redman (Honda)<br>2 L Taveri (Honda)<br>3 A Shepherd (MZ)<br>4 H Fischer (MZ)<br>5 F Perris (Suzuki)<br>6 J Peteja (MZ)<br>Fastest lap – A Shepherd (MZ) | 65.24mph<br>(105.03km/h)<br><br><br><br><br>68.23mph<br>(109.16km/h) |
| **Argentine GP Buenos Aires October 14** | | | | | |
| 1 H Anderson (Suzuki<br>2 V Kissling (DKW)<br>3 M Itoh (Suzuki<br>4 L Moreira (Bultaco)<br>5 M Chizzini (Bultaco)<br>6 P.Rosenthal (Tohatsu) | 69.38mph<br>(111.66km/h) | | | | |

## 1962 250CC

| Spanish GP Montjuich Park May 6 | | French GP Clermont-Ferrand May 13 | | TT Races Isle of Man June 4 | |
|---|---|---|---|---|---|
| 1 J Redman (Honda)<br>2 R McIntyre (Honda)<br>3 T Phillis (Honda)<br>4 D Shorey (Bultaco)<br>5 A Pagani (Aermacchi)<br>6 M Toussaint (Benelli)<br>Record lap – T Phillis (Honda) | 71.17mph<br>(114.62km/h)<br><br><br><br><br>72.43mph<br>(116.56km/h) | 1 J Redman (Honda)<br>2 R McIntyre (Honda)<br>3 T Phillis (Honda)<br>4 D Shorey (Bultaco)<br>5 J-P Beltoise (Morini)<br>6 B Savoye (Mondial)<br>Fastest lap – T Phillis (Honda) | 71.87mph<br>(115.65km/h)<br><br><br><br><br>75.17mph<br>(120.97km/h) | 1 D Minter (Honda)<br>2 J Redman (Honda)<br>3 T Phillis (Honda)<br>4 A Wheeler (Guzzi)<br>5 A Pagani (Aermacchi)<br>6 D Shorey (Bultaco)<br>Fastest lap – R McIntyre (Honda) | 96.68mph<br>(155.59km/h)<br><br><br><br><br>99.06mph<br>(159.42km/h) |
| **Dutch TT Assen June 30** | | **Belgian GP Spa Francorchamps July 8** | | **West German GP Solitude July 15** | |
| 1 J Redman (Honda)<br>2 R McIntyre (Honda)<br>3 T Provini (Morini)<br>4 B Swart (Honda)<br>5 F Perris (Suzuki)<br>6 A Wheeler (Guzzi)<br>Fastest lap – T Provini (Morini) | 82.94mph<br>(133.48km/h)<br><br><br><br><br>85.54mph<br>(137.98km/h) | 1 R McIntyre (Honda)<br>2 J Redman (Honda)<br>3 L Taveri (Honda)<br>4 G Beer (Adler)<br>5 A Wheeler (Guzzi)<br>6 P Vervroegen (Aermacchi)<br>Fastest lap – R McIntyre (Honda) | 113.44mph<br>(182.56km/h)<br><br><br><br><br>114.31mph<br>(184.38km/h) | 1 J Redman (Honda)<br>2 R McIntyre (Honda)<br>3 T Tanaka (Honda)<br>4 G Beer (Honda)<br>5 A Wheeler (Guzzi)<br>6 M Schneider (NSU)<br>Fastest lap – J Redman (Honda) | 90.47mph<br>(145.75km/h)<br><br><br><br><br>91.41mph<br>(147.21km/h) |
| **Ulster GP Dundrod August 11** | | **East German GP Sachsenring August 19** | | **Italian GP Monza September 9** | |
| 1 T Robb (Honda)<br>2 J Redman (Honda)<br>3 L Taveri (Honda)<br>4 A Wheeler (Guzzi)<br>5 J Donaghy (Ducati)<br>6 S Graham (Aermacchi)<br>Fastest lap – L Taveri (Honda) | 88.38mph<br>(142.24km/h)<br><br><br><br><br>90.85mph<br>(146.54km/h) | 1 J Redman (Honda)<br>2 M Hailwood (MZ)<br>3 W Musiol (MZ)<br>4 M Kitano (Honda)<br>5 N Sevostianov (S250)<br>6 D Shorey (Bultaco)<br>Record lap – M Hailwood (MZ) | 98.29mph<br>(158.18km/h)<br><br><br><br><br>100.72mph<br>(162.79km/h) | 1 J Redman (Honda)<br>2 T Provini (Morini)<br>3 A Pagani (Honda)<br>4 M Kitano (Honda)<br>5 G Milani (Aermacchi)<br>6 P Campanelli (Benelli)<br>Fastest lap – J Redman (Honda) | 110.78mph<br>(178.28km/h)<br><br><br><br><br>112.53mph<br>(181.09km/h) |

| Argentine GP Buenos Aires October 14 | | | | | |
|---|---|---|---|---|---|
| 1 A Wheeler (Guzzi)<br>2 U Masetti (Morini)<br>3 R Kaiser (NSU)<br>4 J Terengo (Ducati)<br>5 C Marefetan (Parilla)<br>6 M Dietrich (Aermacchi)<br>Fastest lap – A Wheeler (Guzzi) | 82.31mph<br>(132.47km/h)<br><br><br><br><br>n/a | | | | |

## 1962 350CC

| TT Races Isle of Man June 8 | | Dutch TT Assen June 30 | | Ulster GP Dundrod August 11 | |
|---|---|---|---|---|---|
| 1 M Hailwood (MV)<br>2 G Hocking (MV)<br>3 F Stastny (Jawa)<br>4 R Ingram (Norton)<br>5 M Duff (AJS)<br>6 H Anderson (AJS)<br>Record lap – M Hailwood (MV) | 99.59mph<br>(160.27km/h)<br><br><br><br><br>101.58mph<br>(163.47km/h) | 1 J Redman (Honda)<br>2 M Hailwood (MV)<br>3 S Grassetti (Bianchi)<br>4 F Stastny (Jawa)<br>5 D Minter (Norton)<br>6 P Read (Norton)<br>Fastest lap – S Grassetti (Bianchi) | 85.97mph<br>(138.35km/h)<br><br><br><br><br>87.33mph<br>(140.86km/h) | 1 J Redman (Honda)<br>2 F Stastny (Jawa)<br>3 T Robb (Honda)<br>4 A Shepherd (AJS)<br>5 G Havel (Jawa)<br>6 M Duff (AJS)<br>Fastest lap – M Hailwood (MV) | 93.76mph<br>(150.89km/h)<br><br><br><br><br>94.86mph<br>(153.01km/h) |
| **East German GP Sachsenring August 19** | | **Italian GP Monza September 9** | | **Finnish GP Tampere September 23** | |
| 1 J Redman (Honda)<br>2 M Hailwood (MV)<br>3 T Robb (Honda)<br>4 G Havel (Jawa)<br>5 M Duff (AJS)<br>6 N Sevostianov (S360)<br>Record lap – J Redman (Honda) | 98.12mph<br>(157.91km/h)<br><br><br><br><br>99.33mph<br>(159.85km/h) | 1 J Redman (Honda)<br>2 T Robb (Honda)<br>3 S Grassetti (Bianchi)<br>4 F Stastny (Jawa)<br>5 G Havel (Jawa)<br>6 A Wheeler (Guzzi)<br>Fastest lap – J Redman (Honda) | 112.37mph<br>(180.85km/h)<br><br><br><br><br>114.33mph<br>(183.99km/h) | 1 T Robb (Honda)<br>2 J Redman (Honda)<br>3 A Shepherd (MZ)<br>4 S Gunnarsson (Norton)<br>5 H Kuparinen (AJS)<br>6 M Kitano (Honda)<br>Fastest lap – T Robb (Honda) | 66.42mph<br>(106.96km/h)<br><br><br><br><br>68.04mph<br>(108.86km/h) |

## 1962 500CC

| TT Races Isle of Man June 8 | | Dutch TT Assen June 30 | | Belgian GP Spa Francorchamps July 8 | |
|---|---|---|---|---|---|
| 1 G Hocking (MV)<br>2 E Boyce (Norton)<br>3 F Stevens (Norton)<br>4 B Schneider (Norton)<br>5 R Ingram (Norton)<br>6 B Setchell (Norton)<br>Record lap – G Hocking (MV) | 103.51mph<br>(166.68km/h)<br><br><br><br><br>105.75mph<br>(170.78km/h) | 1 M Hailwood (MV)<br>2 D Minter (Norton)<br>3 P Read (Norton)<br>4 A Shepherd (Matchless)<br>5 B Schneider (Norton)<br>6 T Godfrey (Norton)<br>Record lap – M Hailwood (MV) | 87.35mph<br>(140.57km/h)<br><br><br><br><br>89.65mph<br>(144.61km/h) | 1 M Hailwood (Honda)<br>2 A Shepherd (Matchless)<br>3 T Godfrey (Norton)<br>4 P Driver (Norton)<br>5 J Findlay (Norton)<br>6 F Stevens (Norton)<br>Fastest lap – M Hailwood (MV) | 119.35mph<br>(192.07km/h)<br><br><br><br><br>120.03mph<br>(193.60km/h) |
| **Ulster GP Dundrod August 11** | | **East German GP Sachsenring August 19** | | **Italian GP Monza September 9** | |
| 1 M Hailwood (MV)<br>2 A Shepherd (Matchless)<br>3 P Read (Norton)<br>4 R Langston (Norton)<br>5 T Godfrey (Norton)<br>6 M Spence (Norton)<br>Record lap – M Hailwood (MV) | 96.55mph<br>(155.38km/h)<br><br><br><br><br>99.76mph<br>(160.91km/h) | 1 M Hailwood (MV)<br>2 A Shepherd (Matchless)<br>3 B Schneider (Norton)<br>4 F Stastny (Jawa)<br>5 P Driver (Norton)<br>6 R Foll (Matchless<br>Record lap – M Hailwood (MV) | 102.09mph<br>(164.31km/h)<br><br><br><br><br>104.43mph<br>(168.17km/h) | 1 M Hailwood (MV)<br>2 R Venturi (MV)<br>3 S Grassetti (Bianchi)<br>4 P Read (Norton)<br>5 P Driver (Norton)<br>6 B Schneider (Norton)<br>Fastest lap – R Venturi (MV) | 116.65mph<br>(187.56km/h)<br><br><br><br><br>118.98mph<br>(191.48km/h) |
| **Finnish GP Tampere September 23** | | **Argentine GP Buenos Aires October 14** | | | |
| 1 A Shepherd (Matchless)<br>2 S Gunnarsson (Norton)<br>3 F Stastny (Jawa)<br>4 A,Resko (Matchless)<br>5 H Karlsson (Norton)<br>6 R Foll (Matchless)<br>Fastest lap – A Shepherd (Matchless) | 68.04mph<br>(109.50km/h)<br><br><br><br><br>72.02mph<br>(115.23km/h) | 1 B Caldarella (Matchless)<br>2 J Salatino (Norton)<br>3 E Salatino (Norton)<br>4 P Gamberini (Matchless)<br>5 A Pomesano (Norton)<br>6 F Soler (Norton)<br>Fastest lap – B Caldarella (Matchless) | 90.25mph<br>(145.24km/h)<br><br><br><br><br>n/a | | |

## 1962 SIDECARS

| Spanish GP Montjuich Park May 6 | |
|---|---|
| 1 M Deubel/E Horner (BMW) | 67.17mph |
| 2 F Camathias/H Burkhardt (BMW) | (108.110km/h |
| 3 O Kolle/D Hess (BMW) | |
| 4.A Butscher/H Vester (BMW) | |
| 5 H Scholes/R Lindsay (BMW) | |
| 6 C Vincent/E Bliss (BSA) | |
| Fastest lap – Deubel/Horner (BMW) | 68.32mph |
| | (110.20km/h) |

| French GP Clermont-Ferrand May 13 | |
|---|---|
| 1 M Deubel/E Horner (BMW) | 67.35mph |
| 2 F Camathias/H Burkhardt (BMW) | (108.40km/h) |
| 3 C Vincent/E Bliss (BSA) | |
| 4 O Kolle/D Hess (BMW) | |
| 5 C Lambert/A Herzig (BMW) | |
| 6 E Pickup/K Scott (BMW) | |
| Fastest lap – Camathias/Burkhardt | 69.41mph |
| | (111.96km/h) |

| TT Races Isle of Man June 4 | |
|---|---|
| 1 C Vincent/E Bliss (BSA) | 83.57mph |
| 2 O Kolle/D Hess (BMW) | (134.49km/h) |
| 3 C Seeley/W Rawlings (Matchless) | |
| 4 C Lambert/A Herzig (BMW) | |
| 5 H Luthringshauser/H Knopp (BMW) | |
| 6 G Auerbacher/E Dein (BMW) | 90.49mph |
| Fastest lap – Deubel/Horner (BMW) | (145.96km/h |

| Dutch TT Assen June 30 | |
|---|---|
| 1 F Scheidegger/J Robinson (BMW) | 76.88mph |
| 2 M Deubel/E Horner (BMW) | (123.81km/h) |
| 3 O Kolle/D Hess (BMW) | |
| 4 A Rohsiepe/L Bottcher (BMW) | |
| 5 E Strub/G Rufenacht (BMW) | |
| 6 C Lambert/A Herzig (BMW) | |
| Fastest lap – Camathias/Winter(BMW) | 78.52mph |
| | (126.65km/h) |

| Belgian GP Spa Francorchamps July 8 | |
|---|---|
| 1 F Camathias/H Winter (BMW) | 105.29mph |
| 2 F Scheidegger/J Robinson (BMW) | (169.45km/h) |
| 3 M Deubel/E Horner (BMW) | |
| 4 E Strub/G Rufenacht (BMW) | |
| 5 A Rohsiepe/L Bottcher (BMW) | |
| 6 C Lambert/A Herzig (BMW) | |
| Fastest lap – Camathias/Winter (BMW) | 105.92mph |
| | (170.85km/h) |

| West German GP Solitude July 15 | |
|---|---|
| 1 M Deubel/E Horner (BMW) | 88.05mph |
| 2 F Camathias/H Winter (BMW) | (141.70km/h) |
| 3 F Scheidegger/J Robinson (BMW) | |
| 4 C Lambert/A Herzig (BMW) | |
| 5 A Rohsiepe/L Bottcher (BMW) | |
| 6 F Breu/J Burkhardt (BMW) | |
| Fastest lap – Deubel/Horner (BMW) | 89.21mph |
| | (143.90km/h) |

## 1963 50CC

| Spanish GP Montjuich Park May 5 | |
|---|---|
| 1 H-G. Anscheidt (Kreidler) | 63.04mph |
| 2 H Anderson (Suzuki) | (101.45km/h) |
| 3 J Busquets (Derbi) | |
| 4 I Morishita (Suzuki) | |
| 5 A Pagani (Kreidler) | |
| 6 J Garcia (Ducson) | |
| Record lap – Anscheidt (Kreidler) | 63.85mph |
| | (102.74km/h) |

| West German GP Hockenheim May 26 | |
|---|---|
| 1 H Anderson (Suzuki) | 89.04mph |
| 2 I Morishita (Suzuki) | (143.30km/h) |
| 3 E Degner (Suzuki) | |
| 4 H-G Anscheidt (Kreidler) | |
| 5 M Itoh (Suzuki) | |
| 6 M Ichino (Suzuki) | |
| Record lap – I Morishita (Suzuki) | 90.51mph |
| | (145.75km/h) |

| French GP Clermont-Ferrand June 2 | |
|---|---|
| 1 H-G Anscheidt (Kreidler) | 60.41mph |
| 2 E Degner (Suzuki) | (97.21km/h) |
| 3 M Ichino (Suzuki) | |
| 4 J Busquets (Derbi) | |
| 5 J-P Beltoise (Kreidler) | |
| 6 A Pagani (Kreidler) | |
| Fastest lap – Anscheidt (Kreidler) | 62.05mph |
| | (99.85km/h) |

| TT Races Isle of Man June 12 | |
|---|---|
| 1 M Itoh (Suzuki) | 78.81mph |
| 2 H Anderson (Suzuki) | (126.82km/h) |
| 3 H-G Anscheidt (Kreidler) | |
| 4 I Morishita (Suzuki) | |
| 5 M Ichino (Suzuki) | |
| 6 I Plumridge (Honda) | |
| Record lap – E Degner (Suzuki) | 79.10mph |
| | (127.29km/h) |

| Dutch TT Assen June 29 | |
|---|---|
| 1 E Degner (Suzuki) | 73.92mph |
| 2 H Anderson (Suzuki) | (118.96km/h) |
| 3 M Ichino (Suzuki) | |
| 4 I Morishita (Suzuki) | |
| 5 M Itoh (Suzuki) | |
| 6 H-G Anscheidt (Kreidler) | |
| Record lap – E Degner (Suzuki) | 76.29km/h |
| | (122.77km/h) |

| Belgian GP Spa Francorchamps July 7 | |
|---|---|
| 1 I Morishita (Suzuki) | 87.92mph |
| 2 E Degner (Suzuki) | (141.49km/h) |
| 3 H-G Anscheidt (Kreidler) | |
| 4 H Anderson (Suzuki) | |
| 5 M Itoh (Suzuki) | |
| 6 J-P Beltoise (Kreidler) | |
| R ecord lap – H-G Anscheidt (Kreidler) | 88.92mph |
| | (143.10km/h) |

| Finnish GP Tampere September 1 | |
|---|---|
| 1 H-G Anscheidt (Kreidler) | 63.73mph |
| 2 M Itoh (Suzuki) | (101.77km/h) |
| 3 H Anderson (Suzuki) | |
| 4 I Morishita (Suzuki) | |
| 5.A Pagani (Kreidler) | |
| 6 M Salonen (Prykija) | |
| Record lap – H Anderson (Suzuki) | 65.78mph |
| | (104.92km/h) |

| Argentine GP Buenos Aires October 6 | |
|---|---|
| 1 H Anderson (Suzuki) | 67.21mph |
| 2 E Degner (Suzuki) | (108.17km/h) |
| 3 A Pagani (Kreidler) | |
| 4 V Kissling (Kreidler) | |
| 5 P Samardijan (Suzuki) | |
| 6 G Biscia (Suzuki) | |
| Record lap – H Anderson (Suzuki) | 68.90mph |
| | (111.04km/h) |

| Japanese GP Suzuka November 10 | |
|---|---|
| 1 L Taveri (Honda) | 76.83mph |
| 2 H Anderson (Suzuki) | (123.65km/h) |
| 3 S Masuda (Suzuki) | |
| 4 M Ichino (Suzuki) | |
| 5 S Shimazaki (Honda) | |
| 6 M Itoh (Suzuki) | |
| Record lap – L Taveri (Honda) | 76.83mph |
| | (123.65km/h) |

## 1963 125 CC

| Spanish GP Montjuich Park May 5 | | West German GP Hockenheim May 26 | | French GP Clermont-Ferrand June 2 | |
|---|---|---|---|---|---|
| 1 L Taveri (Honda) | 68.26mph | 1 E Degner (Suzuki) | 105.63mph | 1 H Anderson (Suzuki) | 72.59mph |
| 2 J Redman (Honda) | (109.86km/h) | 2 H Anderson (Suzuki) | (170.00km/h) | 2 J Redman (Honda) | (116.81km/h) |
| 3 K Takahashi (Honda) | | 3 L Szabo (MZ) | | 3 L Taveri (Honda) | |
| 4 .P Inchley (EMC) | | 4 L Taveri (Honda) | | 4 F Perris (Suzuki) | |
| 5 F Gonzales (Bultaco) | | 5 K Takahashi (Honda) | | 5 T Robb (Honda) | |
| 6 M Duff (Bultaco) | | 6 A Shepherd (MZ) | | 6 E Degner (Suzuki) | |
| Fastest lap – L Taveri (Honda) | 69.26mph | Record lap – E Degner (Suzuki) | 107.40mph | Record lap – H Anderson (Suzuki) | 73.60mph |
| | (111.47km/h) | | (172.84km/h) | | (118.45km/h) |

| TT Races Isle of Man June 12 | | Dutch TT Assen June 29 | | Belgian GP Spa Francorchamps July 7 | |
|---|---|---|---|---|---|
| 1 H Anderson (Suzuki) | 89.27mph | 1 H Anderson (Suzuki) | 82.23mph | 1 B Schneider (Suzuki) | 105.03mph |
| 2 F Perris (Suzuki) | (143.66km/h) | 2 F Perris (Suzuki) | (132.42km/h) | 2 H Anderson (Suzuki) | (169.02km/h) |
| 3 E Degner (Suzuki) | | 3 L Taveri (Honda) | | 3 L Taveri (Honda) | |
| 4 L Taveri (Honda) | | 4 B Schneider (Suzuki) | | 4 G Vicenzi (Honda) | |
| 5 B Schneider (Suzuki) | | 5 K Takahashi (Honda) | | 5 T Robb (Honda) | |
| 6 J Redman (Honda) | | 6 T Robb (Honda) | | 6 J-P Beltoise (Bultaco) | |
| Record lap – H Anderson (Suzuki) | 91.32mph | Record lap – B Schneider (Suzuki) | 85.01mph | Record lap – E Degner (Suzuki) | 108.05mph |
| | (146.96km/h) | | (136.88km/h) | | (173.88km/h) |

| Ulster GP Dundrod August 10 | | East German GP Sachsenring August 18 | | Finnish GP Tampere September 1 | |
|---|---|---|---|---|---|
| 1 H Anderson (Suzuki) | 85.84mph | 1 H Anderson (Suzuki) | 93.09mph | 1 H Anderson (Suzuki) | 72.87mph |
| 2 B Schneider (Suzuki) | (138.14km/h) | 2 A Shepherd (MZ) | (149.89km/h) | 2 L Taveri (Honda) | (117.32km/h) |
| 3 L Taveri (Honda) | | 3 B Schneider (Suzuki) | | 3 A Shepherd (MZ) | |
| 4 T Robb (Honda) | | 4 L Taveri (Honda) | | 4 L Szabo (MZ) | |
| 5 K Takahashi (Honda) | | 5 M Duff (MZ) | | 5 J Redman (Honda) | |
| 6 F Perris (Suzuki) | | 6 W Musiol (MZ) | | 6 G Dickinson (Honda) | |
| Fastest lap – B Schneider (Suzuki) | 87.93mph | Record lap – H Anderson (Suzuki) | 94.06mph | Record lap – H Anderson (Suzuki) | 74.58mph |
| | (141.60km/h) | | (151.47km/h) | | (119.19km/h) |

| Italian GP Monza September 15 | | Argentine GP Buenos Aires October 6 | | Japanese GP Suzuka November 10 | |
|---|---|---|---|---|---|
| 1 L Taveri (Honda) | 97.22mph | 1 J Redman (Honda) | 71.20mph | 1 F Perris (Suzuki) | 84.15mph |
| 2 J Redman (Honda) | (156,46km/h) | 2 H Pochettino (Bultaco) | (114.65km/h) | 2 J Redman (Honda) | (135.43km/h) |
| 3 K Takahashi (Honda) | | 3 B Caldarella (Bultaco) | | 3 E Degner (Suzuki) | |
| 4 G Vicenzi (Honda) | | 4 R Gomez (Zanella) | | 4 T Robb (Honda) | |
| 5 J Grace (Bultaco) | | 5 J Salatino (Zanella) | | 5 H Anderson (Suzuki) | |
| 6 S Malina (CZ) | | 6 S Maffia (Ducati) | | 6 M Itoh (Suzuki) | |
| Fastest lap – Redman/Taveri | 99.09mph | Record lap – J Redman (Hnda) | 72.90mph | Record lap – J Redman (Honda) | 85.40mph |
| (Honda) | (159.46km/h) | | (117.38km/h) | | (137.58km/h) |

## 1963 250CC

| Spanish GP Montjuich Park May 5 | | West German GP Hockenheim May 26 | | TT Races Isle of Man June 10 | |
|---|---|---|---|---|---|
| 1 T Provini (Morini) | 72.74mph | 1 T Provini (Morini) | 116.26mph | 1 J Redman (Honda) | 94.85mph |
| 2 J Redman (Honda) | (117.05km/h) | 2 T Robb (Honda) | (187.10km/h) | 2 F Ito (Yamaha) | (152.65km/h) |
| 3 T Robb (Honda) | | 3 J Redman (Honda) | | 3 W A.Smith (Honda) | |
| 4 K Takahashi (Honda) | | 4 S Grassetti (Benelli) | | 4 H Hasegawa (Yamaha) | |
| 5 L Taveri (Honda) | | 5 A Shepherd (MZ) | | 5 T Robb (Honda) | |
| 6 G Milani (Aermacchi) | | 6 S Malina (CZ) | | 6 J Kidson (Guzzi) | |
| Record lap – T Provini (Morini) | | Record lap – T Provini (Morini) | 118.27mph | Fastest lap – J Redman (Honda) | |
| | 73.83mph | | (190.33km/h) | | 97.23mph |
| | (118.81km/h) | | | | (156.47km/h) |

| Dutch TT Assen June 29 | | Belgian GP Spa Francorchamps July 7 | | Ulster GP Dundrod August 10 | |
|---|---|---|---|---|---|
| 1 J Redman (Honda) | 86.19mph | 1 F Ito (Yamaha) | 115.49mph | 1 J Redman (Honda) | 86.64mph |
| 2 F Ito (Yamaha) | (138.71km/h) | 2 Y Sunako (Yamaha) | (185.85km/h) | 2 T Provini (Morini) | (139.43km/h) |
| 3 T Provini (Morini) | | 3 T Provini (Morini) | | 3 T Robb (Honda) | |
| 4 Y Sunako (Yamaha) | | 4 L Taveri (Honda) | | 4 K Takahashi (Honda) | |
| 5 T Robb (Honda) | | 5 T Robb (Honda) | | 5 J Findlay (Mondial) | |
| 6 D Swart (Honda) | | 6 K Takahashi (Honda) | | 6 C Anderson (Aermacchi) | |
| Fastest lap – J Redman (Honda) | 87.61mph | Record lap – F Ito (Yamaha) | 117.82mph | Fastest lap – T Provini (Morini) | 89.23mph |
| | (141.01km/h) | | (189.61km/h) | | (143.60km/h) |

| East German GP Sachsenring August 18 | | Italian GP Monza September 15 | | Argentine GP Buenos Aires | |
|---|---|---|---|---|---|
| 1 M Hailwood (MZ) | 98.23mph | 1 T Provini (Morini) | 111.60mph | 1 T Provini (Morini) | 78.80mph |
| 2 A Shepherd (MZ) | (158.19km/h) | 2 J Redman (Honda) | (179.60km/h) | 2 J Redman (Honda) | (126.90km/h) |
| 3 J Redman (Honda) | | 3 L Taveri (Honda) | | 3 U Masetti (Morini) | |
| 4 L Szabo (MZ) | | 4 A Shepherd (MZ) | | 4 R Kissling (NSU) | |
| 5 L Taveri (Honda) | | 5 S Malina (CZ) | | 5 V Schumann (NSU) | |
| 6 S Malina (CZ) | | 6 T Robb (Honda) | | 6 C Marfetan (Parilla) | |
| Fastest lap – M Hailwood (MZ) | 100.19mph | Fastest lap – T Provini (Morini) | 113.23mph | Record lap – T Provini (Morini) | 81.60mph |
| | (161.33km/h) | | (182.22km/h) | | (131.38km/h) |

| Japanese GP Suzuka November 10 | | | | | |
|---|---|---|---|---|---|
| 1 J Redman (Honda) | 87.25mph | | | | |
| 2 F Ito (Yamaha) | (140.42km/h) | | | | |
| 3 P Read (Yamaha) | | | | | |
| 4 T Provini (Morini) | | | | | |
| 5 L Taveri (Honda) | | | | | |
| 6 I Kasuya (Honda) | | | | | |
| Record lap – F Ito (Yamaha) | 88.71mph | | | | |
| | (142.76km/h) | | | | |

## 1963 350CC

| West German GP Hockenheim May 26 | | TT Races Isle of Man June 14 | | Dutch TT Assen June 29 | |
|---|---|---|---|---|---|
| 1 J Redman (Honda) | 121.85mph | 1 J Redman (Honda) | 94.91mph | 1 J Redman (Honda) | 86.95mph |
| 2 R Venturi (Bianchi) | (196.10km/h) | 2 J Hartle (Gilera) | (152.74km/h) | 2 M Hailwood (MV) | (139.93km/h) |
| 3 P Read (Gilera) | | 3 F Stastny (Jawa) | | 3 L Taveri (Honda) | |
| 4 G Havel (Jawa) | | 4 S Mizen (AJS) | | 4 F Stastny (jawa) | |
| 5 G Milani (Aermacchi) | | 5 J Ahearn (Norton) | | 5 J Ahearn (Norton) | |
| 6 F Stevens (Norton) | | 6 M Duff (AJS) | | 6 G Havel (Jawa) | |
| Record lap – J Redman (Honda) | 123.23mph | Fastest lap – J Redman (Honda) | 101.58mph | Record lap – J Redman (Honda) | 88.11mph |
| | (198.31km/h) | | (163.02km/h) | | (141.77km/h) |
| **Ulster GP Dundrod August 10** | | **East German GP Sachsenring August 18** | | **Finnish GP Tampere September 1** | |
| 1 J Redman (Honda) | 93.78mph | 1 M Hailwood (MV) | 99.85mph | 1 M Hailwood (MV) | 75.33mph |
| 2 M Hailwood (MV) | (150.91km/h) | 2 L Taveri (Honda) | (165.34km/h) | 2 J Redman (MV) | (117.36km/h) |
| 3 L Taveri (Honda) | | 3 J Redman (Honda) | | 3 S Gunnarsson (Norton) | |
| 4 M Duff (AJS) | | 4 G Havel (Jawa) | | 4 N Sevostianov (S360) | |
| 5 F Stevens (Norton) | | 5 N Sevostianov (S360) | | 5 L Taveri (Honda) | |
| 6 L Ireland (Norton) | | 6 M Duff (AJS) | | 6 S Mizen (AJS) | |
| Record lap – J Redman (Honda) | 95.83mph | Record lap – M Hailwood (MV) | 102.67mph | Record lap – M Hailwood (MV) | 75.85mph |
| | (154.22km/h) | | (165.48km/h) | | (120.99km/h) |
| **Italian GP Monza September 15** | | **Japanese GP Suzuka November 10** | | | |
| 1 J Redman (Honda) | 113.41mph | 1 J Redman (Honda) | 84.53mph | | |
| 2 A Shepherd (MZ) | (182.51km/h) | 2 I Yamashita (Honda) | (136.34km/h) | | |
| 3 T Robb (Honda) | | 3 L Taveri (Honda) | | | |
| 4 F Slavicek (Jawa) | | | | | |
| 5 D Shorey (AJS) | | *This race did not count towards | | | |
| 6 F Stevens (Norton) | | the | | | |
| Record lap – J Redman (Honda) | 114.95mph | World Championships. | | | |
| | (184.81km/h) | | | | |

## 1963 500CC

| TT Races Isle of Man June 14 | | Dutch TT Assen June 29 | | Belgian GP Spa Francorchamps July 7 | |
|---|---|---|---|---|---|
| 1 M Hailwood (MV) | 104.64mph | 1 J Hartle (Gilera) | 88.11mph | 1 M Hailwood (MV) | 123.99mph |
| 2 J Hartle (Gilera) | (168.34km/h) | 2 P Read (Gilera) | (141.79km/h) | 2 P Read (Gilera) | (199.53km/h) |
| 3 P Read (Gilera) | | 3 A Shepherd (Matchless) | | 3 A Shepherd (Matchless) | |
| 4 M Duff (Matchless) | | 4 J Ahearn (Norton) | | 4 F Stevens (Norton) | |
| 5 J Dunphy (Norton) | | 5 F Stevens (Norton) | | 5 J Ahearn (Norton) | |
| 6 F Stevens (Norton) | | 6 S Gunnarsson (Norton) | | 6 G Marsovsky (Matchless) | |
| Record lap – M Hailwood (MV) | 106.41mph | Fastest lap – J Hartle (Gilera) | 89.71mph | Record lap – M Hailwood (MV) | 125.61mph |
| | (171.25km/h) | | (144.38km/h) | | (202.14km/h) |
| **Ulster GP Dundrod August 10** | | **East German GP Sachsenring August 18** | | **Finnish GP Tampere September 1** | |
| 1 M Hailwood (MV) | 99.27mph | 1 M Hailwood (MV) | 103.16mph | 1 M Hailwood (MV) | 78.73mph |
| 2 J Hartle (Gilera) | (159.97km/h) | 2 D Minter (Gilera) | (166.02km/h) | 2 A Shepherd (Matchless) | (126.78km/h) |
| 3 D Minter (Gilera) | Record | 3 A Shepherd (Matchless) | | 3 M Duff (Matchless) | |
| 4 A Shepherd (Matchless) | | 4 M Duff (Matchless) | | 4 F Stevens (Norton) | |
| 5 R Bryans (Norton) | | 5 J Findlay (Matchless) | | 5 S Mizen (Matchless) | |
| 6 M Duff (Matchless) | | 6 V Cottle (Norton) | | 6 N Sevostianov (CKB) | |
| Record lap – M Hailwood (MV) | 101.28mph | Record lap – M Hailwood (MV) | 104.65mph | Record lap – M Hailwood (MV) | 80.62mph |
| | (162.99km/h) | | (168.53km/h) | | (129.48km/h) |
| **Italian GP Monza September 15** | | **Argentine GP Buenos Aires October 6** | | | |
| 1 M Hailwood (MV) | 118.07mph | 1 M Hailwood (MV) | 80.05mph | | |
| 2 J Findlay (Matchless) | (190.00km/h) | 2 J Kissling (Norton) | (139.45km/h) | | |
| 3 F Stevens (Norton) | Record | 3 B Caldarella (Matchless) | | | |
| 4 .W A.Smith (Norton) | | 4 N Minguzzi (Matchless) | | | |
| 5 L Richter (Norton) | | 5 F Villavelran (Norton) | | | |
| 6 V Loro (Norton) | | 6 G Costa (Norton) | | | |
| Record lap – M Hailwood (MV) | 119.99mph | Fastest lap – M Hailwood (MV) | 81.70mph | | |
| | (193.08km/h) | | (141.62km/h) | | |

## 1963 SIDECARS

| Spanish GP Montjuich Park May 5 | | West German GP Hockenheim May 26 | | TT Races Isle of Man June 10 | |
|---|---|---|---|---|---|
| 1 M Deubel/E Horner (BMW)<br>2 O Kolle/D Hess (BMW)<br>3 F Camathias/A Herzig (BMW)<br>4 A Birch/P Birch (BMW)<br>5 G Auerbacher/B Heim (BMW)<br>6 .C Seeley/W Rawlings (Matchless)<br>Record lap – Deubel/Horner (BMW) | 66.41mph<br>(106.88km/h)<br><br><br><br><br>68.83mph<br>(110.77km/h) | 1 F Camathias/A Herzig (BMW)<br>2 M Deubel/E Horner (BMW)<br>3 G Auerbacher/B Heim (BMW)<br>4 A Butscher/H Vester (BMW)<br>5 F Breu/H Golsch (BMW)<br>6 C Lambert/G Rufenacht (BMW)<br>Record lap – Camathias/Herzig | 109.67mph<br>(176.50km/h)<br><br><br><br><br>111.47mph<br>(179.18km/h) | 1 F Camathias/A Herzig (BMW)<br>2 F Scheidegger/J Robinson (BMW)<br>3 A Birch/P Birch (BMW)<br>4 O Kolle/D Hess (BMW)<br>5 G Auerbacher/B Heim (BMW)<br>6 C Seeley/W Rawlings (Matchless)<br>Fastest lap – Camathias/Herzig | 88.38mph<br>(142.23km/h)<br><br><br><br><br>89.42mph<br>(143.91km/h |
| **Dutch TT Assen June 29** | | **Belgian GP Spa Francorchamps July 7** | | | |
| 1 M Deubel/E Horner (BMW)<br>2 F Scheidegger/J Robinson (BMW)<br>3 F Camathias/A Herzig (BMW)<br>4 O Kolle/D Hess (BMW)<br>5 G Auerbacher/B Heim (BMW)<br>6 C Vincent/K/Scott (BSA)<br>Record lap – Deubel/Horner (BMW) | 78.41mph<br>(126.18km/h)<br><br><br><br><br>79.33mph<br>(127.78km/h) | 1 F Scheidegger/J Robinson (BMW)<br>2 M Deubel/E Horner (BMW)<br>3 G Auerbacher/B Heim (BMW)<br>4 J Beeton/E Bulgin (BMW)<br>5 O Kolle/D Hess (BMW)<br>6 A Birch/P Birch (BMW)<br>Record lap – Camathias/Herzig BMW | 107.13mph<br>(172.41km/h)<br><br><br><br><br>109.86mph<br>(176.80km/h) | | |

## 1964 50CC

| United States GP Daytona February 1 | | Spanish GP Montjuich Park May 3 | | French GP Clermont Ferrand May 17 | |
|---|---|---|---|---|---|
| 1 H Anderson (Suzuki)<br>2 I Morishita (Suzuki)<br>3 M Itoh (Suzuki)<br>4 H-G Anscheidt (Kreidler)<br>5 J-P Beltoise (Kreidler)<br>6 D Allen (Ducati)<br>Fastest lap – H Anderson (Suzuki) | 78.93mph<br>(127.03km/h)<br><br><br><br><br>79.82mph<br>(128.75km/h) | 1 H-G Anscheidt (Kreidler)<br>2 H Anderson (Suzuki)<br>3 M Itoh (Suzuki)<br>4 I Morishita (Suzuki)<br>5 A Nieto (Derbi)<br>6 L Taveri (Kreidler)<br>Record lap –Anscheidt (Kreidler) | 64.23mph<br>(103.37km/h)<br><br><br><br><br>65.58mph<br>(105.54km/h) | 1 H Anderson (Suzuki)<br>2 H-G Anscheidt (Kreidler)<br>3.J-P Beltoise (Kreidler)<br>4 J Busquets (Derbi)<br>5 I Morishita (Suzuki)<br>6 T Provini (Kreidler)<br>Record lap – H Anderson (Suzuki) | 65.79mph<br>(105.87k mh)<br><br><br><br><br>66.46mph<br>(106.96km/h) |
| **TT Races Isle of Man June 10** | | **Dutch TT Assen June 27** | | **Belgian GP Spa Francorchamps July 5** | |
| 1 H Anderson (Suzuki)<br>2 R Bryans (Honda)<br>3 I Morishita (Suzuki)<br>4 H-G Anscheidt (Kreidler)<br>5 M Itoh (Suzuki)<br>6 N Taniguchi (Honda)<br>Record lap – H Anderson (Suzuki) | 80.64mph<br>(129.77km/h)<br><br><br><br><br>81.13mph<br>(130.57km/h) | 1 R Bryans (Honda)<br>2 I Morishita (Suzuki)<br>3 M Itoh (Suzuki)<br>4 H-G Anscheidt (Kreidler)<br>5 C VanDongen (Kreidler)<br>Only 5 finishers<br>Record lap – R Bryans (Honda) | 75.34mph<br>(121.24km/h)<br><br><br><br><br>76.49mph<br>(123.03km/h) | 1 R Bryans (Honda)<br>2 H-G Anscheidt (Kreidler)<br>3 H Anderson (Suzuki)<br>4 M Itoh (Suzuki)<br>5 I Morishita (Suzuki)<br>6 R Kunz (Kreidler)<br>Record lap – R Bryans (Honda) | 91.71mph<br>(147.59km/h)<br><br><br><br><br>92.46mph<br>(148.79km/h) |
| **West German GP Solitude July 19** | | **Finnish GP Imatra August 30** | | **Japanese GP Suzuka November 1** | |
| 1 R Bryans (Honda)<br>2 I Morishita (Suzuki)<br>3 M Itoh (Suzuki)<br>4 H-G Anscheidt (Kreidler)<br>5 P Eser (Honda)<br>6 F Bairle (Kreidler)<br>Record lap – R Bryans (Honda) | 74.97mph<br>(120.66km/h)<br><br><br><br><br>76.05mph<br>(122.39km/h) | 1 H Anderson (Suzuki)<br>2 H-G Anscheidt (Kreidler)<br>3 L Taveri (Kreidler)<br>4 I Morishita (Suzuki)<br>5 R Kunz (Kreidler)<br>6 C Mates (Honda)<br>Fastest lap – H Anderson (Suzuki) | 68.31mph<br>(109.91km/h)<br><br><br><br><br>69.31mph<br>(110.99km/h) | 1 R Bryans (Honda)<br>2 L Taveri (Honda)<br>3 N Taniguchi (Honda)<br>4 A Itoh (Honda)<br>Record lap – R Bryans (Honda)<br><br>This race did not count towards the Championship due to only 4 starters | 76.76mph<br>(123.52km/h)<br><br><br>77.90mph<br>(125.30km/h) |

## 1964 125CC

| United States GP Daytona February 1 | | Spanish GP Montjuich Park May 3 | | French GP Clermont Ferrand May 17 | |
|---|---|---|---|---|---|
| 1 H Anderson (Suzuki)<br>2 M Itoh (Suzuki)<br>3 B Schneider (Suzuki)<br>4 I Morishita (Suzuki)<br>5 J-P Beltoise (Bultaco)<br>6 R Dickinson (Honda)<br>Fastest lap – H Anderson (Suzuki) | 88.30mph<br>(142.43km/h)<br><br><br><br><br>89.80mph<br>(144.84km/h) | 1 L Taveri (Honda)<br>2 J Redman (Honda)<br>3 R Avery (EMC)<br>4 B Schneider (Suzuki)<br>5 H Anderson (Suzuki)<br>6 C Vincent (Honda)<br>Record lap – L Taveri (Honda) | 69.92mph<br>(112.52km/h)<br><br><br><br><br>71.18mph<br>(114.39km/h) | 1 L Taveri (Honda)<br>2 B Schneider (Suzuki)<br>3 F Perris (Suzuki)<br>4 K Takahashi (Honda)<br>5 J-P Beltoise (Butaco)<br>6 R Foll (Honda)<br>Record lap – L Taveri (Honda) | 73.27mph<br>(117.89km/h)<br><br><br><br><br>74.64mph<br>(120.12km/h) |

| TT Races Isle of Man June 10 | | Dutch TT Assen June 27 | | West German GP Solitude July 19 | |
|---|---|---|---|---|---|
| 1 L Taveri (Honda) | 92.14mph | 1 J Redman (Honda) | 84.09mph | 1 J Redman (Honda) | 83.80mph |
| 2 J Redman (Honda) | (148.28km/h) | 2 P Read (Yamaha) | (135.33km/h) | 2 L Taveri (Honda) | (134.80km/h) |
| 3 R Bryans (Honda) | | 3 R Bryans (Honda) | | 3 W Scheimann (Honda) | |
| 4 S Malina (CZ) | | 4 B Schneider (Suzuki) | | 4 B Schneider (Suzuki) | |
| 5 W Scheimann (Honda) | | 5 H Anderson (Suzuki) | | 5 J Thomas (Honda) | |
| 6 B Beale (Honda) | | 6 F Perris (Suzuki) | | 6 P Eser (Honda) | |
| Record lap – L Taveri (Honda) | 94.18mph | Record lap – J Redman (Honda) | 85.40mph | Record lap – H Anderson (Suzuki) | 91.99mph |
| | (150.57km/h) | | (137.35km/h) | | (148.04km/h) |
| **East German GP Sachsenring July 26** | | **Ulster GP Dundrod August 8** | | **Finnish GP Imatra August 30** | |
| 1 H Anderson (Suzuki) | 94.27mph | 1 H Anderson (Suzuki) | 91.53mph | 1 L Taveri (Honda) | 78.20mph |
| 2 L Taveri (Honda) | (151.71km/h) | 2 L Taveri (Honda) | (147.30km/h) | 2 R Bryans (Honda) | (125.84km/h) |
| 3 J Redman (Honda) | | 3 R Bryans (Honda) | | 3 J Redman (Honda) | |
| 4 H Rosner (MZ) | | 4 F Perris (Suzuki) | | 4 B Schneider (Suzuki) | |
| 5 F Kohlar (MZ) | | 5 B Schneider (Suzuki) | | 5 K Enderlein (MZ) | |
| 6 B Beale (Honda) | | 6 R Torras (Bultaco) | | 6 D Krumpholz (MZ) | |
| Record lap – H Anderson (Suzuki) | 93.91mph | Record lap – H Anderson (Suzuki) | 93.67mph | Fastest lap – L Taveri (Honda) | 79.72mph |
| | (154.33km/h) | | (150.74km/h) | | (127.55/mh) |
| **Italian GP Monza September 13** | | **Japanese GP Suzuka November 1** | | | |
| 1 L Taveri (Honda) | 105.24mph | 1 E Degner (Suzuki) | 85.18mph | | |
| 2 H Anderson (Suzuki) | (169.36km/h) | 2 L Taveri (Honda) | (137.08km/h) | | |
| 3 E Degner (Suzuki) | | 3 Y Katayama (Suzuki) | | | |
| 4 R Bryans (Honda) | | 4 T Tanaka (Honda) | | | |
| 5 F Perris (Suzuki) | | 5 I Matsushima (Yamaha) | | | |
| 6 J Redman (Honda) | | 6 A Motohashi (Yamaha) | | | |
| Record lap – H Anderson (Suzuki) | 107.01mph | Record lap – H Anderson (Suzuki) | 86.59mph | | |
| | (172.21km/h) | | (139.27km/h) | | |

## 1964 250CC

| United States GP Daytona February 2 | | Spanish GP Montjuich Park May 3 | | French GP Clermont Ferrand May 17 | |
|---|---|---|---|---|---|
| 1 A Shepherd (MZ) | 91.19mph | 1 T Provini (Benelli) | 71.78mph | 1 P Read (Yamaha) | 75.35mph |
| 2 .R Grant (Parilla) | (146.75km/h) | 2 J Redman (Honda) | (115.51km/h) | 2 L Taveri (Honda) | (121.26km/h) |
| 3 B Ghering (Bultaco) | | 3 P read (Yamaha) | | 3 B Schneider (Suzuki) | Record |
| 4 J Rocket (Ducati) | | 4 I Kasuya (Honda) | | 4 B Beale (Honda) | |
| 5 D Brown (Ducati) | | 5 H Anderson (Suzuki) | | 5 R Foll (Honda) | |
| 6 R Hamilton (Ducati) | | 6 J Sirera (Montesa) | | 6 R Mailles (Morini) | |
| Fastest lap – A Shepherd (MZ) | 94.37mph | Fastest lap – T Provini (Benelli) | 72.97mph | Record lap – Read & Redman | 77.37mph |
| | (152.21km/h) | | (117.42km/h) | | (124.50km/h) |
| **TT Races Isle of Man June 8** | | **Dutch TT Assen June 27** | | **Belgian GP Spa Francorchamps July 5** | |
| 1 J Redman (Honda) | 97.45mph | 1 J Redman (Honda) | 88.43mph | 1 M Duff (Yamaha) | 118.41mph |
| 2 A Shepherd (MZ) | (156.83km/h) | 2 P Read (Yamaha) | (142.31km/h) | 2 J Redman (Honda) | (190.56km/h) |
| 3 A Pagani (Paton) | | 3 T Robb (Yamaha) | Record | 3 A Shepherd (MZ) | Record |
| 4 S Malina (CZ) | | 4 T Provini (Benelli) | | 4 T Robb (Yamaha) | |
| 5 R Boughey (Yamaha) | | 5 M Duff (Yamaha) | | 5 T Provini (Benelli) | |
| 6 C Hunt (Aermacchi) | | 6 G Milani (Aermacchi) | | 6 I Kasuya (Honda) | |
| Fastest lap – P Read (Yamaha) | 99.42mph | Record lap – J Redman (Honda) | 89.29mph | Record lap – M Duff (Yamaha) | 120.29mph |
| | (160.98km/h) | | (143.61km/h) | | (193.60km/h) |
| **West German GP Solitude July 19** | | **East German GP Sachsenring July 26** | | **Ulster GP Dundrod August 8** | |
| 1 P Read (Yamaha) | 97.00mph | 1 P Read (Yamaha) | 99.64mph | 1 P Read (Yamaha) | 85.91mph |
| 2 J Redman (Honda) | (156.11km/h) | 2 J Redman (Honda) | (160.36km/h) | 2 J Redman (Honda) | (138.26km/h) |
| 3 M Duff (Yamaha) | Record | 3 B Beale (Honda) | Record | 3 R Bryans (Honda) | |
| 4 G Agostini (Morini) | | 4 G Milani (Aermacchi) | | 4 A Shepherd (MZ) | |
| 5 T Provini (Benelli) | | 5 A Pagani (Paton) | | 5 B Beale (Honda) | |
| 6 L Taveri (Honda) | | 6 K Gast (MZ) | | 6 B Schneider (Suzuki) | |
| Record lap – P Read (Yamaha) | 99.37mph | Record lap – M Hailwood (MZ) | 102.06mph | Fastest lap – P Read (Yamaha) | 87.42mph |
| | (159.92km/h) | | (164.24km/h) | | (140.68km/h) |
| **Italian GP Monza September 13** | | **Japanese GP Suzuka October 1** | | | |
| 1 P Read (Yamaha) | 113.91mph | 1 J Redman (Honda) | 87.26mph | | |
| 2 M Duff (Yamaha) | (183.31km/h) | 2 I Kasuya (Honda) | (141.43km/h) | | |
| 3.J .Redman (Honda) | Record | 3 H Hasegawa (Yamaha) | Record | | |
| 4 G Agostini (Morini) | | 4 L Taveri (Honda) | | | |
| 5 A Shepherd (MZ) | | 5 M Hailwood (MZ) | | | |
| 6 L Taveri (Honda) | | Only 5 finishers | | | |
| Record lap – M Duff (Yamaha) | 116.08mph | Fastest lap – J Redman (Honda) | 88.77mph | | |
| | (186.81km/h) | | (142.76km/h) | | |

## 1964 350CC

| TT Races Isle of Man June 12 | | Dutch TT Assen June 27 | | West German GP Solitude July 19 | |
|---|---|---|---|---|---|
| 1 J Redman (Honda) | 98.50mph | 1 J Redman (Honda) | 87.41mph | 1 J Redman (Honda) | 94.90mph |
| 2 P Read (AJS) | (158.52km/h) | 2 M Hailwood (MV) | (140.66km/h) | 2 B Beale (Honda) | (152.77km/h) |
| 3 M Duff (AJS) | Record | 3 R Venturi (Bianchi) | Record | 3 M Duff (AJS) | Record |
| 4 D Minter (Norton) | | 4 P Driver (AJS) | | 4 G Milani (Aermacchi) | |
| 5 D Woodman (AJS) | | 5 M Duff (AJS) | | 5 P Driver (AJS) | |
| 6 J Dunphy (Norton) | | 6 D Minter (Norton) | | 6 V Cottle (AJS) | |
| Fastest lap – J Redman (Honda) | 100.76mph | Record lap – J Redman (Honda) | 88.97mph | Record lap – J Redman (Honda) | |
| | (162.16km/h) | | (143.10km/h) | | 99.79mph |
| | | | | | (160.61km/h) |
| **East German GP Sachsenring July 26** | | **Ulster GP Dundrod August 8** | | **Finnish GP Imatra August 30** | |
| 1 J Redman (Honda) | 96.82mph | 1 J Redman (Honda) | 93.82mph | 1 J Redman (Honda) | 82.77mph |
| 2 G Havel (Jawa) | (155.81km/h) | 2 M Duff (AJS) | (150.88km/h) | 2 B Beale (Honda) | (132.50km/h) |
| 3 M Duff (AJS) | | 3 G Havel (Jawa) | Record | 3 E Kiisa (SKEB) | |
| 4 B Beale (Honda) | | 4 B Beale (Honda) | | 4 A Shepherd (MZ) | |
| 5 V Cottle (AJS) | | 5 C Conn (Norton) | | 5 M Duff (AJS) | |
| 6 F Stevens (AJS) | | 6 F Stevens (AJS) | | 6 D Woodman (AJS) | |
| Fastest lap – J Redman (Honda) | 97.91mph | Record lap – J Redman (Honda) | 96.10mph | Fastest lap – J Redman (Honda) | 84.25mph |
| | (157.55km/h) | | (154.67km/h) | | (134.99km/h) |
| **Italian GP Monza September 13** | | **Japanese GP Suzuka October 1** | | | |
| 1 J Redman (Honda) | 112.35mph | 1 J Redman (Honda) | 86.00mph | | |
| 2 B Beale (Honda) | (180.81km/h) | 2 M Hailwood (MZ) | (138.72km/h) | | |
| 3 S Malina (CZ) | | 3 I Kasuya (Honda) | | | |
| 4 R Passolini (Aermacchi) | | 4 I Yamashita (Yamaha) | | | |
| 5 M Duff (AJS) | | 5 N Nagamatsu (Honda) | | | |
| 6 J Ahearn (Norton) | | Only 5 finishers | | | |
| Record lap – R Venturi (Bianchi) | 116.61mph | Record lap – J Redman (Honda) | 87.82mph | | |
| | (187.84km/h) | | (141.65km/h) | | |

## 1964 500CC

| United States GP Daytona February 2 | | TT Races Isle of Man June 12 | | Dutch TT Assen June 27 | |
|---|---|---|---|---|---|
| 1 M Hailwood (MV) | 100.16mph | 1 M Hailwood (MV) | 100.92mph | 1 M Hailwood (MV) | 87.58mph |
| 2 P Read (Matchless) | (161.20km/h) | 2 D Minter (Norton) | (162.42km/h) | 2 R Venturi (Bianchi) | (140.95km/h) |
| 3 J Hartle (Norton) | | 3 F Stevens (Matchless) | | 3 P Driver (Matchless) | |
| 4 M Duff (Matchless) | | 4 D Woodman (Matchless) | | 4 J Ahearn (Norton) | |
| 5 P Driver (Matchless ) | | 5 G Jenkins (Norton) | | 5 F Stevens (Matchless) | |
| 6 B Parriott (Norton) | | 6 B McCosh (Matchless) | | 6 P Read (Matchless) | |
| Record lap – M Hailwood (MV) | 103.07mph | Fastest lap – M Hailwood (MV) | 102.51mph | Record lap – M Hailwood (MV) | 89.95mph |
| | (166.25km/h) | | (164.97km/h) | | (144.66km/h) |
| **Belgian GP Spa Francorchamps July 5** | | **West German GP Solitude July 19** | | **East German GP Sachsenring July 26** | |
| 1 M Hailwood (MV) | 122.90mph | 1 M Hailwood (MV) | 97.68mph | 1 M Hailwood (MV) | 101.33mph |
| 2 P Read (Matchless) | (197.79km/h) | 2 J Ahearn (Norton) | (157.20km/h) | 2 M Duff (Matchless) | (163.08km/h) |
| 3 P Driver (Matchless) | | 3 P Read (Matchless) | | 3 P Driver (Matchless) | |
| 4 J Ahearn (Norton) | | 4 G Marsovsky (Matchless) | | 4 N Sevostianov (SKEB) | |
| 5 J Findlay (Matchless) | | 5 M Low (Norton) | | 5 D Woodman (Matchless) | |
| 6 D Woodman (Matchless) | | 6 F Stevens (Norton) | | 6 J Ahearn (Norton) | |
| Fastest lap – M Hailwood (MV) | 123.36mph | Fastest lap – M Hailwood (MV) | 99.42mph | Fastest lap – M Hailwood (MV) | 103.87mph |
| | (198.97km/h) | | (160.36km/h) | | (166.27km/h) |
| **Ulster GP Dundrod August 8** | | **Finnish GP Imatra August 30** | | **Italian GP Monza September 13** | |
| 1 P Read (Norton) | 82.24mph | 1 J Ahearn (Norton) | 81.62mph | 1 M Hailwood (MV) | 119.15mph |
| 2 D Creith (Norton) | (132.35km/h) | 2 M Duff (Matchless) | (131.35km/h) | 2 B Caldarella (Gilera) | (191.75km/h) |
| 3 J Ahearn (Norton) | | 3 G Marsovsky (Matchless) | | 3 J Ahearn (Norton) | Record |
| 4 R Fitton (Norton) | | 4 N Sevostianov (SKEB) | | 4 M Duff (Matchless) | |
| 5 C Conn (Norton) | | 5 P Driver (Matchless) | | 5 J Findlay (Matchless) | |
| 6 F Stevens (matchless) | | 6 L Young (Matchless) | | 6 W Scheimann (Norton) | |
| Fastest lap – P Read (Norton) | 83.97mph | Fastest lap – M Duff (Matchless) | 82.45mph | Record lap – B Caldarella (Gilera) | 121.80mph |
| | (135.45km/h) | | (132.99km/h) | | (196.02km/h) |

## 1964 SIDECARS

| Spanish GP Montjuich Park May 3 | | French GP Clermont Ferrand May 17 | | TT Races Isle of Man June 8 | |
|---|---|---|---|---|---|
| 1 F Camathias/R Foll (Gilera) | 66.43mph | 1 F Scheidegger/J Robinson (BMW) | 67.65mph | 1 M Deubel/E Horner (BME) | 89.12mph |
| 2 O Kolle/D Hess (BMW) | (106.91km/h) | 2 M Deubel/E Horner (BMW) | (108.87km/h) | 2 C Seeley/W Rawlings (FCS/BMW) | (143.42km/h) |
| 3 G Auerbacher/B Heim (BMW) | Record | 3 G Auerbacher/B Heim (BMW) | Record | 3 G Auerbacher/B Heim (BMW) | Record |
| 4 M Deubel/E Horner (BMW) | | 4 C Seeley/W Rawlings (FCS/BMW) | | 4 A Butscher/W Kalauch (BMW) | |
| 5 C Vincent/K Scott (BMW) | | 5 A Butscher/W/Kalauch (BMW) | | 5 T Vinicombe/G Golder (Triumph) | |
| 6 L Hahn/G Schafer (BMW) | | 6 J Duhem/F Fernandez (BMW) | | 6 T Jackson/P Hartil (BMW) | |
| Fastest lap – O Kolle (BMW) | 67.81mph | Fastest lap – F Scheidegger (BMW) | 69.11mph | Record lap – M Deubel (BMW) | 89.43mph |
| | (109.38km/h) | | (111.48km/h) | | (144.25km/h) |
| **Dutch TT Assen June 27** | | **Belgian GP Spa Francorchamps July 5** | | **West German GP Solitude July 19** | |
| 1 C Seeley/W Rawlings (FCS/BMW) | 78.74mph | 1 M Deubel/E Horner (BMW) | 106.42mph | 1 F Scheidegger/J Robinson (BMW) | 87.55mph |
| 2 C Vincent/K/Scott (BMW) | (126.78km/h) | 2 F Scheidegger/J Robinson (BMW) | (171.26km/h) | 2 M Deubel/E Horner (BMW) | (140.90km/h) |
| 3 F Scheidegger/J Robinson (BMW) | Record | 3 G Auerbacher/B Heim (BMW) | | 3 G Auerbacher/B Heim (BMW) | |
| 4 M Deubel/E Horner (BMW) | | 4 P Harris/R Campbell (BMW) | | 4 A Butscher/W Kalauch (BMW) | |
| 5 O Kolle/H Marquardt (BMW) | | 5 O Kolle/D Hess (BMW) | | 5 A Wolf/W Zielaff (BMW) | |
| 6 G Auerbacher/B Heim (BMW) | | 6 A Butscher/W Kalauch (BMW) | | 6 G Selbmann/L Ronsdorf (BMW) | |
| Record lap – Seeley & Vincent (BMW) | 79.63mph | Fastest lap – F Camathias (BMW) | 107.22mph | Fastest lap – M Deubel (BMW) | 881.6mph |
| | (128.45km/h) | | (172.94km/h) | | (142.20km/h) |

## 1965 50CC

| United States GP Daytona March 20 | | German GP Nurburgring South April 25 | | Spanish GP Montjuich Park May 9 | |
|---|---|---|---|---|---|
| 1 E Degner (Suzuki | 77.55mph | 1 R Bryans (Honda) | 73.46mph | 1 H Anderson (Suzuki) | 64.58mph |
| 2 H Anderson (Suzuki) | (124.80km/h) | 2 L Taveri (Honda) | (118.22km/h) | 2 R Bryans (Honda) | (103.93km/h) |
| 3 M Ichino (Suzuki) | Record | 3 H Anderson (Suzuki) | Record | 3 J Busquets (Derbi) | |
| 4 H Koshino (Suzuki) | | 4 M Itoh (Suzuki) | | 4 L Taveri (Honda) | |
| 5 J Roca (Derbi) | | 5 A Nieto (Derbi) | | 5 H-G Anscheidt (Kreidler) | |
| 6 G Biscia (Suzuki) | | 6 H-G Anscheidt (Kreidler) | | 6 B Smith (Derbi) | |
| Fastest lap – H Anderson (Suzuki) | 80.86mph | Record lap – L Taveri (Honda) | 75.46mph | Record lap – H Anderson (Suzuki) | 66.48mph |
| | (130.10km/h) | | (121.46km/h) | | (106.95km/h) |
| **French GP Rouen May 16** | | **TT Races Isle of Man June 16** | | **Dutch TT Assen June 26** | |
| 1 R Bryans (Honda) | 79.39mph | 1 L Taveri (Honda) | 79.66mph | 1 R Bryans (Honda) | 76.11mph |
| 2 L Taveri (Honda) | (127.84km/h) | 2 H Anderson (Suzuki) | (128.20km/h) | 2 H Anderson (Honda) | (122.48km/h) |
| 3 E Degner (Suzuki) | | 3 E Degner (Suzuki) | | 3 L Taveri (Honda) | Record |
| 4 M Itoh (Suzuki) | | 4 C Mates (Honda) | | 4 M Itoh (Suzuki) | |
| 5 J Roca (Derbi) | | 5 I Plumridge (Derbi) | | 5 E Degner (Suzuki) | |
| 6 H Anderson (Suzuki) | | 6 E Griffiths (Honda) | | 6 C VanDongen (Kreidler) | |
| Fastest lap – E Degner (Suzuki) | 80.67mph | Fastest lap – L Taveri (Honda) | 80.83mph | Record lap – H Anderson (Suzuki) | 77.60mph |
| | (129.82km/h) | | (130.08km/h) | | (124.88km/h) |
| **BelgianGP Spa Francorchamps July 5** | | **Japanese GP Suzuka October 24** | | | |
| 1 E Degner (Suzki) | 93.93mph | 1 L Taveri (Honda) | 79.51mph | | |
| 2 H Anderson (Suzuki) | (151.35km/h) | 2 R Bryans (Honda) | (128.05km/h) | | |
| 3 L Taveri (Honda) | Record | 3 M Itoh (Suzuki) | Record | | |
| 4 M Itoh (Suzuki) | | 4 H-G Anscheidt (Kreidler) | | | |
| 5 R Bryans (Honda) | | 5 M Ichino (Suzuki) | | | |
| 6 C VanDongen (Kreidler) | | 6 A Itoh (Honda) | | | |
| Record lap – L Taveri (Honda) | 95.54mph | Record lap – H Anderson (Suzuki) | 80.76mph | | |
| | (153.86km/h) | | (130.47k?mh) | | |

## 1965 125CC

| United States GP Daytona March 20 | | West German GP Nurburgring South April 25 | | Spanish GP Montjuich Park May 9 | |
|---|---|---|---|---|---|
| 1 H Anderson (Suzuki) | 89.14mph | 1 H Anderson (Suzuki) | 78.12mph | 1 H Anderson (Suzuki) | 69.93mph |
| 2 E Degner (Suzuki) | (143.76km/h) | 2 F Perris (Suzuki) | (125.81km/h) | 2 F Perris (Suzuki) | (112.54km/h) |
| 3 F Perris (Suzuki) | Record | 3 R Torras (Bultaco) | | 3 D Woodman (MZ) | |
| 4 R Schell (Honda) | | 4 E Degner (Suzuki) | | 4 B Spaggiari (Ducati) | |
| 5 J Tate (Honda) | | 5 D Woodman (MZ) | | 5 K Enderlein (MZ) | |
| 6 B Ghering (Bultaco) | | 6 W Scheimann (Honda) | | 6 A Fegbli (Honda) | |
| Record lap – H Anderson (Suzuki) | 91.47mph | Record lap – H Anderson (Suzuki) | 79.61mph | Fastest lap – F Perris (Suzuki) | 71.05mph |
| | (147.21km/h) | | (128.34km/h) | | (114.34km/h) |

| French GP Rouen May 16 | | TT Races Isle of Man June 16 | | Dutch TT Assen June 26 | |
|---|---|---|---|---|---|
| 1 H Anderson (Suzuki) | 92.06mph | 1 P Read (Yamaha) | 94.28mph | 1 M Duff (Yamaha) | 83.77mph |
| 2 E Degner (Suzuki) | (148.24km/h) | 2 L Taveri (Honda) | (151.73km/h) | 2 Y Katayama (Suzuki) | 134.81km/h) |
| 3 F Perris (Suzuki) | | 3 M Duff (Yamaha) | Record | 3 H Anderson (Suzuki) | |
| 4 D Woodman (MZ) | | 4 D Woodman (MZ) | | 4 B Ivy (Yamaha) | |
| 5 Beale (Honda) | | 5 H Anderson (Suzuki) | | 5 L Taveri (Honda) | |
| 6 G Vicenzi (Honda) | | 6 R Bryans (Honda) | | 6 G Vicenzi (Honda) | |
| Fastest lap – H Anderson (Suzuki) | 94.42mph | Record lap – H Anderson (Suzuki) | 96.02mph | Record lap – H Anderson (Suzuki) | 86.60mph |
| | (151.93km/h) | | (154.52km/h | | (139.36km/h) |

| East German GP Sachsenring July 18 | | Czechoslovak GP Brno July 25 | | Ulster GP Dundrod August 7 | |
|---|---|---|---|---|---|
| 1 F Perris (Suzuki) | 86.74mph | 1 F Perris (Suzuki) | 86.63mph | 1 E Degner (Suzuki) | 86.41mph |
| 2 D Krumpholz (MZ) | (139.69km/h) | 2 D Woodman (MZ) | (139.50km/h) | 2 K Enderlein (MZ) | (139.06km/h) |
| 3 D Woodman (MZ) | | 3 H Rosner (MZ) | | 3 D Woodman (MZ) | |
| 4 J Leiter (MZ) | | 4 J Leiter (MZ) | | 4 R Bryans (Honda) | |
| 5 B Beale (Honda) | | 5 R Rentsch (MZ) | | 5 B Beale (Honda) | |
| 6 J Lenk (MZ) | | 6 F Bocek (CZ) | | 6 T Robb (Bultaco) | |
| Fastest lap – F Perris (Suzuki) | 88.78mph | Record lap – H Anderson (Suzuki) | 88.99mph | Fastest lap – E Degner (Suzuki) | 90.81mph |
| | (142.87km/h) | | (143.29km/h) | | (146.14km/h) |

| Finnish GP Imatra August 22 | | Italian GP Monza September 5 | | Japanese GP Suzuka October 24 | |
|---|---|---|---|---|---|
| 1 H Anderson (Suzuki) | 80.11mph | 1 H Anderson (Suzuki) | 94.26mph | 1 H Anderson (Suzuki) | 85.52mph |
| 2 F Perris (Suzuki) | (129.03km/h) | 2 F Perris (Suzuki) | (151.77km/h) | 2 L Taveri (Honda) | (137.70km/h) |
| 3 J Leiter (MZ) | Record | 3 D Woodman (MZ) | | 3 R Bryans (Honda) | Record |
| 4 R Bryans (Honda) | | 4 K Enderlein (MZ) | | 4 B Ivy (Yamaha) | |
| 5 R Rentsch (MZ) | | 5 H-G Anscheidt (Kreidler/MZ) | | 5 M Yasawa (Honda) | |
| 6 G Vicenzi (Honda) | | 6 G Molloy (Bultaco) | | 6 I Matsushima (Yamaha) | |
| Record lap – H Anderson (Suzuki) | 82.78mph | Fastest lap – H Anderson (Suzuki) | 98.21mph | Record lap – L Taveri (Honda) | 86.99mph |
| | (133.28km/h) | | (158.13km/h) | | (139.18km/h) |

## 1965 250CC

| United States GP Daytona March 21 | | West German GP Nurburgring South April 25 | | Spanish GP Montjuich Park May 9 | |
|---|---|---|---|---|---|
| 1 P Read (Yamaha) | 97.46mph | 1 P Read (Yamaha) | 83.96mph | 1 P Read (Yamaha) | 72.81mph |
| 2 M Duff (Yamaha) | (156.85km/h) | 2 M Duff (Yamaha) | (135.26km/h) | 2 R Torras (Bultaco) | (117.13km/h) |
| 3 S Grassetti (Morini) | Rercord | 3 R Torras (Bultaco) | Record | 3 M Duff (Yamaha) | |
| 4 F Perris (Suzuki) | | 4 G Vicenzi (Honda) | | 4 D Woodman (MZ) | |
| 5 J Busquets (Montesa) | | 5 G Beer (Honda) | | 5 K Cass (Cotton) | |
| 6 S Buckner (Yamaha) | | 6 G Milani (Aermacchi) | | 6 A Pagani (Aermacchi) | |
| Record lap – P Read (Yamaha) | 98.76mph | Record lap – P Read (Yamaha) | 86.11mph | Record lap – P Read (Yamaha) | 73.87mph |
| | (158.94km/h) | | (139.72km/h) | | (118.88km/h) |

| French GP Rouen May 16 | | TT Races Isle of Man June 14 | | Dutch TT Assen June 26 | |
|---|---|---|---|---|---|
| 1 P Read (Yamaha) | 96.01mph | 1 J Redman (Honda) | 97.19mph | 1 P Read (Yamaha) | 87.28mph |
| 2 B Beale (Honda) | (154.60km/h) | 2 M Duff (Yamaha) | (156.41km/h) | 2 J Redman (Honda) | (140.46km/h) |
| 3 B Smith (Bultaco) | | 3 F Perris (Suzuki) | | 3 M Duff (Yamaha) | |
| 4 J-C Guenard (Bultaco) | | 4 T Provini (Benelli) | | 4 Y Katayama (Suzuki) | |
| 5 R Avery (Bultaco) | | 5 F Stastny (CZ) | | 5 B Beale (Honda) | |
| 6 A Barbaroux (Aermacchi) | | 6 D Williams (Mondial) | | 6 D Woodman (MZ) | |
| Fastest lap – J Redman (Honda) | 98.35mph | Record lap – J Redman (Honda) | 100.09mph | Fastest lap – P Read (Yamaha) | 88.79mph |
| | (158.29km/h) | | (161.07km/h) | | (142.89km/h) |

| Belgian GP Spa Francorchamps July 4 | | East German GP Sachsenring July 18 | | Czechoslovak GP Brno July 25 | |
|---|---|---|---|---|---|
| 1 J Redman (Honda) | 120.12mph | 1 J Redman (Honda) | 91.32mph | 1 P Read (Yamaha) | 95.62mph |
| 2 Read (Yamaha) | (193.43km/h) | 2 P Read (Yamaha) | (147.38km/h) | 2 M Duff (Yamaha) | (153.50km/h) |
| 3 M Duff (Yamaha) | Record | 3 D Woodman (MZ) | | 3 J Redman (Honda) | |
| 4 Y Katayama (Suzuki) | | 4 F Stastny (CZ) | | 4 D Woodman (MZ0 | |
| 5 F Perris (Suzuki) | | 5 B Beale (Honda) | | 5 H Rosner (MZ) | |
| 6 B Beale (Honda) | | 6 H Rosner (MZ) | | 6 F Stastny (CZ) | |
| Record lap – P Read (Yamaha) | 121.85mph | Fastest lap – J Redman (Honda) | 93.52mph | Record lap – M Duff (Yamaha) | 95.63mph |
| | (193.60km/h) | | (150.52km/h) | | (153.99km/h) |

| Ulster GP Dundrod August 7 | | Finnish GP Imatra August 22 | | Italian GP Monza September 5 | |
|---|---|---|---|---|---|
| 1 P Read (Yamaha) | 86.04mph | 1 M Duff (Yamaha) | 82.84mph | 1 T Provini (Benelli) | 94.47mph |
| 2 M Duff (Yamaha) | (138.40km/h) | 2 H Rosner (MZ) | (133.41km/h) | 2 H Rosner (MZ) | (152.12km/h) |
| 3 D Woodman (MZ) | | 3 R Bryans (Honda) | | 3 R Venturi (Benelli) | |
| 4 H Rosner (MZ) | | 4 B Beale (Honda) | | 4 G Molloy (Bultaco) | |
| 5 R Bryans (Honda) | | 5 G Vicenzi (Aermacchi) | | 5 F Stastny (CZ) | |
| 6 G Molloy (Bultaco) | | 6 B Coulter (Bultaco) | | 6 G Beer (Honda) | |
| Fastest lap – P Read (Yamaha) | 87.88mph | Record lap – M Duff (Yamaha) | 83.90mph | Fastest lap – T Provini (Benelli) | 99.57mph |
| | (141.42km/h) | | (135.08km/h) | | (160.33km/h) |

| Japanese GP Suzuka October 24 | | | | | |
|---|---|---|---|---|---|
| 1 M Hailwood (Honda)<br>2 I Kasuya (Honda)<br>3 B Ivy (Yamaha)<br>4 I Yamashita (Honda)<br>5 H Hasegawa (Yamaha)<br>Only 5 finishers<br>Record lap – M Hailwood (Honda) | 86.85mph<br>(139.86km/h)<br><br><br><br><br>88.78mph<br>(142.94km/h) | | | | |

## 1965 350CC

| West German GP Nurburgring South April 25 | | TT Races Isle of Man June18 | | Dutch TT Assen June 26 | |
|---|---|---|---|---|---|
| 1 G Agostini (MV)<br>2 M Hailwood (MV)<br>3 G Havel (jawa)<br>4 R Passolini (Aermacchi)<br>5 E Kiisa (Vostok)<br>6 P Driver (AJS)<br>Record lap – G Agostini (MV) | 84.68mph<br>(136.38km/h)<br>Record<br><br><br><br>87.79mph<br>141.49km/h) | 1 J Redman (Honda)<br>2 P Read (Yamaha)<br>3 G Agostini (MV)<br>4 B Beale (Honda)<br>5 G Jenkins (Norton)<br>6 G Milani (Aermacchi)<br>Record lap – M Hailwood (MV) | 100.72mph<br>(162.09km/h)<br><br><br><br><br>102.85mph<br>(165.52km/h) | 1 J Redman (Honda)<br>2 M Hailwood (MV)<br>3 G Agostini (MV)<br>4 R Passolini (Aermacchi)<br>5 G Milani (Aermacchi)<br>6 J Cooper (Norton)<br>Record lap – J Redman (Honda) | 88.22mph<br>(141.98km/h)<br>Record<br><br><br><br>89.71mph<br>(144.37km/h) |
| **East German GP Sachsenring July 18** | | **Czechoslovak GP Brno July 25** | | **Ulster GP Dundrod August 7** | |
| 1 J Redman (Honda)<br>2 D Woodman (MZ)<br>3 G Havel (Jawa)<br>4 F Stastny (Jawa)<br>5 F Bocek (Jawa)<br>6 D Shorey (Norton)<br>Fastest lap – G Agostini (MV) | 98.68mph<br>(158.80km/h)<br><br><br><br><br>101.41mph<br>(163.22km/h) | 1 J Redman (Honda)<br>2 D Woodman (MZ)<br>3 N Sevostianov (Vostok)<br>4 G Milani (Aermacchi)<br>5 R Passolini (Aermacchi)<br>6 D Shorey (Norton)<br>Record lap – J Redman (Honda) | 94.58mph<br>(152.30km/h)<br><br><br><br><br>96.50mph<br>(155.39km/h) | 1 F Stastny (Jawa)<br>2 B Beale (Honda)<br>3 G Havel (Jawa)<br>4 C Conn (Norton)<br>5 J Cooper (Norton)<br>6 G Jenkins (Norton)<br>Fastest lap – J Redman (Honda) | 91.01mph<br>(146.61km/h)<br><br><br><br><br>99.54mph<br>(160.19km/h |
| **Finnish GP Imatra August 22** | | **Italian GP Monza September 5** | | **Japanese GP Suzuka October 24** | |
| 1 G Agostini (MV)<br>2 B Beale (Honda)<br>3 F Bocek (Jawa)<br>4 K Carlsson (AJS)<br>5 L Young (AJS)<br>6 E Hinton (Norton)<br>Record lap – G Agostini (MV) | 84.27mph<br>(137.10km/h)<br>Record<br><br><br><br>85.64mph<br>(137.87km/h) | 1 G Agostini (MV)<br>2 S Grassetti (Bianchi)<br>3 T Provini (Benelli)<br>4 F Stastny (Jawa)<br>5 D Woodman (MZ)<br>6 R Passolini (Aermacchi)<br>Record lap – G Agostini (MV) | 112.96mph<br>(181.90km/h)<br>Record<br><br><br><br>117.61mph<br>(189.38km/h) | 1 M Hailwood (MV)<br>2 J Redman (Honda)<br>3 I Kasuya (Honda)<br>4 I Yamashita (Honda)<br>5 G Agostini (MV)<br>6 W A.Smith (Honda)<br>Record lap – M Hailwood (MV) | 88.04mph<br>(141.74km/h)<br><br><br><br><br>90.09mph<br>(145.14km/h) |

## 1965 500CC

| United States GP Daytona March 1 | | West German GP Nurburgring South April 25 | | TT Races Isle of Man June 18 | |
|---|---|---|---|---|---|
| 1 M Hailwood (MV)<br>2 B Parriott (Norton)<br>3 R Beaumont (Norton)<br>4 K King (Norton)<br>5 E LaBelle (Norton)<br>6 D Loyd (Norton)<br>Fastest lap – M Hailwood (MV) | 99.64mph<br>(160.35km/h)<br><br><br><br><br>101.45mph<br>(166.25km/h) | 1 M Hailwood (MV)<br>2 G Agostini (MV)<br>3 W Scheimann (Norton)<br>4 J Findlay (Matchless)<br>5 E Lenz (Norton)<br>6 B Nelson (Norton)<br>Record lap – M Hailwood (MV) | 86.13mph<br>(138.69km/h)<br><br><br><br><br>89.71mph<br>(144.50km/h) | 1 M Hailwood (MV)<br>2 J Dunphy (Norton)<br>3 M Duff (Matchless)<br>4 I Burne (Norton)<br>5 S Griffiths (Matchless)<br>6 B McCosh (Matchless)<br>Fastest lap – M Hailwood (MV) | 91.69mph<br>(147.56km/h)<br><br><br><br><br>95.11mph<br>(153.06km/h) |
| **Dutch TT Assen June 26** | | **Belgian GP Spa Francorchamps July 4** | | **East German GP Sachsenring July 18** | |
| 1 M Hailwood (MV)<br>2 G Agostini (MV)<br>3 P Driver (Matchless )<br>4 J Cooper (Norton)<br>5 J Ahearn (Norton)<br>6 D Shorey (Norton)<br>Record lap – M Hailwood (MV) | 88.39mph<br>(142.50km/h)<br>Record<br><br><br><br>90.23mph<br>(145.21km/h) | 1 M Hailwood (MV)<br>2 G Agostini (MV)<br>3 D Minter (Norton)<br>4 P Driver (Matchless)<br>5 F Stevens (Matchless)<br>6 G Marsovsky (Matchless)<br>Fastest lap – M Hailwood (MV) | 120.51mph<br>(194.07km/h)<br><br><br><br><br>123.04mph<br>(198.12km/h) | 1 M Hailwood (MV)<br>2 G Agostini (MV)<br>3 P Driver (Matchless)<br>4 J Ahearn (Norton)<br>5 F Stevens (Matchless)<br>6 I Burne (Norton)<br>Fastest lap – M Hailwood (MV) | 93.62mph<br>(150.71km/h)<br><br><br><br><br>95.57mph<br>(153.80km/h) |
| **Czechoslovak GP Brno July 25** | | **Ulster GP Dundrod August 7** | | **Finnish GP Imatra August 22** | |
| 1 M Hailwood (MV)<br>2 .G Agostini (MV)<br>3 J Ahearn (Norton)<br>4 P Driver (Matchless)<br>5 F Stevens (Matchless)<br>6 F Stastny (Jawa)<br>Record lap – M Hailwood (MV) | 94.95mph<br>(152.90km/h)<br><br><br><br><br>96.25mph<br>(154.99km/h) | 1 D Creith (Norton)<br>2 P Driver (Matchless)<br>3 C Conn (Norton)<br>4 J Findlay (Matchless)<br>5 F Stevens (Matchless)<br>6 R Fitton (Norton)<br>Fastest lap – P Driver (Matchless) | 86.20mph<br>(138.72km/h)<br><br><br><br><br>91.49mph<br>(147.23km/h) | 1 G Agostini (MV)<br>2 P Driver (Matchless)<br>3 F Stevens (Matchless)<br>4 O Reihanen (Matchless)<br>5 J Findlay (Matchless)<br>6 L Young (Matchless)<br>Record lap – G Agostini (MV) | 85.14mph<br>(137.10km/h)<br>Record<br><br><br><br>87.62mph<br>(141.09km/h) |

| Italian GP Monza September 5 | | | | | |
|---|---|---|---|---|---|
| 1 M Hailwood (MV)<br>2 G Agostini (MV)<br>3 F Stastny (Jawa)<br>4 F Stevens (Matchless)<br>5 G Mandolini (Guzzi)<br>6 G Marsovsky (Matchless)<br>Fastest lap – M Hailwood (MV) | 97.43mph<br>(156.89km/h)<br><br><br><br><br>103.58mph<br>(166.79km/h) | | | | |

## 1965 SIDECARS

| West German GP Nurburgring South April 25 | | Spanish GP Montjuich Park May 9 | | French GP Rouen May 16 | |
|---|---|---|---|---|---|
| 1 F Scheidegger/J Robinson (BMW)<br>2 S Schazu/H Schneider (BMW)<br>3 A Butscher/W Kalauch (BMW)<br>4 A Wolf/L Ronsdorf (BMW)<br>5 F Huber/J Huber (BMW)<br>6 T Davies/M Merrick (Matchless)<br>Fastest lap – F Scheidegger (BMW) | 70.23mph<br>(113.03km/h)<br><br><br><br><br>75.30mph<br>(121.46km/h) | 1 M Deubel/E Horner (BMW)<br>2 F Scheidegger/J Robinson (BMW)<br>3 A Butscher/W Kalauch (BMW)<br>3 O Kolle/H Marquardt (BMW)<br>4 G Auerbacher/P Rykers (BMW)<br>6 B Thompson/R Bradley (BMW)<br>Fastest – M Deubel (BMW) | 63.59mph<br>(102.34km/h)<br><br><br><br><br>67.41mph<br>(108.74km/h) | 1 F Camathias/F/Ducret (BMW)<br>2 F Scheidegger/J Robinson (BMW)<br>3 M Deubel/E Horner (BMW)<br>4 G Auerbacher/P Rykers (BMW)<br>5 B Thompson/R Bradley (BMW)<br>6 C Seeley/W Rawlings (BMW)<br>Fastest lap – F Camathias (BMW) | 87.96mph<br>(141.56km/h)<br><br><br><br><br>89.16mph<br>(143.85km/h) |
| **TT Races Isle of Man June 14** | | **Dutch TT Assen June 26** | | **Belgian GP Spa Francorchamps July 4** | |
| 1 M Deubel/E Horner (BMW)<br>2 F Scheidegger/J Robinson (BMW)<br>3 G Auerbacher/P Rykers (BMW)<br>4 H Luthringshauser/H Hahn (BMW)<br>5 C Vincent/T Harrison (BMW)<br>6 C Freeman/B Nelson (Norton)<br>Fastest lap – M Deubel (BMW) | 90.57mph<br>(145.76mph)<br><br><br><br><br>91.59mph<br>(147.74km/h) | 1 F Scheidegger/J Robinson (BMW)<br>2 C Vincent/F Roche (BMW)<br>3 C Seeley/W Rawlings (BMW)<br>4 H Luthringshauser/H Hahn (BMW)<br>5 B Thompson/R/Bradley (BMW)<br>6 O Kolle/H Marquardt (BMW)<br>Fastest lap – F Scheidegger (BMW) | 78.81mph<br>(172.57km/h)<br><br><br><br><br>80.87mph<br>(130.45km/h) | 1 F Scheidegger/J Robinson (BMW)<br>2 M Deubel/E Horner (BMW)<br>3 P Harris/R Campbell (BMW)<br>4 H Luthringshauser/H Hahn (BMW)<br>5 F Camathias/F Ducret (BMW)<br>6 C Seeley/W Rawlings (BMW)<br>Fastest lap – F Scheidegger (BMW) | 107.23mph<br>(172.57km/h)<br><br><br><br><br>108.22mph<br>(174.55km/h) |
| **Italian GP Monza September 5** | | | | | |
| 1 F Scheidegger/J Robinson (BMW)<br>2 G Auerbacher/P Rykers (BMW)<br>3 O Kolle/H Marquardt (BMW)<br>4 G Dal-Toe/A Ramoli (BMW)<br>5 B Thompson/R Bradley (BMW)<br>6 A Butscher/W Kalauch (BMW)<br>Fastest lap – F Scheidegger (BMW) | 92.37mph<br>(148.65km/h)<br><br><br><br><br>94.01mph<br>(151.64km/h) | | | | |

## 1966 50CC

| Spanish GP Montjuich Park May 8 | | West German GP Hockenheim May 22 (New circuit) | | Dutch TT Assen June 25 | |
|---|---|---|---|---|---|
| 1 L Taveri (Honda)<br>2 H-G Anscheidt (Kreidler)<br>3 R Bryans (Honda)<br>4 H Anderson (Suzuki)<br>5 A Nieto (Derbi)<br>6 B Smith (Derbi)<br>Record lap – H-G Anscheidt (Kreidler) | 67.44mph<br>(109.01km/h)<br><br><br><br><br>69.01mph<br>(111.22km/h) | 1 H-G Anscheidt (Kreidler)<br>2 R Bryans (Honda)<br>3 H Anderson (Suzuki)<br>4 L Taveri (Honda)<br>5 O Dittrich (Kreidler)<br>6 C Van Dongen (Kreidler)<br>Fastest lap – H-G Anscheidt (Kreidler) | 89.47mph<br>(144.81km/h)<br><br><br><br><br>91.49mph<br>(147.23km/h) | 1 L Taveri (Honda)<br>2 R Bryans (Honda)<br>3 H Anderson (Suzuki)<br>4 H-G Anscheidt (Kreidler)<br>5 Y Katayama (Suzuki)<br>6 I Morishita (Suzuki)<br>Record lap – L Taveri (Honda) | 77.49mph<br>(124.78km/h)<br>Record<br><br><br><br>79.08mph<br>(127.34km/h) |
| **TT Races Isle of Man August 31** | | **Italian GP Monza September 11** | | **Japanese GP Fisco October 17** | |
| 1 R Bryans (Honda)<br>2 L Taveri (Honda)<br>3 H Anderson (Suzuki)<br>4 E Degner (Suzuki)<br>5 B Gleed (Honda)<br>6 D Simmonds (Honda)<br>Record lap – R Bryans (Honda) | 85.66mph<br>(137.83km/h)<br>Record<br><br><br><br>86.49mph<br>(139.18km/h) | 1 H-G Anscheidt (Kreidler)<br>2 R Bryans (Honda)<br>3 L Taveri (Honda)<br>4 H Anderson (Suzuki)<br>5 B Smith (Derbi)<br>6 A Roth (Kreidler)<br>Record lap – Anscheidt (Kreidler) | 94.50mph<br>(152.17km/h)<br>Record<br><br><br><br>96.87mph<br>(155.99km/h) | 1 Y Katayama (Suzuki)<br>2 H-G Anscheidt (Kreidler)<br>3 H Anderson (Suzuki)<br>4 M Itoh (Suzuki)<br>5 T Robb (Bridgestone)<br>6 J Findlay (Bridgestone)<br>Fastest lap – Y Katayama (Suzuki) | 89.83mph<br>(144.89km/h)<br><br><br><br><br>91.38mph<br>(147.40km/h) |

## 1966 125CC

| Spanish GP Montjuich Park May 8 | | West German GP Hockenheim May 22 (New circuit) | | Dutch TT Assen June 25 | |
|---|---|---|---|---|---|
| 1 B Ivy (Yamaha)<br>2 L Taveri (Honda)<br>3 R Bryans (Honda)<br>4 P Read (Yamaha)<br>5 F Villa (Montesa)<br>6 J Medrano (Bultaco)<br>Record lap – P Read (Yamaha) | 69.91mph<br>(112.57km/h)<br><br><br><br><br>68.83mph<br>(116.46km/h) | 1 L Taveri (Honda)<br>2 R Bryans (Honda)<br>3 P Read (Yamaha)<br>4 F Perris (Suzuki)<br>5 H-G Anscheidt (Suzuki)<br>6 H Mann (MZ)<br>Fastest lap – L Taveri (Honda) | 100.97mph<br>(162.50km/h)<br><br><br><br><br>103.07mph<br>(165.92km/h) | 1 B Ivy (Yamaha)<br>2 L Taveri (Honda)<br>3 P Read (Yamaha)<br>4 H Anderson (Suzuki)<br>5 A Motohashi (Yamaha)<br>6 M Duff (Yamaha)<br>Fastest lap – Taveri & Read | 84.59mph<br>(136.21k/mh)<br><br><br><br><br>86.21mph<br>(138.82km/h) |
| **East German GP Sachsenring July 17** | | **Czechoslovak GP Brno July 24** | | **Finnish GP Imatra August 7** | |
| 1 L Taveri (Honda)<br>2 Y Katayama (Suzuki)<br>3 B Ivy (Yamaha)<br>4 P Read (Yamaha)<br>5 F Perris (Suzuki)<br>6 R Bryans (Honda)<br>Record lap – L Taveri (Honda) | 96.53mph<br>(155.44km/h)<br>Record<br><br><br><br>97.70mph<br>(157.23km/h) | 1 L Taveri (Honda)<br>2 R Bryans (Honda)<br>3 B Ivy (Yamaha)<br>4 H Anderson (Suzuki)<br>5 F Perris (Suzuki)<br>6 F Kohlar (MZ)<br>Record lap – B Ivy (Yamaha) | 86.32mph<br>(139.01km/h)<br><br><br><br><br>89.73mph<br>(144.50km/h) | 1 P Read (Yamaha)<br>2 L Taveri (Honda)<br>3 R Bryans (Honda)<br>4 H Anderson (Suzuki)<br>5 Y Katayama (Suzuki)<br>6 H Bischoff (MZ)<br>Record lap – L Taveri (Honda) | 83.21mph<br>(134.11km/h)<br><br><br><br><br>85.33mph<br>(137.38km/h) |
| **Ulster GP Dundrod August 20** | | **TT Races Isle of Man September 2** | | **Italian GP Monza September 11** | |
| 1 L Taveri (Honda)<br>2 R Bryans (Honda)<br>3 .P Read (Yamaha)<br>4 T Robb (Yamaha)<br>5 H Anderson (Suzuki)<br>6 F Perris (Suzuki)<br>Record lap – R Bryans (Honda) | 92.38mph<br>(148.64km/h)<br><br><br><br><br>94.45mph<br>(152.00km/h) | 1 B Ivy (Yamaha)<br>2 P Read (Yamaha)<br>3 H Anderson (Suzuki)<br>4 M Duff (Yamaha)<br>5 F Perris (Suzuki)<br>6 M Hailwood (Honda)<br>Record lap – B Ivy (Yamaha) | 97.66mph<br>(156.10km/h)<br><br><br><br><br>98.55mph<br>(158.60km/h) | 1 L Taveri (Honda)<br>2 R Bryans (Honda)<br>3 B Ivy (Yamaha)<br>4 P Read (Yamaha)<br>5 P Williams (EMC)<br>6 W Scheimann (Honda)<br>Record lap – L Taveri (Honda) | 110.14mph<br>(177.65km/h)<br>(Record)<br><br><br><br>111.97mph<br>(180.31km/h) |
| **Japanese GP Fisco October 17** | | | | | |
| 1 B Ivy (Yamaha)<br>2 Y Katayama (Suzuki)<br>3 M Itoh (Suzuki)<br>4 A Motohashi (Yamaha)<br>5 P Read (Yamaha)<br>6 M Yuzawa (Yamaha)<br>Fastest lap – B Ivy (Yamaha) | 100.78mph<br>(162.55km/h)<br><br><br><br><br>102.62mph<br>(165.52km/h) | | | | |

## 1966 250CC

| Spanish GP Montjuich Park May 8 | | West German GP Hockenheim May 22 (New Circuit) | | French GP Clermont-Ferrand May 29 | |
|---|---|---|---|---|---|
| 1 M Hailwood (Honda)<br>2 D Woodman (MZ)<br>3 R Passolini (Aermacchi)<br>4 J Findlay (Bultaco)<br>5 H Rosner (MZ)<br>6 J Blanco (Bultaco)<br>Record lap – M Hailwood (Honda) | 70.99mph<br>(118.32km/h)<br><br><br><br><br>75.11mph<br>(121.26km/h) | 1 M Hailwood (Honda)<br>2 J Redman (Honda)<br>3 B Ivy (Yamaha)<br>4 D Woodman (MZ)<br>5 F Stastny (Jawa)<br>6 G Beer (Honda)<br>Fastest lap – J Redman (Honda) | 109.23mph<br>(175.86km/h)<br><br><br><br><br>111.08mph<br>(178.78km/h) | 1 M Hailwood (Honda)<br>2 J Redman (Honda)<br>3 P Read (Yamaha)<br>4 D Woodman (MZ)<br>5 H Rosner (MZ)<br>6 .D Lheraud (Yamaha)<br>Record lap – M Hailwood (Honda) | 79.61mph<br>(128.20km/h)<br>Record<br><br><br><br>80.97mph<br>(130.38km/h) |
| **Dutch TT Assen June 25** | | **Belgian GP Spa Francorchamps July 3** | | **East German GP Sachsenring July 17** | |
| 1 M Hailwood (Honda)<br>2 P Read (Yamaha)<br>3 J Redman (Honda)<br>4 D Woodman (MZ)<br>5 RHF Anderson (Yamaha)<br>6 T Robb (Bultaco)<br>Fastest lap – M Hailwood (Honda) | 83.28mph<br>(134.11km/h)<br><br><br><br><br>85.14mph<br>(137.10km/h) | 1 M Hailwood (Honda)<br>2 P Read (Yamaha)<br>3 J Redman (Honda)<br>4 D Woodman (MZ)<br>5 M Duff (Yamaha)<br>6 B Ivy (Yamaha)<br>Record lap – P Read (Yamaha) | 122.33mph<br>(196.87km/h)<br>Record<br><br><br><br>124.08mph<br>(199.68km/h) | 1 M Hailwood (Honda)<br>2 P Read (Yamaha)<br>3 M Duff (Yamaha)<br>4 S Graham (Honda)<br>5 H Rosner (MZ)<br>6 F Stastny (Jawa)<br>Record lap – M Hailwood (Honda) | 103.76mph<br>(167.09km/h)<br>Record<br><br><br><br>105.58mph<br>(169.91km/h) |
| **Czechoslovak Gp Brno July 24** | | **Finnish GP Imatra August 7** | | **Ulster GP Dundrod August 20** | |
| 1 M Hailwood (Honda)<br>2 P Read (Yamaha)<br>3 H Rosner (MZ)<br>4 M Duff (Yamaha)<br>5 G Marsovsky (Bultaco)<br>6 F Stastny (Jawa)<br>Fastest lap – M Hailwood (Honda) | 92.34mph<br>(148.70km/h)<br><br><br><br><br>95.51mph<br>(154.97km/h) | 1 M Hailwood (Honda)<br>2 S Graham (Honda)<br>3 F Stastny (Jawa)<br>4 J Findlay (Bultaco)<br>5 B Beale (Honda)<br>6 K Andersson (HVA)<br>Record lap – M Hailwood (Honda) | 82.41mph<br>(132.75km/h)<br><br><br><br><br>87.19mph<br>(140.22km/h) | 1 G Molloy (Bultaco)<br>2 G Marsovsky (Bultaco)<br>3 K Cass (Bultaco)<br>4 S Griffiths (Royal Enfield)<br>5 J Curry (Honda)<br>6 L Atlee (Cotton)<br>Fastest lap – P Read (Yamaha) | 87.03mph<br>(140.03km/h)<br><br><br><br><br>92.81mph<br>(149.36km/h) |

| TT Races Isle of Man August 28 | | Italian GP Monza September 11 | | Japanese GP Fisco October 17 | |
|---|---|---|---|---|---|
| 1 M Hailwood (Honda) | 101.79mph | 1 M Hailwood (Honda) | 113.59mph | 1 H Hasegawa (Yamaha) | 104.29mph |
| 2 S Graham (Honda) | (163.81km/h) | 2 H Rosner (MZ) | (182.91km/h) | 2 P Read (Yamaha) | (168.22km/h) |
| 3 P Inchley (Villiers) | | 3 A Pagani (Aermacchi) | | 3 A Motohashi (Yamaha) | |
| 4 F Stastny (Jawa) | | 4 J Findlay (Bultaco) | | 4.J .Findlay (Bultaco) | |
| 5 J Findlay (Bultaco) | | 5 B Beale (Honda) | | 5 T Robb (Bultaco) | |
| 6 B Smith (Bultaco) | | 6 G Vicenzi (Aermacchi) | | 6 K Andersson (HVA) | |
| Record lap – M Hailwood (Honda) | 104.29mph | Record lap – M Hailwood (Honda) | 116.86mph | Fastest lap – P Read (Yamaha) | 106.39mph |
| | (167.83km/h) | | (188.18km/h) | | (171.61km/h) |

## 1966 350CC

| West German GP Hockenheim May 22 (New Circuit) | | French GP Clermont-Ferrand May 29 | | Dutch TT Assen June 25 | |
|---|---|---|---|---|---|
| 1 M Hailwood (Honda) | 107.37mph | 1 M Hailwood (Honda) | 79.28mph | 1 M Hailwood (Honda) | 82.63mph |
| 2 T Provini (Benelli) | (172.81km/h) | 2 G Agostini (MV) | (127.66km/h) | 2 G Agostini (MV) | (133.14km/h) |
| 3 B Beale (Honda) | | 3 J Redman (Honda) | | 3 R Passolini (Aermacchi) | |
| 4 S Grassetti (Bianchi) | | 4 G Milani (Aermacchi) | | 4 S Graham (AJS) | |
| 5 G Havel (Jawa) | | 5 R Passolini (Aermacchi) | | 5.G Havel (Jawa) | |
| 6 F Bocke (CZ) | | 6 B Beale (Honda) | | 6 F Stastny (Jawa) | |
| Fastest lap – M Hailwood (Honda) | 110.43mph | Record lap – M Hailwood (Honda) | 80.93mph | Fastest lap – M Hailwood (Honda) | 84.31mph |
| | (177.73km/h) | | (130.32km/h) | | (135.74km/h) |
| **East German GP Sachsenring July 17** | | **Czechoslovak GP Brno July 24** | | **Finnish GP Imatra August 7** | |
| 1 G Agostini (MV) | 104.13mph | 1 M Hailwood (Honda) | 96.81mph | 1 M Hailwood (Honda) | 89.11mph |
| 2 F Stastny (Jawa) | (167.68km/h) | 2 G Agostini (MV) | (155.67km/h) | 2 H Rosner (MZ) | (143.50km/h) |
| 3 G Havel (Jawa) | Record | 3 H Rosner (MZ) | Record | 3 J Ahearn (Norton) | |
| 4 R Passolini (Aermacchi) | | 4 F Stastny (Jawa) | | 4 K Carruthers (Norton) | |
| 5 A Pagani (Aermacchi) | | 5 R Passolini (Aermacchi) | | 5 B Beale (Honda) | |
| 6 J Ahearn (Norton) | | 6 A Pagani (Aermacchi) | | 6 F Stastny (Jawa) | |
| Record lap – G Agostini (MV) | 107.22mph | Record lap – M Hailwood (Honda) | 99.36mph | Record lap – M Hailwood (Honda) | 91.16mph |
| | (172.71km/h) | | (160.01km/h) | | (146.75km/h) |
| **Ulster GP Dundrod August 20** | | **TT Races Isle of Man September 2** | | **Italian GP Monza September 11** | |
| 1 M Hailwood (Honda) | 95.50mph | 1 G Agostini (MV) | 100.87mph | 1 G Agostini (MV) | 115.50mph |
| 2 G Agostini (MV) | (153.66km/h) | 2 P Williams (AJS) | (162.34km/h) | 2 R Passolini (Aermacchi) | (185.98km/h) |
| 3 T Robb (Bultaco) | | 3 C Conn (Norton) | | 3 A Pagani (Aermacchi) | |
| 4 G Havel (Jawa) | | 4 J Ahearn (Norton) | | 4 S Grassetti (Bianchi) | |
| 5 D Simmonds (Honda-Norton) | | 5 F Bocek (CZ) | | 5 F Stastny (Jawa) | |
| 6 J Dunphy (Norton) | | 6 J Blanchard (AJS) | | 6 G Havel (Jawa) | |
| Fastest lap – M Hailwood (Honda) | 97.21mph | Record lap – G Agostini (MV) | 103.09mph | Record lap – G Agostini (MV) | 119.24mph |
| | (156.33km/h) | | (165.80km/h) | | (192.02km/h) |
| **Japanese GP Fisco October 17** | | | | | |
| 1 P Read (Yamaha) | 103.28mph | | | | |
| 2 B Ivy (Yamaha) | (166.59km/h) | | | | |
| 3 A Pagani (Aermacchi) | | | | | |
| 4 B Black (Honda) | | | | | |
| 5 Y Muromachi (Honda) | | | | | |
| 6 K Anderson (Husqvarna) | | | | | |
| Fastest lap – B Ivy (Yamaha) | 105.53mph | | | | |
| | (170.21km/h) | | | | |

## 1966 500CC

| West German GP Hockenheim May 22 (New circuit) | | Dutch TT Assen June 25 | | Belgian GP Spa Francorchamps July 3 | |
|---|---|---|---|---|---|
| 1 J Redman (Honda) | 110.42mph | 1 J Redman (Honda) | 89.05mph | 1 G Agostini (MV) | 98.90mph |
| 2 G Agostini (MV) | (177.70km/h) | 2 G Agostini (MV) | (143.39km/h) | 2 S Graham (Matchless) | (159.88km/h) |
| 3 G Marsovsky (Matchless) | | 3 F Stastny (Jawa) | Record | 3 J Ahearn (Norton) | |
| 4 S Graham (Matchless) | | 4 J Cooper (Norton) | | 4 G Marsovsky (Matchless) | |
| 5 L Young (Matchless) | | 5 S Graham (Matchless) | | 5 J Mawby (Norton) | |
| 6 E Lenz (Matchless) | | 6 J Findlay (McIntyre Matchless) | | 6 R Chandler (Matchless) | |
| Fastest lap – J Redman (Honda) | 112.99mph | Record lap – M Hailwood (Honda) | 92.26mph | Fastest lap – M Hailwood (Honda) | 105.38mph |
| | (181.83km/h) | | (148.54km/h) | | (169.54km/h) |
| **East German GP Sachsenring July 17** | | **Czechoslovak GP Brno July 24** | | **Finnish GP Imatra August 7** | |
| 1 F Stastny (Jawa) | 98.75mph | 1 M Hailwood (Honda) | 88.93mph | 1 G Agostini (MV) | 82.22mph |
| 2 J Findlay (McIntyre Matchless) | (159.90km/h) | 2 G Agostini (MV) | (143.21km/h) | 2 M Hailwood (Honda) | (132.49km/h) |
| 3 J Ahearn (Norton) | | 3 G Marsovsky (Matchless) | | 3 .J Findlay (McIntyre Matchless) | |
| 4 R Chandler (Matchless) | | 4 J Findlay (McIntyre Matchless) | | 4 J Ahearn (Norton) | |
| 5 G Marsovsky (Matchless) | | 5 J Ahearn (Norton) | | 5 M Stanton (Norton) | |
| 6 J Dodds (Norton) | | 6 E Hinton (Norton) | | 6 L Young (Matchless) | |
| Record lap – G Agostini (MV) | 109.71mph | Fastest lap – M Hailwood (Honda) | 91.66mph | Fastest lap – G Agostini (MV) | 87.13mph |
| | (173.34km/h) | | (147.59km/h) | | (140.28km/h) |

| Ulster GP Dundrod August 20 | | TT Races Isle of Man September 2 | | Italian GP Monza September 11 | |
|---|---|---|---|---|---|
| 1 M Hailwood (Honda) | 102.44mph | 1 M Hailwood (Honda) | 103.11mph | 1 G Agostini (MV) | 118.90mph |
| 2 G Agostini (MV) | (164.82km/h) | 2 G Agostini (MV) | (165.90km/h) | 2 P Williams (Matchless) | (191.46km/h) |
| 3 F Stastny (Jawa) | | 3 C Conn (Norton) | | 3 J Findlay (McIntyre Matchless) | |
| 4 .J Findlay (McIntyre Matchless) | | 4 .J Blanchard (Matchless) | | 4 F Stevens (Paton) | |
| 5 C Conn (Norton) | | 5 R Chandler (Matchless) | | 5 W Scheimann (Norton) | |
| 6 P Williams (Matchless) | | 6 F Stastny (Jawa) | | 6 E Lenz (Matchless) | |
| Record lap – M Hailwood (Honda) | 105.03mph<br>(169.02km/h) | Record lap – M Hailwood (Honda) | 107.07mph<br>(172.32km/h) | Record lap – M Hailwood (Honda) | 123.60mph<br>(209.44km/h) |

## 1966 SIDECARS

| West German GP Hockenheim May 22 (New Circuit) | | French GP Clermont-Ferrand May 29 | | Dutch TT Assen June 25 | |
|---|---|---|---|---|---|
| 1 F Scheidegger/J Robinson (BMW) | 96.75mph | 1 F Scheidegger/J Robinson (BMW) | 71.15mph | 1 F Scheidegger/J Robinson (BMW) | 79.32mph |
| 2 M Deubel/E Horner (BMW) | (155.70km/h) | 2 C Seeley/W Rawlings (BMW) | (114.50km/h) | 2 M Deubel/E Horner (BMW) | (127.65km/h) |
| 3 C Seeley/W Rawlings (BMW) | | 3 M Deubel/E Horner (BMW) | Record | 3 O Kolle/R Schmid (BMW) | Record |
| 4 G Auerbacher/E Dein (BMW) | | 4 G Auerbacher/W Kalauch (BMW) | | 4 G Auerbacher/E Dein (BMW) | |
| 5 C Vincent/T Harrison (BMW) | | 5 C Vincent/T Harrison (BMW) | | 5 S Schauzu/H Schneider (BMW) | |
| 6 H Luthringshauser/H Hahn (BMW) | | 6 B Thompson/G Wood (BMW) | | 6 K Enders/R Mannischeff (BMW) | |
| Fastest lap – F Scheidegger (BMW) | 97.91mph<br>(157.92km/h) | Record lap – F Scheidegger (BMW) | 72.19mph<br>(116.45km/h) | Fastest lap – F Scheidegger (BMW) | 79.98mph<br>(129.00km/h) |
| **Belgian GP Spa Francorchamps July 3** | | **TT Races Isle of Man August 28** | | | |
| 1 F Scheidegger/J Robinson (BMW) | 103.86mph | 1 F Scheidegger/J Robinson (BMW) | 90.74mph | | |
| 2 M Deubel/E Horner (BMW) | (167.14km/h) | 2 M Deubel/E Horner (BMW) | (146.03km/h) | | |
| 3 G Auerbacher/W Kalauch (BMW) | | 3 G Auerbacher/E Dein (BMW) | Record | | |
| 4 K Enders/R Mannischeff (BMW) | | 4 K Enders/R Mannischeff (BMW) | | | |
| 5 C Seeley/W Rawlings (BMW) | | 5 C Seeley/W Rawlings (BMW) | | | |
| 6 T Wakefield/G Milton (BMW) | | 6 B Dungworth/N Caddow (BMW) | | | |
| Fastest lap – G Auerbacher (BMW) | 106.70mph<br>(172.10km/h) | Fastest lap – M Deubel (BMW) | 91.42mph<br>(147.46km/h) | | |

## 1967 50CC

| Spanish GP Montjuich Park April 30 | | West German GP Hockenheim May 7 | | French GP Clermont-Ferrand May 21 | |
|---|---|---|---|---|---|
| 1 H-G Anscheidt (Suzuki) | 66.86mph | 1 H-G Anscheidt (Suzuki) | 89.30mph | 1 Y Katayama (Suzuki) | 70.10mph |
| 2 Y Katayama (Suzuki) | (107.67km/h) | 2 R Schmalze (Kreidler) | (143.60km/h) | 2 H-G Anscheidt (Suzuki) | (112.88km/h) |
| 3 B Grau (Derbi) | | 3 J Busquets (Derbi) | | 3 S Graham (Suzuki) | Record |
| 4 J Bordons (Derbi) | | 4 B Smith (Derbi) | | 4 B Smith (Derbi) | |
| 5 D Crivello (Derbi) | | 5 D Gedlich (Kreidler) | | 5 A Nieto (Derbi) | |
| 6 A Nieto (Derbi) | | 6 W Reinhard (Reimo) | | 6 .Crivello (Derbi) | |
| Fastest lap – Y Katayama (Suzuki) | 68.17mph<br>(109.96km/h) | Fastest lap – H-G Anscheidt (Kreidler) | 90.61mph<br>(145.90km/h) | Record lap – Y Katayama (Suzuki) | 71.83mph<br>(115.66km/h) |
| **TT Races Isle of Man June 14** | | **Dutch TT Assen June 24** | | **Belgian GP Spa Francorchamps July 2** | |
| 1 S Graham (Suzuki) | 82.89mph | 1 Y Katayama (Suzuki) | 71.49mph | 1 H-G Anscheidt (Suzuki) | 98.48mph |
| 2 H-G Anscheidt (Suzuki) | (132.62k/mh) | 2 A Nieto (Derbi) | (115.12km/h) | 2 Y Katayama (Suzuki) | (158.55km/h) |
| 3 T Robb (Suzuki) | | 3 B Smith (Derbi) | Record | 3 S Graham (Suzuki) | Record |
| 4 C Walpole (Honda) | | 4 H-G Anscheidt (Suzuki) | | 4 A Nieto (Derbi) | |
| 5 E Griffith (Honda) | | 5.A Toerson (Kreidler) | | 5 A Toerson (Kreidler) | |
| 6 J Lawley (Honda) | | 6 P Lodewijkx (Jamathi) | | 6 P Lodewijkx (Jamathi) | |
| Fastest lap – S Graham (Suzuki) | 85.19mph<br>(137.10km/h) | Fastest lap – Y Katayama (Suzuki) | 74.59mph<br>(120.10km/h) | Record lap – Y Katayama (Suzuki) | 100.01mph<br>(161.04km/h) |
| **Japanese GP Fisco October 10** | | | | | |
| 1 M Itoh (Suzuki) | | | | | |
| 2 S Graham (Suzuki) | | | | | |
| 3 N Kawasaki (Suzuki) | | | | | |
| 4 H-G Anscheidt (Suzuki) | | | | | |
| 5 B Smith (Derbi) | | | | | |
| 6 A Akamatsu (Suzuki) | | | | | |
| Fastest lap – M Itoh (Suzuki) | | | | | |

## 1967 125CC

| Spanish GP Montjuich Park April 30 | |
|---|---|
| 1 B Ivy (Yamaha) | 72.40mph |
| 2 P Read (Yamaha) | (116.59km/h) |
| 3.Y Katayama (Suzuki) | Record |
| 4 S Graham (Suzuki) | |
| 5 F Villa (Montesa) | |
| 6 J Medrano (Bultaco) | |
| Record lap – B Ivy (Yamaha) | 73.78mph<br>(118.80km/h) |

| West German GP Hockenheim May 7 | |
|---|---|
| 1 Y Katayama (Suzuki) | 101.80mph |
| 2 H-G Anscheidt (Suzuki) | (164.09km/h) |
| 3 L Szabo (MZ) | Record |
| 4 F Villa (Montesa) | |
| 5 J Busquets (Montesa) | |
| 6 H Mann (MZ) | |
| Record lap – B Ivy (Yamaha) | 106.89mph<br>(171.49km/h) |

| French GP Clermont-Ferrand May 21 | |
|---|---|
| 1 B Ivy (Yamaha) | 77.40mph |
| 2 P Read (Yamaha) | (124.62km/h) |
| 3 Y Katayama (Suzuki) | Record |
| 4 S Graham (Suzuki) | |
| 5 D Simmonds (Kawasaki) | |
| 6 J Vergenais (Bultaco) | |
| Record lap – B Ivy (Yamaha) | 78.67mph<br>(126.68km/h) |

| TT Races Isle of Man June 14 | |
|---|---|
| 1 P Read (Yamaha) | 97.48mph |
| 2 S Graham (Suzuki) | (156.84km/h) |
| 3 A Motohashi (Yamaha) | |
| 4 D Simmonds (Kawasaki) | |
| 5 K Carruthers (Honda) | |
| 6 J Curry (Honda) | |
| Fastest lap – P Read (Yamaha) | 98.36mph<br>(158.29km/h) |

| Dutch TT Assen June 24 | |
|---|---|
| 1 P Read (Yamaha) | 84.75mph |
| 2 B Ivy (Yamaha) | (136.47km/h) |
| 3 S Graham (Suzuki) | Record |
| 4 Y Katayama (Suzuki) | |
| 5 C VanDongen (Honda) | |
| 6 R Avery (EMC) | |
| Record lap – B Ivy (Yamaha) | 87.12mph<br>(140.28km/h) |

| East German GP Sachsenring July 16 | |
|---|---|
| 1 B Ivy (Yamaha) | 97.14mph |
| 2 P Read (Yamaha) | (156.43km/h) |
| 3 S Graham (Suzuki) | Record |
| 4 K Enderlein (MZ) | |
| 5 T Heuschkel (MZ) | |
| 6 L Szabo (MZ) | |
| Record lap – B Ivy (Yamaha) | 99.37mph<br>(159.92km/h) |

| Czechoslovak GP Brno June 23 | |
|---|---|
| 1 B Ivy (Yamaha) | 91.97mph |
| 2 S Graham (Suzuki) | (148.10km/h) |
| 3 L Szabo (MZ) | |
| 4 T Heuschkel (MZ) | |
| 5 W Scheimann (Honda) | |
| 6 J Curry (Honda) | |
| Record lap – Y Katayama (Suzuki) | 95.08mph<br>(153.09km/h) |

| Finnish GP Imatra August 6 | |
|---|---|
| 1 S Graham (Suzuki) | 81.29mph |
| 2 B Ivy (Yamaha) | (130.91km/h) |
| 3 D Simmonds (Kawasaki) | Record |
| 4 J Lenk (MZ) | |
| 5 K Carruthers (Honda) | |
| 6 H Bischoff (MZ) | |
| Fastest lap – B Ivy (Yamaha) | 85.01mph<br>(136.89km/h) |

| Ulster GP Dundrod August 19 | |
|---|---|
| 1 B Ivy (Yamaha) | 94.81mph |
| 2 P Read (Yamaha) | (152.55km/h) |
| 3 S Graham (Suzuki) | Record |
| 4 K Carruthers (Honda) | |
| 5 K Cass (Bultaco) | |
| 6 G Molloy (Bultaco) | |
| Record lap – B Ivy (Yamaha) | 99.53mph<br>(160.17km/h) |

| Italian GP Monza September 3 | |
|---|---|
| 1 B Ivy (Yamaha) | 103.42mph |
| 2 H-G Anscheidt (Suzuki) | (166.82km/h) |
| 3 L Szabo (MZ) | |
| 4 W Scheimann (Honda) | |
| 5 G Burlando (Honda) | |
| 6 J Curry (Honda) | |
| Fastest lap – B Ivy (Yamaha) | 111.14mph<br>179.26km/h) |

| Canadian GP Mosport Park September 30 | |
|---|---|
| 1 B Ivy (Yamaha) | 79.07mph |
| 2 M Coopey (Yamaha) | (127.22km/h) |
| 3 C Luck (Yamaha) | Record |
| 4 T Ducal (Yamaha) | |
| 5 J Swegan (Yamaha) | |
| 6 I Messina (Yamaha) | |
| Record lap – B Ivy (Yamaha) | 83.51mph<br>(134.36km/h) |

| Japanese GP Fisco October 14 | |
|---|---|
| 1 B Ivy (Yamaha) | 96.47mph |
| 2 S Graham (Suzuki) | (155.34km/h) |
| 3 H Kanaya (Suzuki) | |
| 4 I Morishita (Suzuki) | |
| 5 R Shigeno (Suzuki) | |
| 6 B Smith (Bultaco) | |
| Fastest lap – B Ivy (Yamaha) | 97.80mph<br>(157.39km/h) |

## 1967 250CC

| Spanish GP Montjuich Park April 30 | |
|---|---|
| 1 P Read (Yamaha) | 73.30mph |
| 2 R Bryans (Honda) | (118.03km/h) |
| 3 J Medrano (Bultaco) | |
| 4 G Molloy (Bultaco) | |
| 5 T Robb (Bultaco) | |
| 6 C Giro (Ossa) | |
| Record lap – M Hailwood (Honda) | 77.00mph<br>(123.83km/h) |

| West German GP Hockenheim May 7 | |
|---|---|
| 1 R Bryans (Honda) | 107.20mph |
| 2 P Read (Yamaha) | (172.70km/h) |
| 3 H Rosner (MZ) | |
| 4 J Findlay (Bultaco) | |
| 5 G Marsovsky (Bultaco) | |
| 6 R Schmid (Bultaco) | |
| Record lap – B Ivy (Yamaha) | 111.93mph<br>(179.42km/h) |

| French GP Clermont-Ferrand May 21 | |
|---|---|
| 1 B Ivy (Yamaha) | 78.02mph |
| 2 P Read (Yamaha) | (125.64km/h) |
| 3 M Hailwood (Honda) | |
| 4 R Bryans (Honda) | |
| 5 D Woodman (MZ) | |
| 6 H Rosner (MZ) | |
| Record lap – M Hailwood (Honda) | 83.37mph<br>(134.25km/h) |

| TT Races Isle of Man June 12 | |
|---|---|
| 1 M Hailwood (Honda) | 103.07mph |
| 2 P Read (Yamaha) | (164.90km/h) |
| 3 R Bryans (Honda) | |
| 4 D Simmonds (Kawasaki) | |
| 5 W A.Bill Smith (Kawasaki) | |
| 6 M Chatterton (Yamaha) | |
| Record lap – M Hailwood (Honda) | 104.50mph<br>(168.17km/h) |

| Dutch TT Assen June 24 | |
|---|---|
| 1 M Hailwood (Honda) | 89.60mph |
| 2 B Ivy (Yamaha) | (144.29km/h) |
| 3 R Bryans (Honda) | Record |
| 4 D Woodman (MZ) | |
| 5 D Simmonds (Kawasaki) | |
| 6 G Molloy (Bultaco) | |
| Record lap – M Hailwood (Honda) | 91.37mph<br>(147.09km/h) |

| Belgian GP Spa Francorchamps July 2 | |
|---|---|
| 1 B Ivy (Yamaha) | 122.17mph |
| 2 M Hailwood (Honda) | (196.73km/h) |
| 3 R Bryans (Honda) | |
| 4 D Woodman (MZ) | |
| 5 G Molloy (Bultaco) | |
| 6 G Marsovsky (Bultaco) | |
| Record lap – P Read (Yamaha) | 125.54mph<br>(202.14km/h) |

| East German GP Sachsenring July 16 | |
|---|---|
| 1 P Read (Yamaha) | 103.14mph |
| 2 B Ivy (Yamaha) | (166.09km/h) |
| 3 R Bryans (Honda) | |
| 4 H Rosner (MZ) | |
| 5 G Molloy (Bultaco) | |
| 6 G Marsovsky (Bultaco) | |
| Record lap – P Read (Yamaha) | 105.92mph<br>(170.46km/h) |

| Czechoslovak GP Brno July 23 | |
|---|---|
| 1 P Read (Yamaha) | 96.88mph |
| 2 B Ivy (Yamaha) | (156.60km/h) |
| 3 M Hailwood (Honda) | Record |
| 4 R Bryans (Honda) | |
| 4 H Rosner (MZ) | |
| 6 D Woodman (MZ) | |
| Record lap – B Ivy (Yamaha) | 99.98mph<br>(160.99km/h) |

| Finnish GP Imatra August 6 | |
|---|---|
| 1 M Hailwood (Honda) | 79.67mph |
| 2 B Ivy (Yamaha) | (128.30km/h) |
| 3 D Woodman (MZ) | |
| 4 G Marsovsky (Bultaco) | |
| 5 F Stevens (Paton) | |
| 6 M Stanton (Aermacchi) | |
| Fastest lap – M Hailwood (Honda) | 81.09mph<br>(130.59km/h) |

| Ulster GP Dundrod August 19 | | Italian GP Monza September 3 | | Canadian GP Mosport Park September 30 | |
|---|---|---|---|---|---|
| 1 M Hailwood (Honda) | 104.31mph | 1 P Read (Yamaha) | 119.72mph | 1 M Hailwood (Honda) | 89.90mph |
| 2 R Bryans (Honda) | (167.83km/h) | 2 B Ivy (Yamaha) | (192.78km/h) | 2 P Read (Yamaha) | (144.61km/h) |
| 3 B Ivy (Yamaha) | Record | 3 R Bryans (Honda) | | 3 R Bryans (Honda) | |
| 4 D Woodman (MZ) | | 4 H Rosner (MZ) | | 4 Y DuHamel (Yamaha) | |
| 5 B Steenson (Aermacchi) | | 5 D Woodman (MZ) | | 5 P Carmilleri (Yamaha) | |
| 6 G Marsovsky (Butaco) | | 6 G Molloy (Bultaco) | | 6 R Grant (Yamaha) | |
| Record lap – M Hailwood (Honda) | 105.86mph (170.36km/h) | Record lap – B Ivy (Yamaha) | 121.62mph (195.71km/h) | Record lap – M Hailwood (Honda) | 91.45mph (146.70km/h) |
| **Japanese GP Fisco October 14** | | | | | |
| 1 R Bryans (Honda) | 100.96mph | | | | |
| 2 A Motohashi (Yamaha) | (162.53km/h) | | | | |
| 3 T Hamano (Yamaha) | | | | | |
| 4 T Robb (Bultaco) | | | | | |
| 5 G Milani (Aermacchi) | | | | | |
| 6 B Ivy (Yamaha) | | | | | |
| Fastest lap – H Hasegawa (Yamaha) | 105.12mph (169.17km/h) | | | | |

## 1967 350CC

| West German GP Hockenheim May 7 | | TT Races Isle of Man June 16 | | Dutch TT Assen June 24 | |
|---|---|---|---|---|---|
| 1 M Hailwood (Honda) | 111.20mph | 1 M Hailwood (Honda) | 104.68mph | 1 M Hailwood (Honda) | 87.88mph |
| 2 G Agostini (MV) | (179.06km/h) | 2 G Agostini (MV) | (172.84km/h) | 2 G Agostini (MV) | (141.51km/h) |
| 3 R Passolini (Benelli) | Record | 3 D Woodman (MZ) | | 3 R Passolini (Benelli) | Record |
| 4 A Pagani (Aermacchi) | | 4 A Pagani (Aermacchi) | | 4 F Stevens (Paton) | |
| 5 K Carruthers (Aermacchi) | | 5 C Conn (Norton) | | 5 H Rosner (MZ) | |
| 6 G Milani (Aermacchi) | | 6 G Milani (Aermacchi) | | 6 K Carruthers (Aermacchi) | |
| Record lap – M Hailwood (Honda) | 112.57mph (181.27km/h) | Record lap – M Hailwood (Honda) | 107.73mph (173.34km/h) | Record lap – G Agostini (MV) | 90.27mph (145.40km/h) |
| **East German GP Sachsenring July 16** | | **Czechoslovak GP Brno July 23** | | **Ulster GP Dundrod August 19** | |
| 1 M Hailwood (Honda) | 98.36mph | 1 M Hailwood (Honda) | 103.31mph | 1 G Agostini (MV) | 103.31mph |
| 2 G Agostini (MV) | (158.39km/h) | 2 H Rosner (MZ) | (158.04km/h) | 2 R Bryans (Honda) | (166.22km/h) |
| 3 D Woodman (MZ) | | 3 D Woodman (MZ) | Record | 3 H Rosner (MZ) | Record |
| 4 K Carruthers (Aermacch) | | 4 G Havel (Jawa) | | 4 K Carruthers (Aermacchi) | |
| 5 H Rosner (MZ) | | 5 A Pagani (Aermacchi) | | 5 B Steenson (Aermacchi) | |
| 6 D Shorey (Norton) | | 6 B Stasa (CZ) | | 6 I McGregor (Norton) | |
| Fastest lap – M Hailwood (Honda) | 102.92mph (165.63km/h) | Record lap – M Hailwood (Honda) | 100.60mph (165.63km/h) | Record lap – G Agostini (MV) | 105.11mph (169.15km/h) |
| **Italian GP Monza September 3** | | **Japanese GP Fisco October 14** | | | |
| 1 R Bryans (Honda) | 118.17mph | 1 M Hailwood (Honda) | 98.49mph | | |
| 2 S Grassetti (Benelli) | (191.42km/h) | 2 R Bryans (Honda) | (158.59km/h) | | |
| 3 H Rosner (MZ) | | 3 K Mimuro (Yamaha) | | | |
| 4 A Pagani (Aermacchi) | | 4 J Wada (Yamaha) | | | |
| 5 D Woodman (MZ) | | 5 G Milani (Aermacchi) | | | |
| 6 F Stevens (Paton) | | 6 A Yorino (Yamaha) | | | |
| Record lap – R Bryans (Honda) | 121.62mph (195.71km/h) | Fastest lap – M Hailwood (Honda) | 102.33mph (164.68km/h) | | |

## 1967 500CC

| West German GP Hockenheim May 7 | | TT Races Isle of Man June 16 | | Dutch TT Assen June 24 | |
|---|---|---|---|---|---|
| 1 G Agostini (MV)<br>2 P Williams (Matchless)<br>3 J Findlay (McIntyre Matchless)<br>4 R Fitton (Norton)<br>5 B Nelson (Norton)<br>6 G Jenkins (Norton)<br>Record lap – G Agostini (MV) | 112.30mph<br>(180.81km/h)<br>Record<br>117.12mph<br>(188.59km/h) | 1 M Hailwood (Honda)<br>2 P Williams (Matchless)<br>3 S Spencer (Norton)<br>4 J Cooper (Norton)<br>5 F Stevens (Paton)<br>6 J Hartle (Matchless)<br>Record lap – M Hailwood (Honda) | 105.62mph<br>(168.90km/h)<br>108.77mph<br>(175.04km/h) | 1 M Hailwood (Honda)<br>2 G Agostini (MV)<br>3 P Williams (Matchless)<br>4 D Shorey (Norton)<br>5 G Marsovsky (Matchless)<br>6 C Conn (Norton)<br>Record lap – M Hailwood (Honda) | 90.82mph<br>(146.24km/h)<br>Record<br>92.90mph<br>(149.60km/h) |
| **Belgian GP Spa Francorchamps July 2** | | **East German GP Sachsenring July 16** | | **Czechoslovak GP Brno July 23** | |
| 1 G Agostini (MV)<br>2 M Hailwood (Honda)<br>3 F Stevens (Paton)<br>4 J Findlay (McIntyre Matchless)<br>5 G Marsovsky (Matchless)<br>6 D Minter (Norton)<br>Record lap – G Agostini (MV) | 123.87mph<br>(199.47km/h)<br>128.50mph<br>(206.92km/h) | 1 G Agostini (MV)<br>2 J Hartle (Matchless)<br>3 J Findlay (McIntyre Matchless)<br>4 J Dodds (Norton)<br>5 R Gould (Norton)<br>6 D Shorey (Norton)<br>Record lap – G Agostini (MV) | 105.99mph<br>(170.67km/h)<br>Record<br>109.29mph<br>(175.90km/h) | 1 M Hailwood (Honda)<br>2 G Agostini (MV)<br>3 J Cooper (Norton)<br>4 G Marsovsky (Matchless)<br>5 J Hartle (Matchless)<br>6 J Dodds (Norton)<br>Record lap – M Hailwood (Honda) | 101.47mph<br>(163.40km/h)<br>Record<br>103.71mph<br>(167.00km/h) |
| **Finnish GP Imatra August 6** | | **Ulster GP Dundrod August 19** | | **Italian GP Monza Setember 3** | |
| 1 G Agostini (MV)<br>2 J Hartle (Matchless)<br>3 B Nelson (Norton)<br>4 B Granath (Matchless)<br>5 F Stevens (Paton)<br>6 M Hawthorne (Norton)<br>Fastest lap – G Agostini (MV) | 73.90mph<br>(119.08km/h)<br>77.25mph<br>(124.38km/h) | 1 M Hailwood (Honda)<br>2 J Hartle (Matchless)<br>3 J Findlay (McIntyre Matchless)<br>4 J Blanchard (Fath Seeley)<br>5 S Spencer (Norton)<br>6 J Cooper (Seeley)<br>Record lap – M Hailwood (Honda) | 102.88mph<br>(165.50km/h)<br>Record<br>105.03mph<br>(171.73km/h) | 1 G Agostini (MV)<br>2 M Hailwood (Honda)<br>3 A Bergamonti (Paton)<br>4 F Stevens (Paton)<br>5 G Mandolini (Guzzi)<br>6 J Hartle (Matchless)<br>Record lap – M Hailwood (Honda) | 124.37mph<br>(200.28km/h)<br>126.77mph<br>(204.01km/h) |
| **Canadian GP Mosport Park September 30** | | | | | |
| 1 M Hailwood (Honda)<br>2 G Agostini (MV)<br>3 M Duff (Matchless)<br>4 I Lloyd (Matchless)<br>5 A Georgeades (Velocette)<br>6 J Rockett (Norton)<br>Record lap – M Hailwood (Honda) | 80.32mph<br>(129.20km/h)<br>85.95mph<br>(138.40km/h) | | | | |

## 1967 SIDECARS

| Spanish GP Montjuich Park April 30 | | West German GP Hockenheim May 7 | | French GP Clermont-Ferrand May 21 | |
|---|---|---|---|---|---|
| 1 G Auerbacher/E Dein (BMW)<br>2 K Enders/R Engelhardt (BMW)<br>3 S Schauzu/H Schneider (BMW)<br>4 O Kolle/R Schmid (BMW)<br>5 H Wohlfart/H Vester (BMW)<br>Only 5 finishers<br>Fastest lap – G Auerbacher (BMW) | 68.13mph<br>(109.65km/h)<br>68.94mph<br>(111.20km/h) | 1 K Enders/R Engelhardt (BMW)<br>2 G Auerbacher/E Dein (BMW)<br>3 T Wakefield/G Milton (BMW)<br>4 S Schauzu/H Schneider (BMW)<br>5 B Dungworth/R Wilson (BMW)<br>6 J Attenberger/J Schillinger (BMW)<br>Fastest lap – K Enders (BMW) | 96.87mph<br>(155.90km/h)<br>99.31mph<br>(160.19km/h) | 1 K Enders/R/Engelhardt (BMW)<br>2 S Schauzu/H Schneider (BMW)<br>3 T Wakefield/G Milton (BMW)<br>4 G Auerbacher/E Dein (BMW)<br>5 H Luthringshauser/H Hahn (BMW)<br>6 A Butscher/A Neumann (BMW)<br>Fastest lap – H Fath (Fath URS) | 71.08mph<br>(114.39km/h)<br>72.57mph<br>(117.06km/h) |
| **TT Races Isle of Man June 12** | | **Dutch TT Assen June 24** | | **Belgian GP Spa Francorchamps July 2** | |
| 1 S Schauzu/H Schneider (BMW)<br>2 K Enders/R Engelhardt (BMW)<br>3 C Seeley/R Lindsay (BMW)<br>4 P Harris/J Thornton (BMW)<br>5 B Dungworth/N Caddow (BMW)<br>6 T Vinnicombe/J Flaxman (BSA)<br>Fastest lap – G Auerbacher (BMW) | 90.31mph<br>(145.35km/h)<br>91.49mph<br>(147.57km/h) | 1 K Enders/R Engelhardt (BMW)<br>2 S Schauzu/H Schneider (BMW)<br>3 P Harris/J Thornton (BMW)<br>4 T Wakefield/G Milton (BMW)<br>5 J Attenberger/J Schillinger (BMW)<br>6 A Butscher/A Neumann (BMW)<br>Fastest lap – K Enders (BMW) | 80.06mph<br>(128.85km/h)<br>80.53mph<br>(129.90km/h) | 1 K Enders/R Engelhardt (BMW)<br>2 G Auerbacher/E Dein (BMW)<br>3 S Schauzu/H Schneider (BMW)<br>4 P Harris/J/Thornton (BMW)<br>5 H Luthringshauser/H Hahn (BMW)<br>6 J Attenberger/J Schillinger (BMW)<br>Fastest lap – K Enders (BMW) | 109.47mph<br>(176.18km/h)<br>110.76mph<br>(178.66km/h) |
| **Finnish GP Imatra August 6** | | **Italian GP Monza September 3** | | | |
| 1 K Enders/R Engelhardt (BMW)<br>2 .J Attenberger/J Schillinger (BMW)<br>3 G Auerbacher/E Dein (BMW)<br>4 H Haenni/K Barfuss (BMW)<br>5 B Persson/G Kimsjo (BMW)<br>6 R Bjarnemark/A Ragmo (BMW)<br>Fastest lap – K Enders (BMW) | 71.52mph<br>(115.10km/h)<br>72.96mph<br>(117.69km/h) | 1 G Auerbacher/B Nelson (BMW)<br>2 H Luthringshauser/H Hahn (BMW)<br>3 O Kolle/R Schmid (BMW)<br>4 J Duham/C Maingret (BMW)<br>5 A Butscher/A Neumann (BMW)<br>6 S Schauzu/H Schneider (BMW)<br>Fastest lap – G Auerbacher (BMW) | 101.04mph<br>(162.61km/h)<br>102.69mph<br>(165.63km/h) | | |

## 1968 50CC

| West German GP Nurburgring South April 21 | | Spanish GP Montjuich Park May 4 | | TT Races Isle of Man June 14 | |
|---|---|---|---|---|---|
| 1 H-G Anscheidt (Suzuki) | 74.19mph | 1 H-G Anscheidt (Suzuki) | 63,26mph | 1 B Smith (Derbi) | 72.88mph |
| 2 R Kunz (Kreidler) | (119.40km/h) | 2 A Nieto (Derbi) | (101.81km/h) | 2 C Walpole (Honda) | (117.29km/h) |
| 3 R Schmalze (Kreidler) | | 3 B Smith (Derbi) | | 3 E Griffith (Honda) | |
| 4 L Fassbender (KreidlerO | | 4 P Lodewijkx (Jamathi) | | 4 D Lock (Honda) | |
| 5 C VanDongen (Kreidler) | | 5 C Giro (Derbi) | | 5 J Pink (Honda) | |
| 6 F Stefe (Tomos) | | 6 F Cufi (Derbi) | | 6 R Udall (Honda) | |
| Fastest lap – Anscheidt (Kreidler) | 75.31mph | Fastest lap – A Nieto (Derbi) | 64.72mph | Fastest lap – B Smith (Derbi) | 73.27mph |
| | 121.48km/h) | | (104.84km/h) | | (118.19km/h) |
| **Dutch TT Assen June 29** | | **Belgian GP Spa Francorchamps July 7** | | | |
| 1 P Lodewijkx (Jamathi) | 72.87mph | 1 H-G Anscheidt (Suzuki) | 93.53mph | | |
| 2 H-G Anscheidt (Suzuki) | (117.27km/h) | 2 P Lodewijkx (Jamathi) | (150.52km/h) | | |
| 3 A Toersen (Kreidler) | | 3 A Nieto (Derbi) | | | |
| 4 J DeVries (Kreidler) | | 4 B Smith (Derbi) | | | |
| 5 J Schurgers (Kreidler) | | 5 M Mijwaart (Jamathi) | | | |
| 6 R Schmalze (Kreidler) | | 6 R Schmalze (Kreidler) | | | |
| Fastest lap – P Lodewijkx (Jamathi) | 74.24mph | Fastest lap – Anscheidt (Kreidler) | 94.41mph | | |
| | (119.75km/h) | | (152.29km/h) | | |

## 1968 125CC

| West German GP Nurburgring South April 21 | | Spanish GP Montjuich Park May 4 | | TT Races Isle of Man June 14 | |
|---|---|---|---|---|---|
| 1 P Read (Yamaha) | 84.6mph | 1 S Canellas (Bultaco) | 69.27mph | 1 P Read (Yamaha) | 99.10mph |
| 2 H-G Anscheidt (Suzuki) | (136.41km/h) | 2 G Molloy (Bultaco) | (111.49km/h) | 2 B Ivy (Yamaha) | (159.48km/h) |
| 3 S Mohringer (MZ) | Record) | 3 H Rosner (MZ) | | 3 K Carruthers (Honda) | Record |
| 4 D Braun (MZ) | | 4 W Scheimann (Honda) | | 4 T Robb (Bultaco) | |
| 5 K Andersson (MZ) | | 5 T Robb (Bultaco) | | 5 G Keith (Montesa) | |
| 6 K Carruthers (Honda) | | 6 P Alvarez (Bultaco) | | 6 S Murray (Honda) | |
| Record lap – B Ivy (Yamaha) | 85.6mph | Fastest lap – B Ivy (Yamaha) | 73.10mph | Record lap – B Ivy (Honda) | 100.32mph |
| | (138.09km/h) | | (117.91km/h) | | (161.44km/h) |
| **Dutch TT Assen June 29** | | **East German GP Sachsenring July 14** | | **Czechoslovak GP Brno July 21** | |
| 1 P Read (Yamaha) | 82.66mph | 1 P Read (Yamaha) | 97.32mph | 1 P Read (Yamaha) | 85.45mph |
| 2 G Molloy (Bultaco) | (133.03km/h) | 2 B Ivy (Yamaha) | (156.62km/h) | 2 L Szabo (MZ) | (137.52km/h) |
| 3 J Huberts (MZ) | | 3 G Bartusch (MZ) | Record | 3 G Bartusch (MZ) | |
| 4 S Canellas (Bultaco) | | 4 L Szabo (MZ) | | 4 D Braun (MZ) | |
| 5 D Braun (MZ) | | 5 H Bischoff (MZ) | | 5 L John (MZ) | |
| 6 G Vicenzi (Montesa) | | 6 T Heuschkel (MZ) | | 6 J Reisz (MZ) | |
| Fastest lap – P Read (Yamaha) | 83.00mph | Record lap – B Ivy (Yamaha) | 100.03mph | Fastest lap – B Ivy (Yamaha) | 87.64mph |
| | (133.88km/h) | | (161.34km/h) | | (141.37km/h) |
| **Finnish GP Imatra August 4** | | **Ulster GP Dundrod August 17** | | **Italian GP Monza September 15** | |
| 1 P Read (Yamaha) | 85.38mph | 1 B Ivy (Yamaha) | 99.62mph | 1 B Ivy (Yamaha) | 106.04mph |
| 2 B Ivy (Yamaha) | (137.40km/h) | 2 P Read (Yamaha) | (160.33km/h) | 2 P Read (Yamaha) | (170.66km/h) |
| 3 H Rosner (MZ) | Record | 3 H Rosner (MZ) | Record | 3 H-G Anscheidt (Suzuki) | |
| 4 B Kohlar (MZ) | | 4 G Molloy (Bultaco) | | 4 D Simmonds (Kawasaki) | |
| 5 J Lenk (MZ) | | 5 D,Braun (MZ) | | 5 L Szabo (MZ) | |
| 6 T Heuschkel (MZ) | | 6 K Carruthers (Honda) | | 6 D Braun (MZ) | |
| Record lap – B Ivy (Yamaha) | 87.06mph | Record lap – P Read (Yamaha) | 102.18mph | Fastest lap – B Ivy (Yamaha) | 108.57mph |
| | (140.43km/h) | | (164.82km/h) | | (175.12km/h) |

## 1968 250CC

| West German GP Nurburgring South April 21 | | Spanish GP Montjuich Park May 5 | | TT Races Isle of Man June 10 | |
|---|---|---|---|---|---|
| 1 B Ivy (Yamaha) | 87.86mph | 1 P Read (Yamaha) | 73.45mph | 1 B Ivy (Yamaha) | 99.56mph |
| 2 G Molloy (Butaco) | (141.40km/h) | 2 H Rosner (MZ) | (118.21km/h) | 2 R Passolini (Benelli) | (160.22km/h) |
| 3 K Andersson (Yamaha) | Record | 3 G Molloy (Bultaco) | | 3 H Rosner (MZ) | |
| 4 R Gould (Yamaha/Bultaco) | | 4 C Giro (Ossa) | | 4 M Uphill (Suzuki) | |
| 5 J Findlay (Bultaco) | | 5 C Rocamora (Bultaco) | | 5 R Gould (Yamaha/Bultaco) | |
| 6 S Herrero (Ossa) | | 6 P Eickelberg (Aermacchi) | | 6 W A.Smith (Yamaha) | |
| Record lap – B Ivy (Yamaha) | 89.40mph (144.20km/h) | Fastest lap – P Read (Yamaha) | 74.80mph (121.66km/h) | Record lap – B Ivy (Yamaha) | 105.27mph (169.80km/h) |
| **Dutch TT Assen June 29** | | **Belgian GP Spa Francorchamps July 7** | | **East German GP Sachsenring July 14** | |
| 1 B Ivy (Yamaha) | 88.14mph | 1 P Read (Yamaha) | 116.40mph | 1 B Ivy (Yamaha) | 103.05mph |
| 2 P Read (Yamaha) | (141.85km/h) | 2 H Rosner (MZ) | (187.33km/h) | 2 P Read (Yamaha) | (165.85km/h) |
| 3 R Passolini (Benelli) | | 3 R Gould (Yamaha/Bultaco) | | 3 H Rosner (MZ) | |
| 4 H Rosner (MZ) | | 4 L Szabo (MZ) | | 4 R Gould (Yamaha/Bultaco) | |
| 5 R Gould (Yamaha/Bultaco) | | 5 S Herrero (Ossa) | | 5 G Molloy (Bultaco) | |
| 6 S Herrero (Ossa) | | 6 K Andersson (Yamaha) | | 6 J Findlay (Bultaco) | |
| Fastest lap – B Ivy (Yamaha) | 89.09mph (143.70km/h) | Fastest lap – B Ivy (Yamaha) | 125.12mph (201.82km/h) | Record lap – P Read (Yamaha) | 105.92mph (170.85km/h) |
| **Czechoslovak GP Brno July 21** | | **Finnish GP Imatra August 4** | | **Ulster GP Dundrod August 17** | |
| 1 P Read (Yamaha) | 92.34mph | 1 P Read (Yamaha) | 79.66mph | 1 B Ivy (Yamaha) | 97.47mph |
| 2 B Ivy (Yamaha) | (148.61km/h) | 2 H Rosner (MZ) | (128.20km/h) | 2 H Rosner (MZ) | (156.87km/h) |
| 3 H Rosner (MZ) | | 3 R Gould (Yamaha/Bultaco) | | 3 R Gould (Yamaha/Bultaco) | |
| 4 R Gould (Yamaha/Bultaco) | | 4 G Molloy (Bultaco) | | 4 G Molloy (Bultaco) | |
| 5 G Milani (Aermacchi) | | 5 L Szabo (MZ) | | 5 M Uphill (Suzuki) | |
| 6 G Molloy (Bultaco) | | 6 G Marsovsky (Bultaco) | | 6 K Andersson (Yamaha) | |
| Fastest lap – P Read (Yamaha) | 94.35mph (152.18km/h) | Record lap – P Read (Yamaha) | 84.20mph (135.82km/h) | Fastest lap – B Ivy (Yamaha) | 103.38mph (166.75km/h) |
| **Italian GP Monza September 15** | | | | | |
| 1 P Read (Yamaha) | 110/73mph | | | | |
| 2 B Ivy (Yamaha) | (178.21km/h) | | | | |
| 3 S Herrero (Ossa) | | | | | |
| 4 G Keith (Yamaha) | | | | | |
| 5 J Findlay (Bultaco) | | | | | |
| 6 R Butcher (Suzuki) | | | | | |
| Fastest lap – P Read (Yamaha) | 112.89mph (182.09km/h) | | | | |

## 1968 350CC

| West German GP Nurburgring South April 21 | | TT Races Isle of Man June 14 | | Dutch TT Assen June 29 | |
|---|---|---|---|---|---|
| 1 G Agostini (MV) | 90.80mph | 1 G Agostini (MV) | 104.78mph | 1 G Agostini (MV) | 87.82mph |
| 2 R Passolini (Benelli) | (146.45km/h) | 2 R Passolini (Benelli) | (168.59km/h) | 2 G Molloy (Bultaco) | (141.41km/h) |
| 3 K Carruthers (Aermacchi) | Record | 3 W A.Smith (Honda) | Record | 3 G Milani (Aermacchi) | |
| 4 G Molloy (Bultaco) | | 4 D Woodman (Aermacchi) | | 4 B Stasa (CZ) | |
| 5 D Shorey (Norton) | | 5 J Cooper (Seeley) | | 5 D Woodman (Aermacchi) | |
| 6 B Stasa (CZ) | | 6 J Findlay (Aermacchi) | | 6 D Simmonds (Kawasaki) | |
| Record lap – G Agostini (MV) | 92.62mph (149.39km/h) | Fastest lap – G Agostini (MV) | 106.77mph (171.82km/h) | Fastest lap – G Agostini (MV) | 89.60mph (144.53km/h) |
| **East German GP Sachsenring July14** | | **Czechoslovak GP Brno July 21** | | **Ulster GP Dundrod August 17** | |
| 1 G Agostini (MV) | 102.92mph | 1 G Agostini (MV) | 88.86mph | 1 G Agostini (MV) | 102.74mph |
| 2 H Rosner (MZ) | ((165.71km/h) | 2 H Rosner (MZ) | (143.08km/h) | 2 K Carruthers (Aermacchi) | (165.30km/h) |
| 3 K Carruthers (Aermacchi) | | 3 F Stastny (Jawa) | | 3 B Steenson (Aermacchi) | |
| 4 G Molloy (Bultaco) | | 4 K .Carruthers (Aermacchi) | | 4 F Stastny (Jawa) | |
| 5 D Woodman (Aermacchi) | | 5 K Hoppe (Aermacchi) | | 5 D Woodman (Aermacchi) | |
| 6 B Nelson (Norton) | | 6 B Nelson (Norton) | | 6 B Nelson (Norton) | |
| Fastest lap – G Agostini (MV) | 106.28mph (171.13km/h) | Fastest lap – G Agostini (MV) | 97.05mph (156.36km/h) | Record lap – G Agostini (MV) | 106.37mph (171.18km/h) |
| **Italian GP Monza September 15** | | | | | |
| 1 G Agostini (MV) | 106.27mph | | | | |
| 2 R Passolini (Benelli) | (171.11km/h) | | | | |
| 3 S Grassetti (Benelli) | | | | | |
| 4 B Stasa (CZ) | | | | | |
| 5 B Spaggiari (Ducati) | | | | | |
| 6 F Ststny (Jawa) | | | | | |
| Fastest lap – G Agostini (MV) | 109.77mph (176.65km/h) | | | | |

## 1968 500CC

| West German GP Nurburgring South April 21 | | Spanish GP Montjuich Park May 5 | | TT Races Isle of Man June 14 | |
|---|---|---|---|---|---|
| 1 G Agostini (MV)<br>2 D Shorey (Norton)<br>3 P Williams (Matchless)<br>4 G Marsovsky (Matchless)<br>5 B Stasa (CZ)<br>6 R Gould (Norton)<br>Record lap – G Agostini (MV) | 89.20mph<br>(143.91km/h | 1 G Agostini (MV)<br>2 J Findlay (McIntyre Matchless)<br>3 J Dodds (Norton)<br>4 A Bergamonti (Paton)<br>5 G Marsovsky (Matchless)<br>6 R Butcher (Norton)<br>Record lap – G Agostini (MV) | 74.81mph<br>(119.24km/h)<br>Record<br>75.49mph<br>(121.76km/h) | 1 G Agostini (MV)<br>2 B Ball (Seeley)<br>3 B Randle (Norton)<br>4 W A.Smith (Matchless)<br>5 M Lunde (Matchless)<br>6 K Carruthers (Norton)<br>Fastest lap – G Agostini (MV) | 101.38mph<br>(163.52km/h)<br>104.91mph<br>(168.83km/h) |
| Dutch TT Assen June 29 | | Belgian GP Spa Francorchamps July 7 | | East German GP Sachsenring July 14 | |
| 1 G Agostini (MV)<br>2 J Findlay (McIntyre Matchless)<br>3 J Cooper (Seeley)<br>4 P Williams (Matchless)<br>5 K Carruthers (Norton)<br>6 R Chandler (Seeley)<br>Fastest lap – G Agostini (MV) | 87.83mph<br>(141.43km/h)<br>90.55mph<br>(145.82km/h) | 1 G Agostini (MV)<br>2 J Findlay (McIntyre Matchless)<br>3 D Woodman (Seeley)<br>4 R Fitton (Norton)<br>5 K Carruthers (Norton)<br>6 J Coopoer (Seeley)<br>Record lap – G Agostini (MV) | 124.74mph<br>(200.86km/h)<br>Record<br>129.20mph<br>(208.54km/h) | 1 G Agostini (MV)<br>2 A Pagani (Linto)<br>3 J Findlay (McIntyre Matchless)<br>4 J Cooper (Seeley)<br>5 B Nelson (Paton)<br>6 G Nash (Norton)<br>Record lap – G Agostini (MV) | 105.83mph<br>(170.38km/h)<br>Record<br>109.79mph<br>(176.79km/h) |
| Czechoslovak GP Brno July 21 | | Finnish GP Imatra August 4 | | Ulster GP Dundrod August 17 | |
| 1 G Agostini (MV)<br>2 .J Findlay (McIntyre Matchless)<br>3 G Marsovsky (Matchless)<br>4 .B Nelson (Paton)<br>5 P Williams (Matchless)<br>6 D Shorey (Norton)<br>Fastest lap – G Agostini (MV) | 86.37mph<br>(139.21km/h)<br>97.92mph<br>(157.76km/h) | 1 G Agostini (MV)<br>2 J Findlay (McIntyre Matchless)<br>3 D Woodman (Seeley)<br>4 N Sevostianov (Vostok)<br>5 J Dodds (Noirton)<br>6 G Marsovsky (Matchless)<br>Record lap – G Agostini (MV) | 89.15mph<br>(143.80km/h)<br>Record<br>93.09mph<br>(150.15km/h) | 1 G Agostini (MV)<br>2 R Fitton (Norton)<br>3 J Hartle (Matchless)<br>4 P Tait (Triumph)<br>5 J Findlay (McIntyre Matchless)<br>6 K Carruthers (Norton)<br>Fastest lap – G Agostini (MV) | 94.89mph<br>(152.67km/h)<br>97.57mph<br>(156.99km/h) |
| Italian GP Monza September 15 | | | | | |
| 1 G Agostini (MV)<br>2 R Passolini (Benelli)<br>3 A Bergamonti (Paton)<br>4 A Pagani (Linto)<br>5 .S Berterelli (Paton)<br>6 K Carruthers (Norton)<br>Fastest lap – G Agostini (MV) | 110.69mph<br>(178.24km/h)<br>113.56mph<br>(182.75km/h) | | | | |

## 1968 SIDECARS

| West German GP Nurburgring South April 21 | | TT Races Isle of Man June 8 | | Dutch TT Assen June 29 | |
|---|---|---|---|---|---|
| 1 H Fath/W Kalauch (URS)<br>2 G Auerbacher/H Hahn (BMW)<br>3 S Schauzu/H Schneider (BMW)<br>4 J Attenberger/J Schillinger (BMW)<br>5 H Luthringshauser/L Ronsdorf<br>6 O Kolle/R Schmid (BMW)<br>Fastest lap – K Enders (BMW) | 78.97mph<br>(127.10km/h)<br>80.77mph<br>(130.29km/h) | 1 S Schauzu/H Schneider (BMW)<br>2 J Attenberger/J Schillinger (BMW)<br>3 H Luthringshauser/G Hughes<br>4 H Fath/W Kalauch (URS)<br>5 J Brandon/C Holland (BMW)<br>6 M Tombs/T Tombs (BMW)<br>Record lap – K Enders (BMW) | 91.07mph<br>(146.56km/h)<br>Record<br>94.09mph<br>(151.76km/h) | 1 J Attenberger/J Schillinger (BMW)<br>2 K Enders/R Engelhardt (BMW)<br>3 S Schauzu/H Schneider (BMW)<br>4 G Auerbacher/H DeWever (BMW)<br>5 H Fath/W Kalauch (URS)<br>6 J-C Castella/A Castella (BMW)<br>Record lap – J Attenberger (BMW) | 80.83mph<br>(130.09km/h)<br>Record<br>82.69mph<br>(133.08km/h) |
| Belgian GP Spa Francorchamps July 7 | | Finnish GP Imatra August 4 | | Italian GP round run at Hockenheim October 13 | |
| 1 G Auerbacher/H Hahn (BMW)<br>2 A Butscher/J Huber (BMW)<br>3 H Lunemann/N Caddow (BMW)<br>4 T Wakefield/G Milton (BMW)<br>5 O Kolle/R Schmid (BMW)<br>6 J-C Castella/A Castella (BMW)<br>Fastest lap – H Fath (URS) | 108.78mph<br>(175.07km/h)<br>110.65mph<br>(178.48km/h) | 1 H Fath/W Kalauch (URS)<br>2 H Luthringshauser/G Hughes<br>3 G Auerbacher/H Hahn (BMW)<br>4 O Kolle/R Schmid (BMW)<br>5 K Calenius/S Vesterinen (BMW)<br>6 R Bjarnemark/A Ragmo (BMW)<br>Fastest lap – H Fath (URS) | 77.98mph<br>(125.50km/h)<br>79.96mph<br>(128.98km/h) | 1 H Fath/W Kalauch (URS)<br>2 K Enders/R Engelhardt (BMW)<br>3 G Auerbacher/H Hahn (BMW)<br>4 S Schauzu/H Schneider (BMW)<br>5 H Luthringshauser/G Hughes (BMW)<br>6 A Butscher/J Huber (BMW)<br>Record lap – H Fath (URS) | 98.52mph<br>(158.56km/h)<br>Record<br>100.51mph<br>(162.12km/h) |

## 1969 50CC

| Spanish GP Jarama May 4 | | West German GP Hockenheim May 11 | | French GP Le Mans May 18 | |
|---|---|---|---|---|---|
| 1 A Toersen (Kreidler)<br>2 A Nieto (Derbi)<br>3 J DeVries (Kreidler)<br>4 G Parlotti (Tomos)<br>5 G Lombardi (Guazzoni)<br>6 J Unterladstatter (KTM)<br>Fastest lap – A Nieto (Derbi) | 54.05mph<br>(86.99km/h)<br><br><br><br><br>55.48mph<br>(89.49km/h) | 1 A Toersen (Kreidler)<br>2 J DeVries (Kreidler)<br>3 B Smith (Derbi)<br>4 W Reinhard (Reimo)<br>5 G Parlotti (Tomos)<br>6 L Fassbender (Kreidler)<br>Fastest lap – A Toersen (Kreidler) | 85.26mph<br>(137.22km/h)<br><br><br><br><br>86.10mph<br>(138.88km/h) | 1 A Toersen (Kreidler)<br>2 A Nieto (Derbi)<br>3 P Lodewijkx (Jamathi)<br>4 G Parlotti (Tomos)<br>5 R Kunz (Kreidler)<br>6 B Smith (Derbi)<br>Fastest lap – A Toersen Kreidler) | 69.41mph<br>(111.71km/h)<br><br><br><br><br>70.10mph<br>(113.07km/h) |
| **Dutch TT Assen June 28** | | **Belgian GP Spa Francorchamps July 6** | | **East German GP Sachsenring July 13** | |
| 1 B Smith (Derbi)<br>2 J DeVries (Kreidler)<br>3 A Toersen (Kreidler)<br>4 P Lodewijkx (Jamathi)<br>5 R Kunz (Kreidler)<br>6 J Schurgers (Kreidler)<br>Fastest lap – A Nieto (Derbi) | 74.39mph<br>(119.72km/h)<br><br><br><br><br>77.06mph<br>(124.30km/h) | 1 B Smith (Derbi)<br>2 S Herrero (Derbi)<br>3 A Toersen (Kreidler)<br>4 C VanDongen (Kreidler)<br>5 L Fassbender (Kreidler)<br>6 M Mijwaart (Jamathi)<br>Fastest lap – B Smith (Derbi) | 89.91mph<br>(144.69km/h)<br><br><br><br><br>90.39mph<br>(145.80km/h) | 1 A Nieto (Derbi)<br>2 S Herrero (Derbi)<br>3.A Toersen (Kreidler)<br>4 R Kunz (Kreidler)<br>5 J DeVries (Kreidler)<br>6 E Lazzarini (Morbidelli)<br>Fastest lap – Nieto & Herrero (Derbi) | 79.32<br>(127.66km/h)<br><br><br><br><br>80.47mph<br>(129.80km/h) |
| **Czechoslovak GP Brno July 20** | | **Ulster GP Dundrod August 16** | | **Italian GP Imola September 7** | |
| 1 P Lodewijkx (Jamathi)<br>2 B Smith (Derbi)<br>3 A Nieto (Derbi)<br>4 A Toersen (Kreidler)<br>5 C VanDongen (Kreidler)<br>6 M Mijwaart (Jamathi)<br>Fastest lap – B Smith (Derbi) | 74.88mph<br>(120.51km/h)<br><br><br><br><br>76.83mph<br>(123.93km/h) | 1 A Nieto (Derbi)<br>2 J DeVries (Kreidler)<br>3 F Whiteway (Suzuki)<br>4 S Aspin (Garelli)<br>5 L Lawlor (Derbi)<br>6 F Redfern (Honda)<br>Fastest lap – P Lodewijkx (Jamathi) | 80.18mph<br>(129.05km/h)<br><br><br><br><br>83.20mph<br>(134.20km/h) | 1 P Lodewijkx (Jamathi)<br>2 B Smith (Derbi)<br>3 A Toersen (Kreidler)<br>4 J DeVries (Kreidler)<br>5 L Fassbender (Kreidler)<br>6 S Berterelli (Minarelli)<br>Fastest lap – A Nieto (Derbi) | 76.30mph<br>(122.79km/h)<br><br><br><br><br>78.96mph<br>(127.37km/h) |
| **Yugoslavia GP Opatija September 14** | | | | | |
| 1 P Lodewijkx (Jamathi)<br>2 A Nieto (Derbi)<br>3 J DeVries (Kreidler)<br>4 M Mijwaart (Jamathi)<br>5 R Kunz (Kreidler)<br>6 J Huberts (Kreidler)<br>Fastest lap – A Nieto (Derbi) | 74.13mph<br>(119.30km/h)<br><br><br><br><br>76.99mph<br>(124.18km/h) | | | | |

## 1969 125CC

| Spanish GP Jarama May 4 | | West German GP Hockenheim May 11 | | French GP Le Mans | |
|---|---|---|---|---|---|
| 1 C VanDongen (Suzuki)<br>2 K Andersson (Maico)<br>3 W Villa (Villa)<br>4 E Escuder (Bultaco)<br>5 B Veigel (Honda)<br>6 K Carruthers (Aermacchi)<br>Fastest lap – S Canellas (Yamaha) | 56.24mph<br>(90.52km/h)<br><br><br><br><br>58.36mph<br>(94.13km/h) | 1 D Simmonds (Kawasaki)<br>2 D Braun (Suzuki)<br>3 H Kriwanek (Rotax)<br>4 L John (Yamaha)<br>5 H Rosner (MZ)<br>6 J Huberts (MZ)<br>Fastest lap – D Braun (Suzuki) | 93.18mph<br>(150.29km/h)<br><br><br><br><br>96.96mph<br>(156.05km/h) | 1 J Aureal (Yamaha)<br>2 D Simmonds (Kawasaki)<br>3.G Molloy (Bultaco)<br>4 J Roca (Derbi)<br>5 J-F Chaffin (Vila)<br>6 P Viura (Maico)<br>Fastest lap – D Simmonds (Kawasaki) | 73.37mph<br>(118.08km/h)<br><br><br><br><br>77.78mph<br>(125.46km/h) |
| **TT Races Isle of Man June 13** | | **Dutch TT Assen June 28** | | **Belgian GP Spa Francorchamps July 6** | |
| 1 D Simmonds (Kawasaki)<br>2 K Carruthers (Aermacchi)<br>3 R J.G Dickinson (Honda)<br>4 S Murray (Honda)<br>5 J Kiddie (Honda)<br>6 C Ward (Bultaco)<br>Fastest lap – D Simmonds (Kawasaki) | 91.06mph<br>(146.55km/h)<br><br><br><br><br>92.24mph<br>(148.79km/h) | 1 D Simmonds (Kawasaki)<br>2 K Andersson (Maico)<br>3 S Bertarelli (Aermacchi)<br>4 G Molloy (Bultaco)<br>5 T Robb (Bultaco)<br>6 J Dodds (Aermacchi)<br>Fastest lap – D Simmonds (Kawasaki) | 81.65mph<br>(131.40km/h)<br><br><br><br><br>82.26mph<br>(132.69km/h) | 1 D Simmonds (Kawasaki)<br>2 D Braun (Suzuki)<br>3 C VanDongen (Suzuki)<br>4 K Andersson (Maico)<br>5 J Huberts (MZ)<br>6 S Lohmann (MZ)<br>Fastest lap – D Braun (Suzuki) | 106.91mph<br>(172.05km/h)<br><br><br><br><br>108.11mph<br>(174.38km/h) |
| **East German GP Sachsenring July 13** | | **Czechoslovak GP Brno July 20** | | **Finnish GP Imatra August 3** | |
| 1 D Simmonds (Kawasaki)<br>2 H Kriwanek (Rotax)<br>3 F Kohlar (MZ)<br>4 R Mankiewicz (MZ)<br>5 C VanDongen (Suzuki)<br>6 T Heuschkel (MZ)<br>Fastest lap – D Braun (Suzuki) | 88.61mph<br>(142.60km/h)<br><br><br><br><br>90.53mph<br>(146.03km/h) | 1 D Simmonds (Kawasaki)<br>2 D Braun (Suzuki)<br>3 C VanDongen (Suzuki)<br>4 F Kohlar (MZ)<br>5 L Szabo (MZ)<br>6 T Heuschkel (MZ)<br>Fastest lap – D Simmonds (Kawasaki) | 86.58mph<br>(139.34km/h)<br><br><br><br><br>87.13mph<br>(140.54km/h) | 1 D Simmonds (Kawasaki)<br>2 G Bartusch (MZ)<br>3 C VanDongen (Suzuki)<br>4 D Braun (Suzuki)<br>5 T Heuschkel (MZ)<br>6 C Mortimer (Villa)<br>Fastest lap – D Simmonds (Kawasaki) | 79.62mph<br>(128.14km/h)<br><br><br><br><br>80.58mph<br>(129.98km/h) |

| Italian GP Imola September 7 | | Yugoslavia GP Opatija | | | |
|---|---|---|---|---|---|
| 1 D Simmonds (Kawasaki) | 86.81mph | 1 D Braun (Suzuki) | 76.50mph | | |
| 2 L Szabo (MZ) | (140.02km/h) | 2 D Simmonds (Kawasaki) | (123.11km./h) | | |
| 3 F Villa (Villa) | | 3 R Mankiewicz (MZ) | | | |
| 4 W Villa (Villa) | | 4 L Szabo (MZ) | | | |
| 5 R Mankiewicz (MZ) | | 5 H Kriwanek (Rotax) | | | |
| 6 S Bertarelli (Aermacchi) | | 6 F Kohlar (MZ) | | | |
| Fastest lap – D Simmonds (Kawasaki) | 88.05mph | Fastest lap – D Braun (Suzuki) | 79.91mph | | |
| | (142.02km/h) | | (128.90km/h) | | |

## 1969 250CC

| Spanish GP Jarama May 4 | | West German GP Hockenheim May 11 | | French GP Le Mans May 18 | |
|---|---|---|---|---|---|
| 1 S Herrero (Ossa) | 57.57mph | 1 K Andersson (Yamaha) | 101.29mph | 1 S Herrero (Ossa) | 81.60mph |
| 2 K Andersson (Yamaha) | (92.65km/h) | 2 L John (Yamaha) | (163.10km/h) | 2 R Gould (Yamaha) | (131.32km/h) |
| 3 B Jansson (Kawasaki) | | 3 K Huber (Yamaha) | | 3 K Andersson (Yamaha) | |
| 4 M Personen (Yamaha) | | 4 F Perris (Suzuki) | | 4 L Szabo (MZ) | |
| 5 G Vicenzi (Yamaha) | | 5 T Gruber (Yamaha) | | 5 A Bergamonti (Aermacchi) | |
| 6 H Rosner (MZ) | | 6 A Bergamonti (Aermacchi) | | 6 F Perris (Suzuki) | |
| Fastest lap – R Passolini (Benelli) | 60.59mph | Fastest lap – H Rosner (MZ) | 104.63mph | Fastest lap – S Herrero (Ossa) | 82.17mph |
| | (97.73km/h) | | (168.77km/h) | | (132.54km/h) |
| **TT Races Isle of Man June 9** | | **Dutch TT Assen June 28** | | **Belgian GP Spa Francorchamps July 6** | |
| 1 K Carruthers (Benelli) | 95.93mph | 1 R Passolini (Benelli) | 86.26mph | 1 S Herrero (Ossa) | 117.96mph |
| 2 F Perris (Suzuki) | (154.38km/h) | 2 K Carruthers (Benelli) | (138.83km/h) | 2 R Gould (Yamaha) | (189.83km/h) |
| 3 S Herrero (Ossa) | | 3 S Herrero (Ossa) | | 3 K Carruthers (Benelli) | |
| 4 M Chatterton (Yamaha) | | 4 R Gould (Yamaha) | | 4 K Andersson (Yamaha) | |
| 5 F Whiteway (Suzuki) | | 5.S Grassetti (Yamaha) | | 5 J Aureal (Yamaha) | |
| 6 D Chatterton (Yamaha) | | 6 D Braun (MZ) | | 6 E Hinton (Yamaha) | |
| Fastest lap – K Carruthers (Benelli) | 99.01mph) | Fastest lap – R Passolini (Benelli) | 88.21mph | Fastest lap – K Carruthers (Benelli) | 119.54mph |
| | (159.34km/h) | | (142.29km/h) | | (192.81km/h) |
| **East German GP Sachsenring July 13** | | **Czechoslovak GP Brno July 20** | | **Finnish GP Imatra August 3** | |
| 1 R Passolini (Benelli) | 93.14mph | 1 R Passolini (Benelli) | 92.58mph | 1 K Andersson (Yamaha) | 86.69mph |
| 2 S Herrero (Ossa) | (149.90km/h) | 2 R Gould (Yamaha) | (148.99km/h) | 2 G Bartusch (MZ) | (139.51km/h) |
| 3 H Rosner (MZ) | | 3 K Carruthers (Benelli) | | 3 B Jansson (Kawasaki) | |
| 4 K Andersson (Yamaha) | | 4 H Rosner (MZ) | | 4 K Carruthers (Benelli) | |
| 5 K Carruthers (Benelli) | | 5 S Grassetti (Yamaha) | | 5 D Braun (MZ) | |
| 6 B Jansson (Kawasaki) | | 6 D Braun (MZ) | | 6 S Herrero (Ossa) | |
| Fastest lap – R Passolini (Benelli) | 94.94mph | Fastest lap – R Goud (Yamaha) | 94.76mph | Fastest lap – K Andersson (Yamaha) | 88.47mph |
| | (153.13km/h) | | (152.85km/h) | | (142.70km/h) |
| **Ulster GP Dundrod August 16** | | **Italian GP Imola September 7** | | **Yugoslav GP Opatija September 14** | |
| 1 K Carruthers (Benelli) | 93.59mph | 1 P Read (Yamaha) | 94.28mph | 1 K Carruthers (Benelli) | 81.27mph |
| 2 K Andersson (Yamaha) | (150.62km/h) | 2 K Carruthers (Benelli) | (151.73km/h) | 2 G Parlotti (Benelli) | (130.80km/h) |
| 3 R McCullough (Yamaha) | | 3 K Andersson (Yamaha) | | 3 K Andersson (Yamaha) | |
| 4 B Guthrie (Yamaha) | | 4 B Jansson (Kawasaki) | | 4 B Jansson (Kawasaki) | |
| 5 C Mortimer (Yamaha) | | 5 S Herrero (Ossa) | | 5 S Grassetti (Yamaha) | |
| 6 F Richards (Yamaha) | | 6 H Rosner (MZ) | | 6 G Bartusch (MZ) | |
| Fastest lap – K Carruthers (Benelli) | 98.64mph | Fastest lap – P Read (Yamaha) | 96.52mph | Fastest lap – G Parlotti (Benelli) | 83.81km/h) |
| | (159.11km/h) | | (155.68km/h) | | (135.18km/h) |

## 1969 350CC

| Spanish GP Jarama May 4 | | West German GP Hockenheim May 11 | | TT Races Isle of Man June 13 | |
|---|---|---|---|---|---|
| 1 G Agostini (MV) | 61.71mph | 1 G Agostini (MV) | 111.72mph | 1 G Agostini (MV) | 101.79mph |
| 2 K Carruthers (Aermacchi) | (99.31km/h) | 2 B Ivy (Jawa) | (179.80km/h) | 2 B Steenson (Aermacchi) | (163.81km/h) |
| 3 G Vicenzi (Yamaha) | | 3 F Stastny (Jawa) | | 3 J Findlay (Aermacchi) | |
| 4 G Molloy (Bultaco | | 4 J Findlay (Yamaha) | | 4 T Dickie (Seeley) | |
| 5 J Findlay (Yamaha) | | 5 G Vicenzi (Yamaha) | | 5 T Grotefeld (Yamaha) | |
| 6 H Denzler (Aermacchi) | | 6 K Carruthers (Aermacchi) | | 6 S Griffiths (AJS) | |
| Fastest lap – G Agostini (MV) | 65.96mph | Fastest lap – G Agostini (MV) | 111.74mph | Fastest lap – G Agostini (MV) | 103.76mph |
| | (106.84km/h) | | (180.24km/h) | | (167.37km/h) |
| **Dutch TT Assen June 28** | | **East German GP Sachsenring July 13** | | **Czechoslovak GP Brno July 20** | |
| 1 G Agostini (MV) | 89.22mph | 1 G Agostini (MV) | 92.52mph | 1 G Agostini (MV) | 95.78mph |
| 2 B Ivy (Jawa) | (143.59km/h) | 2 R Gould (Yamaha) | (148.90km/h) | 2 R Gould (Yamaha) | (154.14km/h) |
| 3 S Grassetti (Yamaha) | | 3 H Rosner (MZ) | | 3 S Grassetti (Yamaha) | |
| 4 K Hoppe (Yamaha) | | 4 G Vicenzi (Yamaha) | | 4 H Rosner (MZ) | |
| 5 J Findlay (Yamaha) | | 5 B Stasa (CZ) | | 5 G Vicenzi (Yamaha) | |
| 6 G Vicenzi (Yamaha) | | 6 M Lunde (Yamaha) | | 6 B Stasa (CZ) | |
| Fastest lap – G Agostini (MV) | 91.12mph | Fastest lap – G Agostini (MV) | 94.47mph | Fastest lap – R Gould (Yamaha) | 98.17mph |
| | (146.98km/h) | | (152.38km/h) | | (158.35km/h) |

| Finnish GP Imatra August 3 | | Ulster GP Dundrod August 16 | | Italian GP Imola September 7 | |
|---|---|---|---|---|---|
| 1 G Agostini (MV)<br>2 R Gould (Yamaha)<br>3 G Vicenzi (Yamaha)<br>4 H Rosner (MZ)<br>5 M Pesonen (Yamaha)<br>6 A Ohligschlager (Yamaha)<br>Fastest lap – G Agostini (MV) | 89.23mph<br>(143.60km/h)<br><br><br><br><br>91.56mph<br>(147.68km/h) | 1 G Agostini (MV)<br>2 H Rosner (MZ)<br>3 C Crawford (Aermacchi)<br>4 T Rutter (Yamaha)<br>5 F Stastny (Jawa)<br>6 T Robb (Aermacchi)<br>Fastest lap – G Agostini (MV) | 99.99mph<br>(160.92km/h)<br><br><br><br><br>102.36mph<br>(165.11km/h) | 1 P Read (Yamaha)<br>2 S Grassetti (Jawa)<br>3 W Scheimann (Yamaha)<br>4 S Bertarelli (Aermacchi)<br>5 M Pesonen (Yamaha)<br>6 B Spaggiari (Ducati)<br>Fastest lap – P Read (Yamaha) | 93.89mph<br>(151.10km/h)<br><br><br><br><br>97.99mph<br>(158.05km/h) |
| **Yugoslav GP Opatija September 14** | | | | | |
| 1 S Grassetti (Jawa)<br>2 G Milani (Aermacchi)<br>3 F Stastny (Jawa)<br>4 B Stasa (CZ)<br>5 L Young (Aermacchi)<br>6 A Ohligschlager (Yamaha)<br>Fastest lap – S Grassetti (Jawa) | 87.92mph<br>(141.50km/h)<br><br><br><br><br>91.21mph<br>(147.12km/h) | | | | |

## 1969 500CC

| Spanish GP Jarama May 4 | | West German GP Hockenheim May 11 | | French GP Le Mans May 18 | |
|---|---|---|---|---|---|
| 1 G Agostini (MV)<br>2 A Bergamonti (Paton)<br>3 G Molloy (Bultaco)<br>4 G Marsovsky (Linto)<br>5 G Nash (Norton)<br>6 G Fischer (Matchless)<br>Fastest lap – G Agostini (MV) | 69.37mph<br>(111.64km/h)<br><br><br><br><br>71.79mph<br>(115.80km/h) | 1 G Agostini (MV)<br>2 K Hoppe (Fath URS)<br>3 J Findlay (Linto)<br>4 J Dodds (Linto)<br>5 R Fitton (Norton)<br>6 G Marsovsky (Linto)<br>Fastest lap – G Agostini (MV) | 112.78mph<br>(168.54km/h)<br><br><br><br><br>113.47mph<br>(183.03km/h) | 1 G Agostini (MV)<br>2 B Nelson (Paton)<br>3 K Auer (Matchless)<br>4 T Louwes (Norton)<br>5 G Nash (Norton)<br>6 G Marsovsky (Linto)<br>Fastest lap – G Agostini (MV) | 75.04mph<br>(120.77km/h)<br><br><br><br><br>83.30mph<br>(134.36km/h) |
| **TT Races Isle of Man June 13** | | **Dutch TT Assen June 28** | | **Belgian GP Spa Francorchamps July 6** | |
| 1 G Agostini (MV)<br>2 A Barnett (Kirby-Metisse)<br>3 T Dickie (Seeley)<br>4 D Woodman (Seeley)<br>5 J T.Findlay (Norton)<br>6 R Chandler (Seeley)<br>Fastest lap – G Agostini (MV) | 104.75mph<br>(168.54km/h)<br><br><br><br><br>106.25mph<br>(170.99km/h) | 1 G Agostini (MV)<br>2 P Williams (matchless)<br>3 A Barnett (Kirby-Metisse)<br>4 G Milani (Aermacchi)<br>5 J Findlay (Aermacchi)<br>6 G Marsovsky (Linto)<br>Fastest lap – G Agostini (MV) | 89.09mph<br>(143.37km/h)<br><br><br><br><br>90.73mph<br>(146.35km/h) | 1 G Agostini (MV)<br>2 P Tait (Triumph)<br>3 A Barnett (Kirby-Metisse)<br>4 G Marsovsky (Linto)<br>5 R Chandler (Seeley)<br>6 R Fitton (Norton)<br>Record lap – G Agostini (MV) | 125.85mph<br>(202.53km/h)<br>Record<br><br><br><br>130.52mph<br>(210.53km/h) |
| **East German Gp Sachsenring July 13** | | **Czechoslovak GP Brno July 20** | | **Finnish GP Imatra August 3** | |
| 1 G Agostini (MV)<br>2 B Nelson (Paton)<br>3 S Ellis (Linto)<br>4 W Bergold (Matchless)<br>5 T Dennehy (Honda)<br>6 J O'Brian (Matchless)<br>Fastest lap – G Agostini (MV) | 94.23mph<br>(151.65km/h)<br><br><br><br><br>95.26mph<br>(153.66km/h) | 1 G Agostini (MV)<br>2 G Marsovsky (Linto)<br>3 B Stasa (CZ)<br>4 S Bertarelli (Paton)<br>5 D Shorey (Seeley)<br>6 W Scheimann (Norton)<br>Fastest lap – G Agostini (MV) | 96.18mph<br>(154.78km/h)<br><br><br><br><br>100.92mph<br>(162.78km/h) | 1 G Agostini (MV)<br>2 B Nelson (Paton)<br>3 G Nash (Norton)<br>4 H Kuparinen (Matchless)<br>5 L Young (Matchless)<br>6 P Lehtela (Matchless)<br>Record lap – G Agostini (MV) | 89.35mph<br>(143.80km/h)<br><br><br><br><br>93.76mph<br>(150.89km/h) |
| **Ulster GP Dundrod August 16** | | **Italian GP Imola September 7** | | **Yugoslav GP Opatija September 14** | |
| 1 G Agostini (MV)<br>2 B Steenson (Seeley)<br>3 M Uphill (Norton)<br>4 R Fitton (Norton)<br>5 B Scully (Norton)<br>6 R Chandler (Seeley)<br>Record lap – G Agostini (MV) | 103.72mph<br>(166.92km/h)<br>Record<br><br><br><br>107.66mph<br>(173.26km/h) | 1 A Pagani (Linto)<br>2 G Milani (Aermacchi)<br>3 J Dodds (Linto)<br>4 T Dennehy (Honda)<br>5 B Steenson (Seeley)<br>6 R Chandler (Seeley)<br>Fastest lap – J Dodds (Linto) | 93.48mph<br>(150.44km/h)<br><br><br><br><br>95.40mph<br>(153.88km/h) | 1 G Nash (Norton)<br>2 F Trabalzini (Paton)<br>3 S Ellis (Linto)<br>4 L Young (Matchless)<br>5 K Turner (Linto)<br>6 P Lehtela (Matchless)<br>Fastest lap – G Nash (Norton) | 79.61mph<br>(128.12km/h)<br><br><br><br><br>81.51mph<br>(131.48km/h) |

## 1969 SIDECARS

| West German GP Hockenheim May 11 | | French GP Le Mans May 18 | | TT Races Isle of Man June 9 | |
|---|---|---|---|---|---|
| 1 K Enders/R Engelhardt (BMW)<br>2 F Linnarz/R Kuhnemund (BMW)<br>3 A Butscher/J Huber (BMW)<br>4 H Lunemann/N Caddow (BMW)<br>5 J-C Castella/A Castella (BMW)<br>6 T Wakefield/G Milton (BMW)<br>Record lap – H Fath/W Kalauch (URS) | 97.29mph<br>(156.57km/h)<br><br><br><br><br>102.80mph<br>(165.82km/h) | 1 H Fath/W Kalauch (URS)<br>2 G Auerbacher/H Hahn (BMW)<br>3 S Schauzu/H Schneider (BMW)<br>4 F Linnarz/R Kuhnemund (BMW)<br>5 A Butscher/J Huber (BMW)<br>6 M Hauri/H Hausamann (BMW)<br>Fastest lap – H Fath (URS) | 76.68mph<br>(148.80km/h)<br><br><br><br><br>78.78mph<br>(127.07km/h) | 1 K Enders/R Engelhardt (BMW)<br>2 S Schauzu/H Schneider (BMW)<br>3 H Fath/W Kalauch (URS)<br>4 A Butscher/J Huber (BMW)<br>5 F Linnarz/R Kuhnemund (BMW)<br>6 R Hawes/P/Mann (Seeley)<br>Fastest lap – K Enders (BMW) | 92.46mph<br>(148.80km/h)<br>Record<br><br><br><br>92.54mph<br>(148.92km/h) |
| **Dutch TT Assen June 28** | | **Belgian GP Spa Francorchamps July 6** | | **Finnish GP Imatra August 3** | |
| 1 H Fath/W Kalauch (URS)<br>2 G Auerbacher/H Hahn (BMW)<br>3 H Lunemann/N Caddow (BMW)<br>4 A Butscher/J Huber (BMW)<br>5 F Linnarz/R Kuhnemund (BMW)<br>6 H Luthringshauser/G Hughes<br>Record lap – H Fath (URS) | 80.45mph<br>(129.47km/h)<br><br><br><br><br>82.67mph<br>(133.35km/h) | 1 H Fath/W Kalauch (URS)<br>2 K Enders/R/Engelhardt (BMW)<br>3 G Auerbacher/H/Hahn (BMWO<br>4 F Linnarz/R Kuhnemund (BMW)<br>5 A Butscher/J Huber (BMW)<br>6 G Milton/J Thornton (BMW)<br>Record lap – H Fath (URS) | 111.78mph<br>(179.90km/h)<br>Record<br><br><br><br>112.40mph<br>(181.30km/h) | 1 K Enders/R Engelhardt (BMW)<br>2 H Lunemann/N Caddow (BMW)<br>3 H Luthringshauser/G Hughes<br>4 A Butscher/J Huber (BMW)<br>5 G Auerbacher/H Hahn (BMW)<br>6 J-C Castella/A Castella (BMW)<br>Record lap – H Fath/B Nelson (URS) | 78.10mph<br>(125.70km/h)<br>record<br><br><br><br>80.83mph<br>(130.38km/h) |
| **Ulster GP Dundrod August 16** | | | | | |
| 1 K Enders/R Engelhardt (BMW)<br>2 S Schauzu/H Schneider (BMW)<br>3 F Linnarz/R Kuhnemund (BMW)<br>4 H Luthringshauser/G Hughes<br>5 B Copson/J Graham (BMW)<br>6 J Philpott/W Turrington (Norton)<br>Record lap – K Enders (BMW) | 89.92mph<br>(143.10km/h)<br>Record<br><br><br><br>90.79mph<br>(146.45km/h) | | | | |

# World Championship results 1960-1969

## 1960

| 125cc | 250cc | 350cc | 500cc | Sidecars |
|---|---|---|---|---|
| 1 C Ubbiali (MV)<br>2 G Hocking (MV)<br>3 E Degner (MZ)<br>4 B Spaggiari (MV)<br>5 J Hempleman (MZ)<br>6 L Taveri (MV) | 1 C Ubbiali (MV)<br>2 G Hocking (MV)<br>3 L Taveri (MV)<br>4 J Redman (Honda)<br>5 M Hailwood (Ducati&Mondial)<br>6 T Phillis (Honda) | 1 J Surtees (MV)<br>2 G Hocking (MV)<br>3 J Hartle (MV/Norton)<br>4 F Stastny (Jawa)<br>5 RHF Anderson (Norton)<br>6 RN Brown(Norton) | 1 J Surtees (MV)<br>2 R Venturi (MV)<br>3 J Hartle (MV/Norton)<br>4 RN Brown (Norton)<br>5 E Mendogni (MV)<br>6 M Hailwood (Norton) | 1 H Fath/A Wohlgemuth (BMW)<br>2 F Scheidegger/H Burkhardt (BMW)<br>3 P Harris/R Campbell (BMW)<br>4 H Camathias/J Chisnell/R Foll/"Fiston" (BMW)<br>5 E Strub/H Cecco (BMW)<br>6 M Deubel/H Hohler (BMW) |

## 1961

| 125cc | 250cc | 350cc | 500cc | Sidecars |
|---|---|---|---|---|
| 1 T Phillis (Honda)<br>2 E Degner (MZ)<br>3 L Taveri (Honda)<br>4 J Redman (Honda)<br>5 K Takahashi (Honda)<br>6 M Hailwood (EMC&Honda) | 1 M Hailwood (Honda)<br>2 T Phillis (Honda)<br>3 J Redman (Honda)<br>4 K Takahashi (Honda)<br>5 R McIntyre (Honda)<br>6 S Grassetti (Benelli) | 1 G Hocking (MV)<br>2 F Stastny (Jawa)<br>3 G Havel (Jawa)<br>4 P Read (Norton)<br>5 R McIntyre (Bianchi)<br>6 R Rensen (Norton) | 1 G Hocking (MV)<br>2 M Hailwood (Norton/MV)<br>3 F Perris (Norton)<br>4 R McIntyre (Norton)<br>5 A King (Norton)<br>6 B Schneider (Norton) | 1 M Deubel/E Horner (BMW)<br>2 F Scheidegger/H Burkhardt (BMW)<br>3 E Strub/R Foll/K Huber (BMW)<br>4 A Rohsiepe/L Botscher (BMW)<br>5 A Butscher/E Butscher/M Ludwigheit (BMW)<br>6 O Kolle/D Hess (BMW) |

## 1962

| 50cc | 125cc | 250cc | 350cc | 500cc |
|---|---|---|---|---|
| 1 E Degner (Suzuki) | 1 L Taveri (Honda) | 1 J Redman (Honda) | 1 J Redman (Honda) | 1 M Hailwood (MV) |
| 2 H-G Anscheidt (Kreidler) | 2 J Redman (Honda) | 2 R McIntyre (Honda) | 2 T Robb (Honda) | 2 A Shepherd (Matchless) |
| 3 L Taveri (Honda) | 3 T Robb (Honda) | 3 A Wheeler (Guzzi) | 3 M Hailwood (MV) | 3 P Read (Norton) |
| 4 J Huberts (Kreidler) | 4 K Takahashi (Honda) | 4 T Phillis (Honda) | 4 F Stastny (Jawa) | 4 B Schneider (Norton) |
| 5 M Itoh (Suzuki) | 5 M Haillwood (EMC) | 5 T Provini (Morini) | 5 S Grassetti (Bianchi) | 5 G Hocking (MV) |
| 6 T Robb (Honda) | 6 H Anderson (Suzuki) | 6 D Minter (Honda) | 6 A Shepherd (MZ) | 6 B Calderella (Matchless) |
| Sidecars | | | | |
| 1 M Deubel/E Horner (BMW) | | | | |
| 2 F Camathias/H Burkhardt/H Winter (BMW) | | | | |
| 3 F Scheidegger/J Robinson (BMW) | | | | |
| 4 O Kolle/D Hess (BMW) | | | | |
| 5 C Vincent/E Bliss (BSA) | | | | |
| 6 C Lambert/A Herzig (BMW) | | | | |

## 1963

| 50cc | 125cc | 250cc | 350cc | 500cc |
|---|---|---|---|---|
| 1 H Anderson (Suzuki) | 1 H Anderson (Suzuki) | 1 J Redman (Honda) | 1 J Redman (Honda) | 1 M Hailwood (MV) |
| 2 H-G Anscheidt (Kreidler) | 2 L Taveri (Honda) | 2 T Provini (Morini) | 2 M Hailwood (Honda) | 2 A Shepherd (Matchless) |
| 3 E Degner (Susuki) | 3 J Redman (Honda) | 3 F Ito (Yamaha) | 3 L Taveri (Honda) | 3 J Hartle (Gilera) |
| 4 I Morishita (Suzuki) | 4 F Perris (Suzuki) | 4 T Robb (Honda) | 4 G Havel (Jawa) | 4 P Read (Gilera) |
| 5 M Itoh (Suzuki) | 5 B Schneider (Suzuki) | 5 L Taveri (Honda) | 5 F Stastny (Jawa) | 5 F Stevens (Norton) |
| 6 M Ichino Suzuki) | 6 E Degner (Suzuki) | 6 A Shepherd (MZ) | 6 R Venturi (Bianchi) | 6 M Duff (Matchless) |
| Sidecars | | | | |
| 1 M Deubel/E Horner (BMW) | | | | |
| 2 F Camathias/AHerzig (BMW) | | | | |
| 3 F Scheidegger/J Robinson (BMW) | | | | |
| 4 O Kolle/D Hess (BMW) | | | | |
| 5 G Auerbacher/B Heim (BMW) | | | | |
| 6 A Birch/P Birch (BMW) | | | | |

## 1964

| 50cc | 125cc | 250cc | 350cc | 500cc |
|---|---|---|---|---|
| 1 H Anderson (Suzuki) | 1 L Taveri (Honda) | 1 P Read (Yamaha) | 1 J Redman (Honda) | 1 M Hailwood (MV) |
| 2 R Bryans (Honda) | 2 J Redman (Honda) | 2 J Redman (Honda) | 2 B Beale (Honda) | 2 J Ahearn (Norton) |
| 3 H-G Anscheidt (Kreidler) | 3 H Anderson (Suzuki) | 3 A Shepherd (MZ) | 3 M Duff (AJS&Yamaha) | 3 P Read (Matchless&Norton) |
| 4 I Morishita (Suzuki) | 4 B Schneider (Suzuki) | 4 M Duff (Yamaha) | 4 M Hailwood (MV&MZ) | 4 M Duff (Matchless) |
| 5 M Itoh (Suzuki) | 5 R Bryans (Honda) | 5 T Provini (Benelli) | 5 G Havel (Jawa) | 5 P Driver (Matchless) |
| 6 J-P Beltoise (Kreidler) | 6 E Degner (Suzuki) | 6 L Taveri (Honda) | 6 P Read (Yamaha) | 6 F Stevens (Matchless) |
| Sidecars | | | | |
| 1 M Deubel/E Horner (BMW) | | | | |
| 2 F Scheidegger/J Robinson (BMW) | | | | |
| 3 C Seeley/W Rawlings (FCS BMW) | | | | |
| 4 G Auerbacher/B Heim (BMW) | | | | |
| 5 O Koller/D Hess/H Marquardt (BMW) | | | | |
| 6 A Butscher/W Kalauch (BMW) | | | | |

## 1965

| 50cc | 125cc | 250cc | 350cc | 500cc |
|---|---|---|---|---|
| 1 R Bryans (Honda) | 1 H Anderson (Suzuki) | 1 P Read (Yamaha) | 1 J Redman (Honda) | 1 M Hailwood (MV) |
| 2 L Taveri (Honda) | 2 F Perris (Suzuki) | 2 M Duff (Yamaha) | 2 G Agostini (MV) | 2 G Agostini (MV) |
| 3 H Anderson (Suzuki) | 3 D Woodman (MZ) | 3 J Redman (Honda) | 3 M Hailwood (MV) | 3 P Driver (Matchless) |
| 4 E Degner (Suzuki) | 4 E Degner (Suzuki) | 4 H Rosner (MZ) | 4 B Beale (Honda) | 4 F Stevens (Matchless) |
| 5 M Itoh (Suzuki) | 5 L Taveri (Honda) | 5 D Woodman (MZ) | 5 D Woodman (MZ) | 5 J Ahearn (Norton) |
| 6 M Ichino (Suzuki) | 6 M Duff (Yamaha) | 6 B Beale (Honda) | 6 F Stastny (Jawa) | 6 D Creith (Norton) |
| Sidecars | | | | |
| 1 F Scheidegger/J Robinson (BMW) | | | | |
| 2 M Deubel/E Horner (BMW) | | | | |
| 3 G Auerbacher/P Rykers (BMW) | | | | |
| 4 F Camathias/F Ducret (BMW) | | | | |
| 5 A Butscher/W Kalauch (BMW) | | | | |
| 6 H Luthringshauser/H Hahn (BMW) | | | | |

## 1966

| 50cc | 125cc | 250cc | 350cc | 500cc | |
|---|---|---|---|---|---|
| 1 H-G Anscheidt (Suzuki) | 1 L Taveri (Honda) | 1 M Hailwood (Honda) | 1 M Hailwood (Honda) | 1 G Agostini (MV) | |
| 2 R Bryans (Honda) | 2 B Ivy (Yamaha) | 2 P Read (Yamaha) | 2 G Agostini (MV) | 2 M Hailwood (Honda) | |
| 3 L Taveri (Honda) | 3 R Bryans (Honda) | 3 J Redman (Honda) | 3 R Passolini (Aermacchi) | 3 J Findlay (Matchless) | |
| 4 H Anderson (Suzuki) | 4 P Read (Yamaha) | 4 D Woodman (MZ) | 4 F Stastny (Jawa) | 4 F Stastny (Jawa) | |
| 5 Y Katayama (Suzuki) | 5 H Anderson (Suzuki) | 5 H Rosner (MZ) | 5 G Havel (Jawa) | 5 J Redman (Honda) | |
| 6 B Smith (Derbi) | 6 Y Katayama (Suzuki) | 6 S Graham (Honda) | 6 A Pagani (Aermacchi) | 6 G Marsovsky (Matchless) | |
| Sidecars | | | | | |
| 1 F Scheidegger/J Robinson (BMW) | | | | | |
| 2 M Deubel/E Horner | | | | | |
| 3 C Seeley/W Rawlings (BMW) | | | | | |
| 4 G Auerbacher/E Dein/W Kalauch (BMW) | | | | | |
| 5 K Enders/R Mannischeff (BMW) | | | | | |
| 6 C Vincent/T Harrison (BMW) | | | | | |

## 1967

| 50cc | 125cc | 250cc | 350cc | 500cc |
|---|---|---|---|---|
| 1 H-G Anscheidt (Suzuki) | 1 B Ivy (Yamaha) | 1 M Hailwood (Honda) | 1 M Hailwood (Honda) | 1 G Agostini (MV) |
| 2 Y Katayama (Suzuki) | 2 P Read (Yamaha) | 2 P Read (Yamaha) | 2 G Agostini (MV) | 2 M Hailwood (Honda) |
| 3 S Graham (Suzuki) | 3 S Graham (Suzuki) | 3 B Ivy (Yamaha) | 3 R Bryans (Honda) | 3 J Hartle (Matchless) |
| 4 A Nieto (Derbi) | 4 Y Katayama (Suzuki) | 4 R Bryans (Honda) | 4 H Rosner (MZ) | 4 P Williams (Matchless) |
| 5 B Smith (Derbi) | 5 L Szabo (MZ) | 5 D Woodman (MZ) | 5 D Woodman (MZ) | 5 J Findlay (Matchless) |
| 6 M Itoh (Suzuki) | 6 H-G Anscheidt (Suzuki) | 6 H Rosner (MZ) | 6 A Pagani (Aermacchi) | 6 F Stevens (Paton) |
| Sidecars | | | | |
| 1 K Enders/R Engelhardt (BMW) | | | | |
| 2 G Auerbacher/E Dein/B Nelson | | | | |
| 3 S Schauzu/H Schneider (BMW) | | | | |
| 4 T Wakefield/G Milton (BMW) | | | | |
| 5 J Attenberger/J Schillinger (BMW) | | | | |
| 6 H Luthringshauser/H Hahn (BMW) | | | | |

## 1968

| 50cc | 125cc | 250cc | 350cc | 500cc |
|---|---|---|---|---|
| 1 H-G Anscheidt (Suzuki) | 1 P Read (Yamaha) | 1 P Read (Yamaha) | 1 G Agostini (MV) | 1 G Agostini (MV) |
| 2 P Lodewijkx (Jamathi) | 2 B Ivy (Yamaha) | 2 B Ivy (Yamaha) | 2 R Passolini (Benelli) | 2 J Findlay (Matchless) |
| 3 B Smith (Derbi) | 3 G Molloy (Bultaco) | 3 H Rosner (MZ) | 3 K Carruthers (Aermacchi) | 3 G Marsovsky (Matchless) |
| 4 A Nieto (Derbi) | 4 H Rosner (MZ) | 4 R Gould (Yamaha) | 4 H Rosner (MZ) | 4 R Fitton (Norton) |
| 5 R Kunz (Kreidler) | 5 S Canellas (Bultaco) | 5 G Molloy (Bultaco) | 5 G Molloy (Bultaco) | 5 A Pagani (Linto) |
| 6 C Walpole (Honda) | 6 L Szabo (MZ) | 6 R Passolini (Benelli) | 6 D Woodman (Aermacchi) | 6 P Williams (Matchless) |
| Sidecars | | | | |
| 1 H Fath/W Kalauch (URS) | | | | |
| 2 G Auerbacher/H Hahn/H DeWever (BMW) | | | | |
| 3 S Schauzu/H Schneider (BMW) | | | | |
| 4 J Attenbergen/J Schillinger (BMW) | | | | |
| 5 H Luthringshauser/L Ronsdorf/G Hughes (BMW) | | | | |

## 1969

| 50cc | 125cc | 250cc | 350cc | 500cc |
|---|---|---|---|---|
| 1 A Nieto (Derbi) | 1 D Simmonds (Kawasaki) | 1 K Carruthers (Benelli) | 1 G Agostini (MV) | 1 G Agostini (MV) |
| 2 A Toerson (Kreidler) | 2 D Braun (Suzuki) | 2 K Andersson (Yamaha) | 2 S Grassetti (Yamaha/Jawa) | 2 G Marsovsky (Linto) |
| 3 B Smith (Derbi) | 3 C VanDongen (Suzuki) | 3 S Herrero (Ossa) | 3 G Visenzi (Yamaha) | 3 G Nash (Norton) |
| 4 J DeVries (Kreidler) | 4 K Andersson (Maico) | 4 R Passolini (Benelli) | 4 H Rosner (MZ) | 4 B Nelson (Paton) |
| 5 P Lodewijkx (Jamathi) | 5 H Kriwanek (Rotax) | 5 B Jansson(Kawasaki) | 5 R Gould (Yamaha) | 5 A Barnett (Kirby Metisse) |
| 6 G Parlotti (Tomos) | 6 G Molloy (Bultaco) | 6 R Gould (Yamaha) | 6 J Findlay (Yamaha/ Aermacchi) | 6 S Ellis (Linto) |
| Sidecars | | | | |
| 1 K Enders/R Engelhardt (BMW) | | | | |
| 2 H Fath/W Kalauch (URS) | | | | |
| 3 G Auerbacher/H Hahn (BMW) | | | | |
| 4 S Schauzu/H Schneider (BMW) | | | | |
| 5 F Linnarz/R Kuhnemund (BMW) | | | | |
| 6 A Butscher/J Huber (BMW) | | | | |

# Grand Prix statistics 1960-1969

## INDIVIDUAL WORLD CHAMPIONSHIP WINNERS 1960-1969

| Name | 50cc | 125cc | 250cc | 350cc | 500cc | Sidecar | Total |
|---|---|---|---|---|---|---|---|
| Mike Hailwood – GB | – | – | 3 | 2 | 4 | – | 9 |
| Giacomo Agostini – Italy | – | – | – | 2 | 4 | – | 6 |
| Jim Redman – Rhodesia | – | – | 2 | 4 | – | – | 6 |
| Hugh Anderson – New Zealand | 2 | 2 | – | – | – | – | 4 |
| Phil Read – GB | – | 1 | 3 | – | – | – | 4 |
| Max Deubel pass; Emil Horner – Germany | – | – | – | – | – | 4 | 4 |
| Luigi Taveri – Switzerland | – | 3 | – | – | – | – | 3 |
| Hans-Georg Anscheidt – Germany | 3 | – | – | – | – | – | 3 |
| Gary Hocking – Rhodesia | – | – | – | 1 | 1 | – | 2 |
| John Surtees – GB | – | – | – | 1 | 1 | – | 2 |
| Carlo Ubbiali – Italy | 1 | 1 | – | – | – | – | 2 |
| Klaus Enders pass: Ralf Engelhardt – Germany | – | – | – | – | – | 2 | 2 |
| Helmut Fath pass: Alfred Wohlgemuth, Wolfgang Kalauch – Germany | – | – | – | – | – | 2 | 2 |
| Fritz Scheidegger pass; John Robinson – Switzerland | – | – | – | – | – | 2 | 2 |
| Bill Ivy – GB | – | 1 | – | – | – | – | 1 |
| Ralph Bryans – GB | 1 | – | – | – | – | – | 1 |
| Tom Phillis – Australia | – | 1 | – | – | – | – | 1 |
| Kel Carruthers – Australia | – | – | 1 | – | – | – | 1 |
| Angel Nieto – Spain | 1 | – | – | – | – | – | 1 |
| Dave Simmonds – GB | – | 1 | – | – | – | – | 1 |
| Ernst Degner – East Germany | 1 | – | – | – | – | – | 1 |

## GRAND PRIX WINNERS 1960-1969

| | | | | | | | |
|---|---|---|---|---|---|---|---|
| Mike Hailwood – GB | – | 1 | 21 | 16 | 37 | – | 75 |
| Giacomo Agostini – Italy | – | – | – | 22 | 29 | – | 51 |
| Jim Redman – Rhodesia | – | 4 | 18 | 21 | 2 | – | 45 |
| Phil Read – GB | – | 10 | 22 | 3 | 1 | – | 36 |
| Luigi Taveri – Switzerland | 6 | 22 | 2 | – | – | – | 30 |
| Hugh Anderson – New Zealand | 8 | 17 | – | – | – | – | 25 |
| Bill Ivy – GB | – | 14 | 7 | – | – | – | 21 |
| Gary Hocking – Rhodesia | – | – | 3 | 6 | 8 | – | 17 |
| Fritz Scheidegger/John Robinson – Switzerland/GB | – | – | – | – | – | 15 | 15 |
| Ernst Degner – East Germany | 7 | 8 | – | – | – | – | 14 |
| Hans-Georg Anscheidt – Germany | 14 | – | – | – | – | – | 14 |
| Max Deubel/Emil Horner – Germany | – | – | – | – | – | 12 | 12 |
| Ralph Bryans – GB | 8 | – | 2 | 1 | – | – | 11 |
| Klaus Enders/Ralf Engelhard – Germany | – | – | – | – | – | 9 | 9 |
| Helmut Fath/Alfred Wohlgemuth/Wolfgang Kalauch – Germany | – | – | – | – | – | 8 | 8 |
| Dave Simmonds – GB | – | 8 | – | – | – | – | 8 |
| John Surtees – GB | – | – | – | 2 | 5 | – | 7 |
| Tom Phillis – Australia | – | 4 | 2 | – | – | – | 6 |
| Tarquinio Provini – Italy | – | – | 6 | – | – | – | 6 |
| Florian Camathias/Harry Winter/A.Herzig/R.Foll/F.Ducret – Switzerland | – | – | – | – | – | 5 | 5 |
| Frantisek Stastny – Czechoslovakia | – | – | – | 3 | 1 | – | 4 |
| Kunimitsu Takahashi – Japan | – | 3 | 1 | – | – | – | 4 |
| Yoshimi Katayama – Japan | 3 | 1 | – | – | – | – | 4 |
| Paul Lodewijkx – Holland | 4 | – | – | – | – | – | 4 |
| Aalt Toersen – Holland | 3 | – | – | – | – | – | 3 |
| John Hartle – GB | – | – | – | 1 | 2 | – | 3 |
| Frank Perris – GB | – | 3 | – | – | – | – | 3 |
| Renzo Passolini – Italy | – | – | 3 | – | – | – | 3 |
| Barry Smith – Australia | 3 | – | – | – | – | – | 3 |
| Georg Auerbacher/E.Dein/Billie Nelson/H.Hahn – Germany/GB | – | – | – | – | – | 3 | 3 |
| Santiago Herrero – Spain | – | – | 3 | | – | – | 3 |
| Kel Carruthers – Australia | – | – | 3 | | – | – | 3 |
| Mike Duff – Canada | – | 1 | 2 | – | – | – | 3 |
| Bob McIntyre – GB | – | – | 2 | – | – | – | 2 |
| Kent Anderson – Sweden | – | – | 2 | – | – | – | 2 |
| Stuart Graham – GB | 1 | 1 | – | – | – | – | 2 |
| Jan Huberts – Holland | 2 | – | – | – | – | – | 2 |
| Misuo Ito – Japan | 2 | – | – | – | – | – | 2 |
| Angel Nieto – Spain | 2 | – | – | – | – | – | 2 |
| Tommy Robb – GB | – | – | 1 | 1 | – | – | 2 |
| Sigi Schauzu/Horst Schneider – Germany | – | – | – | – | – | 2 | 2 |
| Alan Shepherd – GB | – | – | 1 | – | 1 | – | 2 |
| Jack Ahearn – Australia | – | – | – | – | 1 | – | 1 |
| Johann Attenberger/Josef Schillinger – Germany | – | – | – | – | – | 1 | 1 |

| | | | | | | | |
|---|---|---|---|---|---|---|---|
| Jean Aureal – France | – | 1 | – | – | – | – | 1 |
| Dieter Braun – Germany | – | 1 | – | – | – | – | 1 |
| Benedicto Calderella – Argentina | – | – | – | – | 1 | – | 1 |
| Dick Creith – GB | – | – | – | – | 1 | – | 1 |
| Fumio Ito – Japan | – | – | 1 | – | – | – | 1 |
| Hiroshi Hasegawa – Japan | – | – | 1 | – | – | – | 1 |
| Pip Harris/Ray Campbell – GB | – | – | – | – | – | 1 | 1 |
| Jorge Kissling – Argentina | – | – | – | – | 1 | – | 1 |
| Derek Minter – GB | – | – | 1 | – | – | – | 1 |
| Ginger Molloy – New Zealand | – | – | 1 | – | – | – | 1 |
| Isao Morishita – Japan | 1 | – | – | – | – | – | 1 |
| Godfrey Nash – GB | – | – | – | – | 1 | – | 1 |
| Alberto Pagani – Italy | – | – | – | – | 1 | – | 1 |
| Bert Schneider – Austria | – | 1 | – | – | – | – | 1 |
| Colin Seeley/Wally Rawlings – GB | – | – | – | – | – | 1 | 1 |
| Teisuke Tanaka – Japan | – | 1 | – | – | – | – | 1 |
| Cees Van Dongen – Holland | – | – | 1 | – | – | – | 1 |
| Remo Venturi – Italy | – | – | – | – | 1 | – | 1 |
| Chris Vincent/Eric Bliss – GB | – | – | – | – | – | 1 | 1 |
| Arthur Wheeler – GB | – | – | 1 | – | – | – | 1 |
| Silvio Grassetti – Italy | – | – | – | 1 | – | – | 1 |
| Salvador Canellas – Spain | – | 1 | – | – | – | – | 1 |

## RIDERS WHO HAVE WON DOUBLE WORLD TITLES 1960-1969

| Rider & Machine | Category | Year |
|---|---|---|
| Gary Hocking (MV) | 350cc & 500cc | 1961 |
| Hugh Anderson (Suzuki) | 50cc & 125cc | 1963 |
| Phil Read (Yamaha) | 125cc & 250cc | 1968 |

## RIDERS WHO HAVE WON BACK TO BACK DOUBLE WORLD TITLES 1960-1969

| Rider & Machine | Category | Year |
|---|---|---|
| Jim Redman (Honda) | 250cc & 350cc | 1962, 1963 |
| Mike Hailwood (Honda) | 250cc & 350cc | 1966, 1967 |
| Giacomo Agostini (MV) | 350cc & 500cc | 1968, 1969 |

## RIDERS WHO HAVE WON CONSECUTIVE WORLD TITLES 1960-1969

| Rider & Machine | Category | Year |
|---|---|---|
| Mike Hailwood (MV) | 500cc | 1962, 1963. 1964, 1965 |
| Jim Redman (Honda) | 350cc | 1962, 1963, 1964, 1965 |
| Giacomo Agostini (MV) | 500cc | 1966, 1967, 1968, 1969 |
| Max Deubel/Emil Horner (BMW) | Sidecar | 1961, 1962, 1963, 1964 |
| Hans-Georg Anscheidt (Suzuki | 50cc | 1966, 1967, 1968 |
| Jim Redman (Honda) | 250cc | 1962, 1963 |
| Hugh Anderson (Suzuki) | 50cc | 1963, 1964 |
| Phil Read (Yamaha) | 250cc | 1964, 1965 |
| Mike Hailwood (Honda) | 250cc | 1966, 1967 |
| Mike Hailwood (Honda) | 350cc | 1966, 1967 |
| Giacomo Agostini (MV) | 350cc | 1968, 1969 |
| Fritz Scheidegger/John Robinson (BMW) | Sidecar | 1965, 1966 |

## RIDERS WHO HAVE WON EVERY ROUND OF THE WORLD CHAMPIONSHIP 1960-1969

| Rider & Machine | Category | Year | Rounds |
|---|---|---|---|
| Giacomo Agostini (MV) | 500cc | 1968 | 10 |
| Jim Redman (Honda) | 350cc | 1964 | 8 |
| Giacomo Agostini (MV) | 350cc | 1968 | 7 |
| Fritz Scheidegger/John Robinson (BMW) | Sidecar | 1966 | 5 |

## RIDERS WHO HAVE WON 10 OR MORE GPS IN A SEASON 1960-1969

| Rider & Machine | Year | 50cc | 125cc | 250cc | 350cc | 500cc | Total |
|---|---|---|---|---|---|---|---|
| Mike Hailwood (Honda) | 1966 | | | 10 | 6 | 3 | 19 |
| Giacomo Agostini | 1969 | | | | 8 | 10 | 18 |
| Giacomo Agostini | 1968 | | | | 7 | 10 | 17 |
| Mike Hailwood (Honda) | 1967 | | | 5 | 6 | 5 | 16 |
| Jim Redman (Honda) | 1964 | | 2 | 3 | 8 | | 13 |
| Gary Hocking (MV) | 1961 | | | 1 | 4 | 7 | 12 |
| Phil Read (Yamaha) | 1968 | | 6 | 5 | | | 11 |
| Bill Ivy (Yamaha) | 1967 | | 8 | 2 | | | 10 |

## GRAND PRIX WINS BY COUNTRIES 1960-1969

| Country | 50cc | 125cc | 250cc | 350cc | 500cc | Sidecar | Total |
|---|---|---|---|---|---|---|---|
| GB | 9 | 37 | 58 | 23 | 47 | 3 | 177 |
| Rhodesia | – | 4 | 21 | 27 | 10 | – | 62 |
| Italy | – | – | 9 | 23 | 29 | – | 61 |
| Germany | 14 | 1 | | | | 35 | 50 |
| Switzerland | 6 | 12 | 2 | | | 20 | 40 |
| New Zealand | 8 | 17 | 1 | | | | 26 |
| East Germany | 7 | 8 | | | | | 15 |
| Japan | 6 | 5 | 3 | | | | 14 |
| Australia | 3 | 4 | 2 | 3 | 1 | | 13 |
| Holland | 9 | | 1 | | | | 10 |
| Spain | 2 | 1 | 3 | | | | 6 |
| Czechoslovakia | | | | 3 | 1 | | 4 |
| Canada | | 1 | 2 | | | | 3 |
| Argentina | | 1 | | | 2 | | 2 |
| Sweden | | 2 | | | | | 2 |
| France | | 1 | | | | | 1 |
| Austria | | 1 | | | | | 1 |

## WORLD CHAMPIONSHIP WINS BY COUNTRIES 1960-1969

| Country | 50cc | 125cc | 250cc | 350cc | 500cc | Sidecar | Total |
|---|---|---|---|---|---|---|---|
| GB | 1 | 3 | 6 | 3 | 5 | | 18 |
| Germany | 3 | | | | | 8 | 11 |
| Italy | | 1 | 1 | 2 | 4 | | 8 |
| Rhodesia | | | 2 | 5 | 1 | | 8 |
| Switzerland | | 3 | | | | 2 | 5 |
| New Zealand | 2 | 2 | | | | | 4 |
| Australia | | 1 | 1 | | | | 2 |
| East Germany | 1 | | | | | | 1 |
| Spain | 1 | | | | | | 1 |

## CONSTRUCTORS' WORLD CHAMPIONSHIPS 1960-1969

| Make | 50cc | 125cc | 250cc | 350cc | 500cc | Sidecar | Total |
|---|---|---|---|---|---|---|---|
| Honda | 2 | 4 | 5 | 6 | 1 | | 18 |
| MV | | 1 | 1 | 4 | 9 | | 15 |
| BMW | | | | | | 11 | 11 |
| Suzuki | 5 | 2 | | | | | 7 |
| Yamaha | | 2 | 3 | | | | 5 |
| Kawasaki | | 1 | | | | | 1 |
| Derbi | 1 | | | | | | 1 |
| Benelli | | | 1 | | | | 1 |

## GP WINS BY MAKES 1960-1969

| Make | 50cc | 125cc | 250cc | 350cc | 500cc | Sidecar | Total |
|---|---|---|---|---|---|---|---|
| Honda | 14 | 33 | 47 | 37 | 10 | | 141 |
| MV | | 4 | 7 | 34 | 74 | | 119 |
| Yamaha | | 26 | 35 | 2 | | | 63 |
| Suzuki | 30 | 28 | | | | | 58 |
| BMW | | | | | | 53 | 53 |
| Kreidler | 11 | | | | | | 11 |
| Benelli | | | 8 | | | | 8 |
| Kawasaki | | 8 | | | | | 8 |
| Norton | | | | 1 | 6 | | 7 |
| MZ | | 4 | 2 | | | | 6 |
| Fath URS | | | | | | 6 | 6 |
| Derbi | 5 | | | | | | 5 |
| Jawa | | | | 4 | 1 | | 5 |
| Morini | | | 4 | | | | 4 |
| Jamathi | 4 | | | | | | 4 |
| Ossa | | | 3 | | | | 3 |
| Bultaco | | 1 | 1 | | | | 2 |
| Gilera | | | | | 1 | 1 | 2 |
| Matchless | | | | | 2 | | 2 |
| Moto Guzzi | | | 1 | | | | 1 |
| BSA | | | | | | 1 | 1 |
| Linto | | | | | 1 | | 1 |

# Grand Prix machines 1960-1969

| Year | Make & model | Type | Cyls | Bore/stroke | Capacity | Gears | Power output/rpm |
|---|---|---|---|---|---|---|---|
| 1960 | MV Agusta | Gear-driven dohc | 1 | 53x56 | 124 | 5 | 20bhp @ 12,500 |
| | Honda RC143 | Bevel driven dohc 8-valve | 2 | 46x37.5 | 124 | 6 | 18ps @ 13,500 |
| | Suzuki RT60 | Piston-ported two-stroke | 2 | 44x41 | 124 | 6 | 13ps @ 11,000 |
| | MZ | Disc-valve two-stroke | 1 | 54x54 | 123.6 | 6 | 23ps @ 10,700 |
| | MV Agusta | Gear-driven dohc | 2 | 53x56.2 | 247 | 7 | 36bhp @ 12,000 |
| | Honda RC161 | Gear-driven dohc 16-valve | 4 | 44x41 | 249.3 | 6 | 38ps @ 13,500 |
| | MV Agusta | Gear-driven dohc | 4 | 47.5x49.3 | 349.3 | 5 | 42bhp @ 11,000 |
| | MV Agusta | Gear-driven dohc | 4 | 63x56.4 | 497 | 5 | 70bhp @ 10,500 |
| 1961 | Honda 2RC143 | Bevel driven dohc, 8-valve | 2 | 44x41 | 124.6 | 6 | 23ps @ 14,000 |
| | MZ | Disc-valve two-stroke | 1 | 54X54 | 123.6 | 6 | 25bhp @ 10,800 |
| | Suzuki RT61 | Disc-valve two-stroke | 2 | 44x41 | 124 | 6 | 20ps @ 12,000 |
| | Yamaha RA41 | Disc-valve two-stroke | 1 | 56x50 | 124 | 6 | 20ps @ 10,000 |
| | Suzuki RV61 | Disc-valve two-stroke | 2 | 56x50.5 | 249 | 6 | 28ps @ 11,000 |
| | Yamaha RD48 | Disc-valve two-stroke | 2 | 56x50.7 | 249 | 6 | 35ps @ 10,000 |
| | Honda RC162 | Gear-driven dohc 16-valve | 4 | 44x41 | 249.2 | 6 | 45ps @ 14,000 |
| | MV Agusta | Gear-driven dohc | 4 | 47.5x49.3 | 349.3 | 5 | 42bhp @ 11,000 |
| | Jawa | Gear-driven dohc | 2 | 59x63.6 | 350 | 5 | 49bhp @ 10,600 |
| | Bianchi | Gear-driven dohc | 2 | 65x52.5 | 348.42 | 5/6 | 48bhp @ 10,600 |
| | MV Agusta | Gear-driven dohc | 4 | 53x56.4 | 497 | 5 | 70bhp @ 10,500 |
| 1962 | Suzuki RM62 | Disc-valve two-stroke | 1 | 40x39.5 | 49.64 | 8 | 8ps@ 10,500 (10/12,000) |
| | Kreidler | Disc-valve two-stroke | 1 | 40x39.7 | 49.90 | 4x3 | 8bhp @ 11,000 |
| | Honda RC111 | Gear-driven dohc 4-valve | 1 | 40x39 | 49 | 9 | 10ps @ 15,000 |
| | Honda RC145 | Gear-driven dohc 8-valve | 2 | 44x41 | 124.6 | 6 | 24ps @ 14,000 |

| Year | Make & model | Type | Cyls | Bore/stroke | Capacity | Gears | Power output/rpm |
|---|---|---|---|---|---|---|---|
| | Suzuki RT62 | Disc-valve two-stroke | 1 | 54x54 | 123.67 | 7 | 24ps @ 11,000 |
| | Honda RC163 | Gear-driven dohc 16-valve | 4 | 44x41 | 249.37 | 6 | 46 ps @ 14,000 |
| | MZ 250 | Disc-valve | 2 | 54x54 | 247 | 6 | 45bhp @ 10,000 |
| | SKEB S-259 | Shaft & bevel dohc | 2 | 55x52 | 248 | 6 | 38bhp @ 11,500 |
| | Honda RC 170 | Gear-driven dohc 16-valve | 4 | 47x41 | 285 | 6 | 49 ps @ 14,000 |
| | Honda RC171 | Gear-driven dohc 16-valve | 4 | 49x45 | 339.26 | 6 | 50ps @ 10,500 |
| | MV Agusta 350 | As per 1961 | | | | | |
| | Jawa | Shaft & bevel dohc | 2 | 59x63.6 | 347 | 5 | 49bhp @ 10,600 |
| | SKEB S-360 | Shaft & bevel dohc | 2 | 62x57.6 | 349 | 6 | 50.5 bhp @ 10,100 |
| | MV Agusta 500 | As per 1961 + ( six-speed g/box) | | | | | |
| 1963 | Suzuki RM63 | Disc-valve two-stroke | 1 | 40x39.5 | 49.64 | 9 | 11ps @ 13,000 |
| | Kreidler | Disc-valve two-stroke | 1 | 40x39.7 | 49.90 | 12 | 12bhp @ 11,000 |
| | Suzuki RT63 | Disc-valve two-stroke | 2 | 43x42.6 | 123.7 | 8 | 26ps @ 12,000 |
| | Honda RC145 | As per 1962 | | | | | |
| | MZ | Disc-valve | 1 | 54x54 | 123.6 | 6 | 25bhp @ 10,800 |
| | Honda RC164 | Gear-driven dohc 16-valve | 4 | 44x41 | 249.37 | 6 | 46ps @ 14,000 |
| | Honda CR72 | Gear-driven dohc | 2 | 54x54 | 249 | 6 | 42ps @ 12,000 |
| | Morini | Dohc four-stroke | 1 | 72x61 | 248.3 | 6 | 38bhp @ 11,000 |
| | Yamaha RD56 | Disc-valve two-stroke a/c | 2 | 56x50.7 | 248 | 7 | 45ps @ 11,000 |
| | MZ | Disc-valve part w/c | 2 | 54x54 | 247 | 6 | Approx 48bhp @ 10,000 |
| | Honda CR77 | Gear-driven dohc | 2 | 60x54 | 305 | 6 | 46ps @ 11,000 |
| | Honda RC172 | Gear-driven dohc 16-valve | 4 | 50x44.5 | 349.3 | 6 | 53ps @ 14,000 |
| | MV Agusta 350 | As per 1961 four-cylinder | | | | | |
| | Gilera | Gear-driven dohc | 4 | 46x52.6 | 349.6 | 5 | 47bhp @ 11,000 |
| | Jawa | Shaft & bevel driven dohc | 2 | 59x63.6 | 348 | 6 | 49bhp @ 10,600 |
| | SKEB S360 | Gear-driven dohc | 2 | 62x57.6 | 349 | 6 | 50bhp @ 10,400 |
| | Gilera | Gear-driven dohc | 4 | 52x58.8 | 499 | 5 | 70bhp @ 11,000 |
| | MV Agusta 500 | As per 1962 four-cylinder | | | | | |
| 1964 | Suzuki RM64 | Disc-valve, two-stroke a/c | 1 | 41.5x36.8 | 49.75 | 9 | 12.5ps @ 14,000 |
| | Honda RC114 | Gear-driven dohc 8-valve | 2 | 33x29.2 | 49.6 | 9 | 14ps @ 20,000 |
| | Kreidler | Disc-valve two-stroke | 1 | 40x39.7 | 49.9 | 6x2 | 14bhp @ 11,000 |
| | Honda 2RC146 | Gear-driven dohc 16-valve | 4 | 35x32 | 124.9 | 7 | 24ps @ 15,000 |
| | Suzuki RT64 | Disc-valve, two-stroke | 2 | 43x42.6 | 123.7 | 8 | 30ps @ 13,000 |
| | Yamaha RA75 | Disc-valve two-stroke a/c | 2 | 44x41 | 124.7 | 8 | 25ps @ 12,000 |
| | CZ | Shaft & bevel driven dohc | 2 | 45x39.2 | 125 | 6 | 24bhp @ 15,000 |
| | Yamaha RD56 | Disc-valve two-stroke, a/c | 2 | 56x50.7 | 248 | 6 | 54ps @ 11,000 |
| | Honda 2RC164 | Gear-driven dohc, 16-valve | 4 | 44x41 | 249.37 | 7 | 49ps @ 14,000 |
| | Honda 3RC164 | Gear-driven dohc 24-valve | 6 | 39x34.8 | 249.43 | 7 | 50ps @ 18,000 |
| | Suzuki RZ64 | Disc-valve two-stroke w/c | Sq4 | 43x42.6 | 246 | 5/6 | 50ps @ 12,000 |
| | MZ | Disc-valve two-stroke w/c | 2 | 54x54 | 247 | 8 | 53bhp @ 10,400 |
| | Benelli | Gear-driven dohc | 4 | 44x40.6 | 246.32 | 7 | 45bhp @ 14,000 |
| | Honda RC172 | Gear-driven dohc, 16-valve | 4 | 50x44.5 | 349.3 | 6 | 53ps @ 14,000 |
| | MV 350 | As per 1961 four-cylinder | | | | | |
| | Vostok S-364 | Gear-driven dohc | 4 | 49x46 | 347 | 6 | 52bhp @ 13,000 |
| | MV 500 | As per 1962 four-cylinder | | | | | |

| Year | Make & model | Type | Cyls | Bore/stroke | Capacity | Gears | Power output/rpm |
|---|---|---|---|---|---|---|---|
| 1965 | Honda RC115 | Gear-driven dohc 8-valve | 2 | 34x27.4 | 49.6 | 9 | 13ps @ 20,000 |
| | Suzuki RK65 | Disc-valve two-stroke w/c | 2 | 32.5x30 | 49.75 | 12 | 14.5ps @ 16,000 |
| | Honda 4RC146 | Gear-driven dohc, 16-valve | 4 | 35x32 | 124.9 | 7 | 28ps @ 18,000 |
| | Yamaha RA75A | Disc-valve two-stroke w/c | 2 | 44x41 | 124.7 | 8 | 28ps @ 13,000 |
| | Suzuki RT65 | Disc-valve two-stroke w/c | 2 | 43x42.6 | 123.7 | 9 | 30ps @ 14,000 |
| | MZ | Disc-valve two-stroke w/c | 2 | 54x54 | 247 | 6 | 54bhp @ 10,900 |
| | Yamaha RD56 | Disc-valve two-stroke a/c | 2 | 56x50.7 | 249.8 | 7 | 50ps @ 11,000 |
| | Honda RC165 | Gear-driven dohc, 24-valve | 6 | 39x34.8 | 249.43 | 7 | 55ps @ 18,000 |
| | Suzuki RZ65 | Disc-valve two-stroke w/c | Sq 4 | 43x42.6 | 247.32 | 7/8 | 56ps @ 12,850 |
| | Benelli | Gear-driven dohc | 4 | 44x40.5 | 246.32 | 7 | 48bhp @ 14,500 |
| | Jawa | Shaft and bevel driven dohc | 2 | 59x63,6 | 348 | 6 | 51bhp @ 11,000 |
| | Honda 2RC172 | Gear-driven dohc, 16-valve | 4 | 50x44.5 | 349 | 6 | 60ps @ 13,000 |
| | MV | Gear-driven dohc | 3 | 52x54.3 | 344 | 7 | 62.5bhp @ 13,500 |
| | MV 500 | As per 1962 four-cylinder | | | | | |
| 1966 | Suzuki RK66 | Disc-valve two-stroke w/c | 2 | 32.5x30 | 49.75 | 14 | 16.5ps @ 17,000 |
| | Honda RC116 | Gear-driven dohc 8-valve | 2 | 35.5x25.14 | 49.77 | 10 | 15ps @ 21,000 |
| | Honda RC149 | Gear-driven dohc 20-valve | 5 | 35.5x25.14 | 124.43 | 8 | 34ps @ 20,500 |
| | Yamaha RA75/97 | Disc-valve two-stroke w/c | 2 | 44x41 | 124.7 | 8 | 30ps @ 13,000 |
| | Suzuki RT66 | Disc-valve two-stroke w/c | 2 | 43x42.6 | 123.7 | 9 | 32ps @ 13,800 |
| | Honda RC166 | Gear-driven dohc 24-valve | 6 | 39x34.8 | 249.43 | 7 | 60ps @ 18,000 |
| | Yamaha RD05 | Disc-valve two-stroke w/c | V4 | 44x40.5 | 249 | 8 | 70ps ? @ 14,000 |
| | Honda RC173 | Gear-driven dohc 16-valve | 4 | 50x44.5 | 349.3 | 6 | 70ps @ 14,000 |
| | Aermacchi | Push rod ohv | 1 | 74x80 | 344 | 5 | N/A |
| | Jawa | Shaft & bevel driven dohc | 2 | 59x63.6 | 347 | 6 | 42bhp @ 9200 |
| | MV | Gear-driven dohc | 3 | 52x54.3 | 344 | 7 | 48bhp @ 12,000 |
| | Honda RC180 | Gear-driven dohc 16-valve | 4 | 57x48 | 489.94 | 6 | 85ps @ 12,000 |
| | MV | Gear-driven dohc | 3 | 62x54 | 490 | 7 | 78bhp @ 12,000 |
| | Paton | Gear-driven dohc | 2 | 72x57.8 | 470.66 | 6 | 52bhp @ 9600 |
| | Jawa | Shaft & Bevel driven dohc | 2 | 66.5x63.6 | 442 | 6 | N/A |
| 1967 | Suzuki RK67 | Disc-valve two-stroke w/c | 2 | 32.5x30 | 49.75 | 14 | 17.5ps @ 17,300 |
| | Derbi | Disc-valve two-stroke w/c | 1 | 38x42 | 49 | | N/A |
| | Yamaha RA97 | Disc-valve two-stroke w/c | 2 | 44x41 | 124.7 | 10 | 35ps @ 14,000 |
| | Suzuki RT67 | Disc-valve two-stroke w/c | 2 | 43x42.6 | 123.7 | 10 | 35ps @ 14,000 |
| | Kawasaki KA-1 | Disc-valve w/c | 2 | 43x42.6 | 123 | 8 | N/A |
| | Honda RC166 | Gear-driven dohc 24-valve | 6 | 41x31.5 | 249.5 | 7 | 63ps @ 18,000 |
| | Yamaha RD05A | Disc-valve two-stroke w/c | V4 | 44x40.5 | 249 | 8 | 70ps @ 15,000 |
| | Honda RC174 | Gear-driven dohc 24-valve | 6 | 41x37.5 | 297.06 | 7 | 65ps @ 17,000 |
| | MV | Gear-driven dohc | 3 | 55x49 | 349 | 7 | 62bhp @ 13,500 |
| | Benelli | Gear-driven dohc | 4 | 51x42 | 343 | 7 | 64bhp @ 13,800 |
| | Aermacchi | Push rod ohv | 1 | 74x80 | 344 | 5 | NA |
| | MV | Gear-driven dohc | 3 | 62x55 | 497.9 | 7 | 80bhp @ 12,000 |
| | Honda RC181 | Gear driven dohc 16 valve | 4 | 57.56x48 | 499 | 6 | 85ps @ 12,000 |

| Year | Make & model | Type | Cyls | Bore/stroke | Capacity | Gears | Power output/rpm |
|---|---|---|---|---|---|---|---|
| 1968 | Suzuki RK67 | As per 1967 | | | | | |
| | Jamathi | Disc-valve two-stroke w/c | 1 | 40x39 | 49 | 9 | N/A |
| | Derbi | Disc-valve two-stroke w/c | 1 | 38x42 | 47.6 | 6 | N/A |
| | Yamaha RA31A | Disc-valve two-stroke w/c | V4 | 35x32.4 | 124.7 | 9 | 44ps @ 18,000 |
| | Suzuki RT67 | As per 1967 | | | | | |
| | MZ | Disc-valve two-stroke | 1 | 54x54 | 125 | 6 | |
| | MZ | Disc-valve two-stroke w/c | 2 | 54x54 | 250 | 6 | 54bhp @ 11,500 |
| | Ossa | Disc-valve two-stroke | 1 | 70x65 | 249 | 6 | 40bhp @ 11,500 |
| | Yamaha RD05A | As per 1967 | | | | | |
| | Benelli | Gear-driven dohc 16-valve | 4 | 52x40.6 | 344 | 7 | 60/14,00 – 64/13,800 |
| | MV | Gear-driven dohc | 3 | 55x49 | 349 | 7 | 62bhp @ 13,500 |
| | Aermacchi | Push rod ohv | 1 | 77x75 | 349 | 6 | 42bhp @ 8400 |
| | MZ | Disc-valve two-stroke w/c | 2 | | 305 | 6 | 56bhp @ 11,000 |
| | Linto | Push rod ohv | 2 | 72x61 | 496 | 6 | NA |
| | Benelli | Gear-driven dohc | 4 | 54x54 | 494 | 6 | NA |
| | Vostok S-565 | Gear-driven dohc | 4 | 55x52 | 494 | 6 | 76bhp @ 12,000 |
| | MV | Gear-driven dohc | 3 | 62x55 | 497.9 | 7 | 80bhp @ 12,000 |
| | | | | | | | |
| 1969 | Derbi | Disc-valve two-stroke w/c | 1 | 38x42 | 47.6 | 6 | N/A |
| | Kreidler Van Veen | Disc-valve two-stroke w/c | 1 | 40x39.7 | 49.8 | 6 | 16bhp @ 16,000 |
| | Kawasaki KA-1 | Disc-valve two-stroke w/c | 2 | 43x42.6 | 124 | 8 | 30ps @ 15,000 |
| | Suzuki RT67 | As per 1967 | | | | | |
| | Benelli | Gear-driven dohc 16-valve | 4 | 44x40.6 | 246.9 | 8 | 55/16,00 64/14,500 |
| | Yamaha TD2 | Piston-ported two-stroke a/c | 2 | 56x50 | 247 | 5 | 44ps @ 10,500 |
| | Ossa | Disc-valve two-stroke a/c | 1 | 70x65 | | 5 | 42bhp |
| | MV | As per 1968 3 cylinder | | | | | |
| | Yamaha TR2 | Piston-ported two-stroke a/c | 2 | 61x59.6 | 348 | 5 | 54ps @ 9500 |
| | Aermacchi | Push rod ohv | 1 | 77x75 | 349 | 6 | 42bhp @ 8500 |
| | Jawa 673 | Disc-valve two-stroke w/c | V4 | 50x44 | 345.6 | 6 | 52bhp @ 13,000 |
| | CZ 860GP | Gear-driven Dohc 16-valve | V4 | 50x44 | 346 | 8 | 53bhp @ 16,000 |
| | Linto | Push rod ohv | 2 | 72x61 | 496.7 | 6 | 64bhp @ 10,000 |
| | Hannah-Paton | Gear-driven dohc 8-valve | 2 | 73.5x57 | 483.68 | 6 | 70bhp |
| | MV | As per 1968 3 cylinder | | | | | |

*NB There is no direct comparison between ps and bhp figures, which are obtained differently (1ps does not equal 1bhp). Generally British and European manufacturers used bhp while Japanese ones used only ps. Regarding the three-cylinder MVs, the bore/stroke figures are only an approximation due to the confusing and often contradictory figures quoted for these machines.*

Circa 1960 to 1965 500cc four-cylinder MV Agusta. (Author collection)

Circa 1964 250cc disc-valve, twin-cylinder MZ. (Author collection)

1963 350cc four-cylinder Honda RC172. (Author collection)

*Circa 1964 250cc twin-cylinder, disc-valve Yamaha RD56. (Courtesy Classic Yams)*

*1967 50cc twin-cylinder, two-stroke Suzuki RK67 with 14-speed gearbox. (Author collection)*

*1966 125cc five-cylinder Honda RC149. (Author collection)*

*Circa 1967 three-cylinder 500cc MV Agusta. (Author collection)*

*1967 250cc, six-cylinder Honda RC166. (Author collection)*

*1967 500cc four-cylinder Honda RC181. (Author collection)*

*1969 250cc twin-cylinder, two-stroke Yamaha TD2. (Author collection)*

*1969 125cc twin-cylinder, two-stroke Kawasaki KA1. (Author collection)*

# GP circuits 1960 to 1969

| Country | Circuit |
|---|---|
| Belgium | Spa Francorchamps 8.74 miles 14.12km |
| Canada | Mosport Park 2.46 miles 3.95km |
| Czechoslovakia | Brno 8.69 miles 13.94km |
| Finland | Tampere 2.24 miles 3.60km |
| Finland | Imatra 3.76 miles 6.03km |
| France | Rouen 4.08 miles 6.54km |
| France | Clermont-Ferrand 5.02 miles 8.05km |
| France | Le Mans 2.64 miles 4.24km |
| Great Britain | Isle of Man 37.76 miles 60.72km |
| Great Britain | Dundrod Ireland 7.52 miles 12.06km |
| Germany | Solitude 7.11 miles 11.44km |
| Germany | Nürburgring 14.25 miles 22.85km |
| Germany | Nürburgring South 4.82 miles 7.74km |
| Germany | Hockenheim (1961 to 1963) 4.81 miles 7.72km |
| Germany | Hockenheim 1964 4.21 miles 6.76km |
| Germany | Sachsenring 5.37 miles 8.61km |
| Holland | Assen Van Drenthe 4.81 miles 7.70km |
| Italy | Monza 3.58 miles 5.75km |
| Italy | Imola 3.13 miles 5.01km |
| Japan | Suzuka 3.76 miles 6.04km |
| Japan | Fisco 3.74 miles 6.0km |
| Spain | Montjuich Park 2.35 miles 3.79km |
| Spain | Jarama 2.12 miles 3.40km |
| Sweden | Kristianstad 4.07 miles 6.53km |
| USA | Daytona 3.10 miles 4.98km |
| Yugoslavia | Opatija 3.73 miles 5.99km |

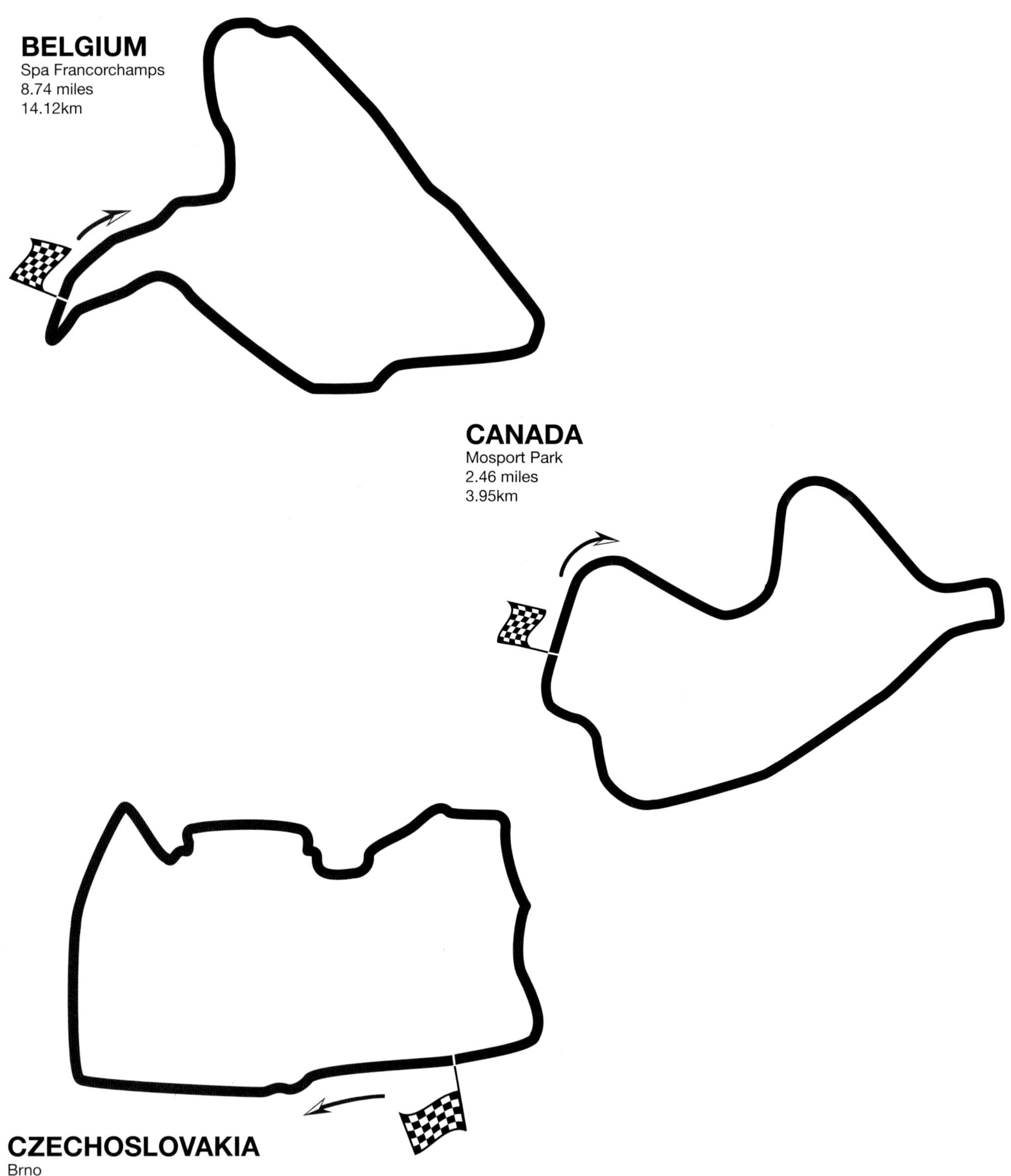
BELGIUM
Spa Francorchamps
8.74 miles
14.12km
CANADA
Mosport Park
2.46 miles
3.95km
CZECHOSLOVAKIA
Brno
8.69 miles
13.94km

## FINLAND
Tampere
2.24 miles
3.6km

## FINLAND
Imatra
3.76 miles
6.03km

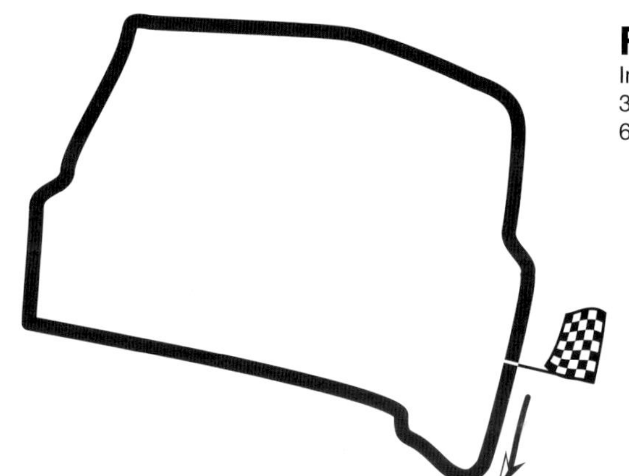

## FRANCE
Rouen
4.08 miles
6.54km

**FRANCE**
Clermont-Ferrand
5.02 miles
8.05km

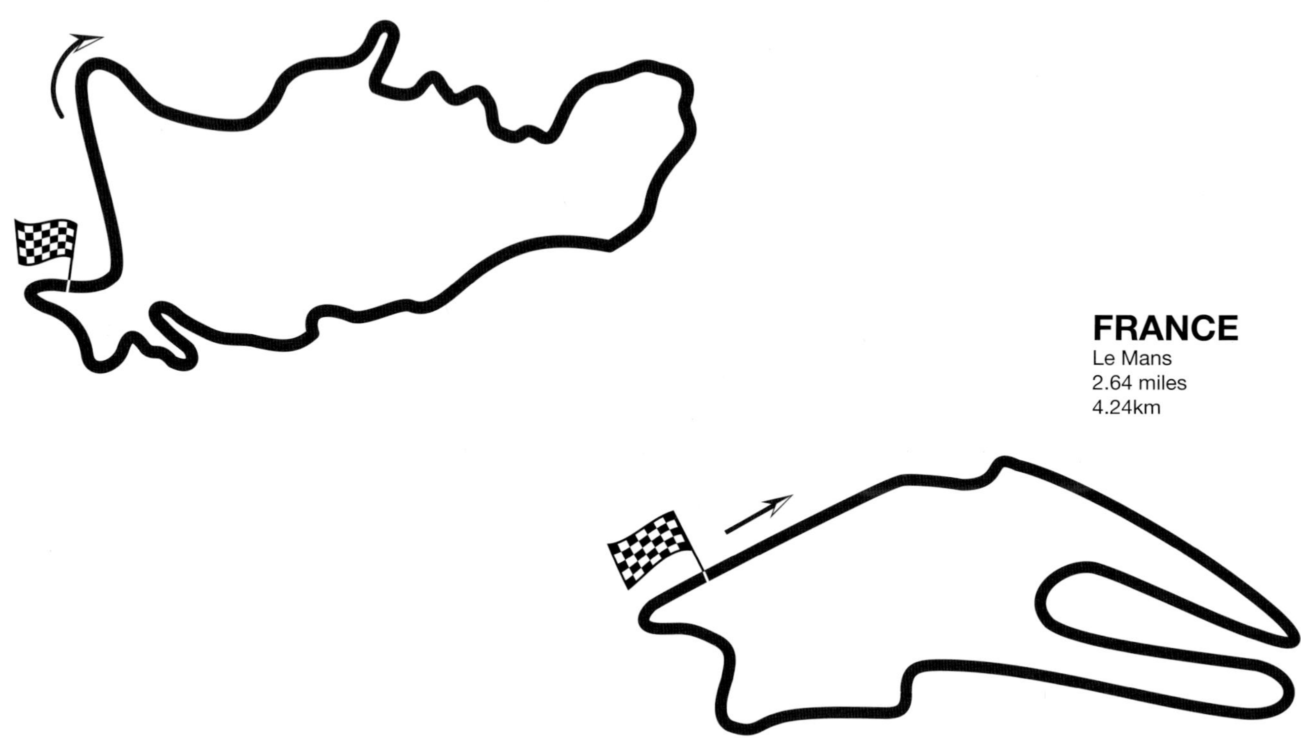

**FRANCE**
Le Mans
2.64 miles
4.24km

**GERMANY**
Solitude
7.11 miles
11.44km

## GERMANY
Nürburgring South
4.82 miles
7.74km

## GERMANY
Nürburgring Nordschleife
14.25 miles
22.85km

## GERMANY
Hockenheim 1961
4.81 miles
7.72km

## GERMANY

Hockenheim 1964
4.21 miles
6.76km

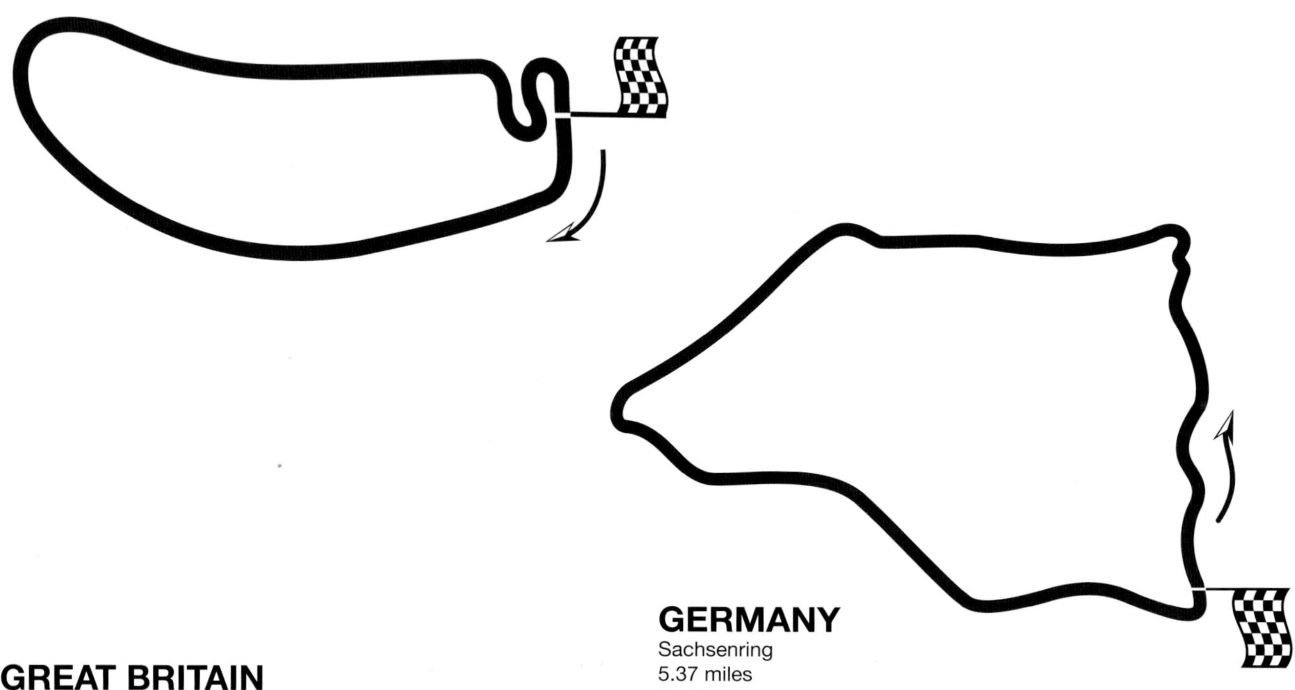

## GERMANY

Sachsenring
5.37 miles
8.61km

## GREAT BRITAIN

Isle of Man
37.76 miles
60.72km

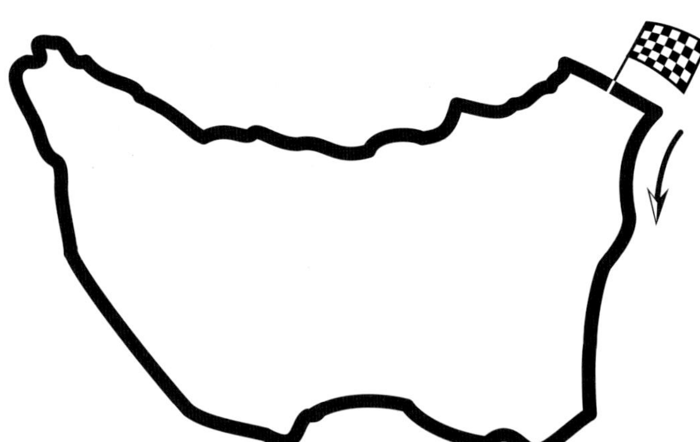

## HOLLAND

Assen
4.81 miles
7.70km

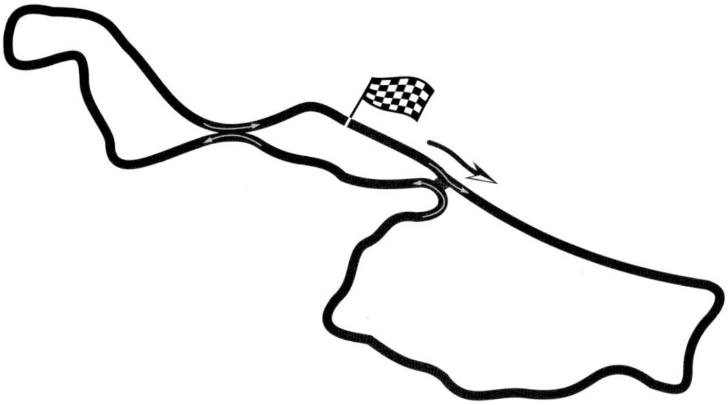

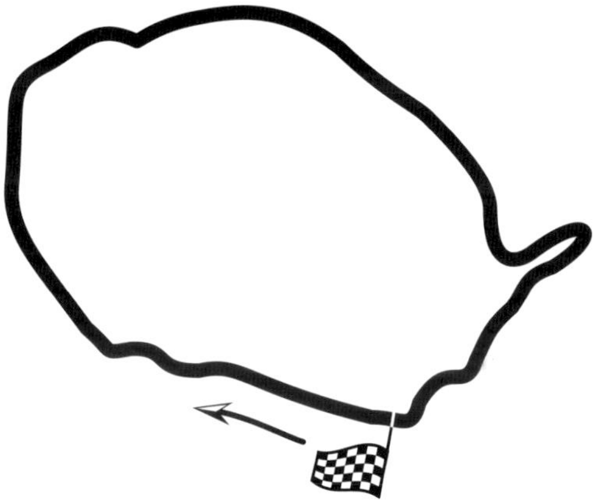

## IRELAND

Dundrod
7.52 miles
12.06km

## ITALY

Monza
3.58 miles
5.75km

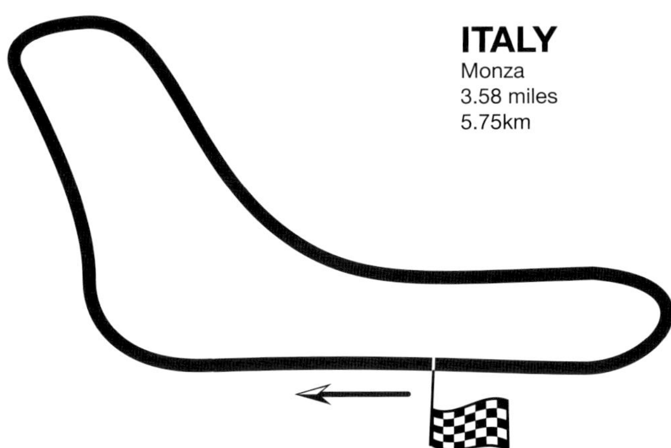

**ITALY**
Imola
3.13 miles
5.01km

**JAPAN**
Suzuka
3.76 miles
6.04km

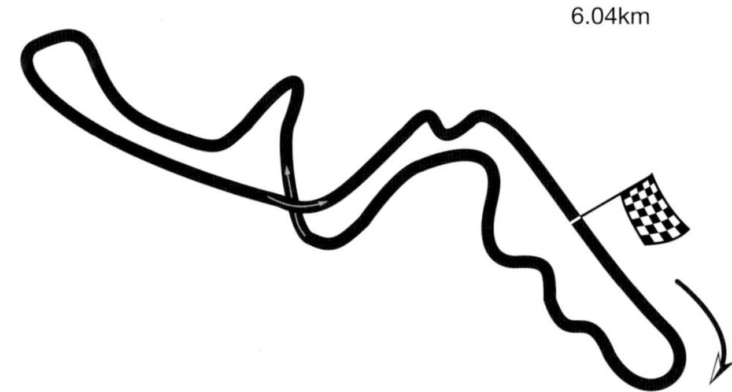

**JAPAN**
Fisco
3.74 & 2.72 miles
6.00km & 4.36km

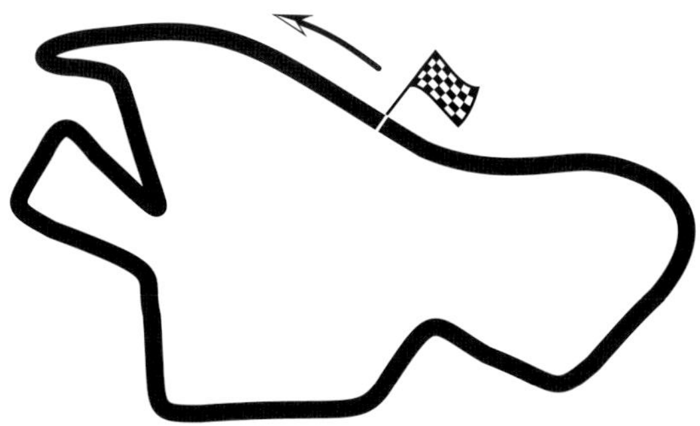

**SPAIN**
Montjuich Park
2.35 miles
3.79km

**SPAIN**
Jarama
2.12 miles
3.40km

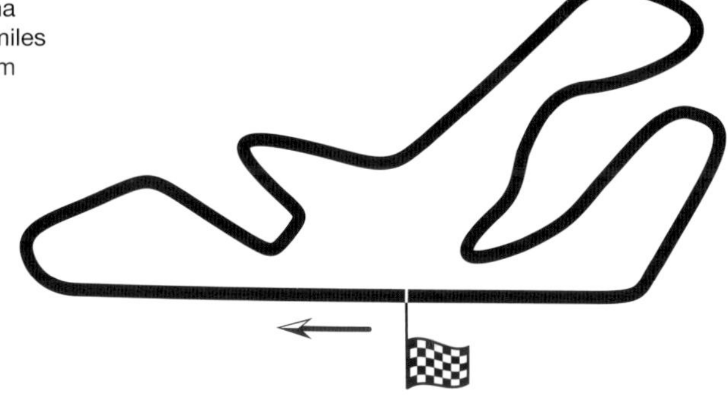

**SWEDEN**
Kristianstad
4.07 miles
6.53km

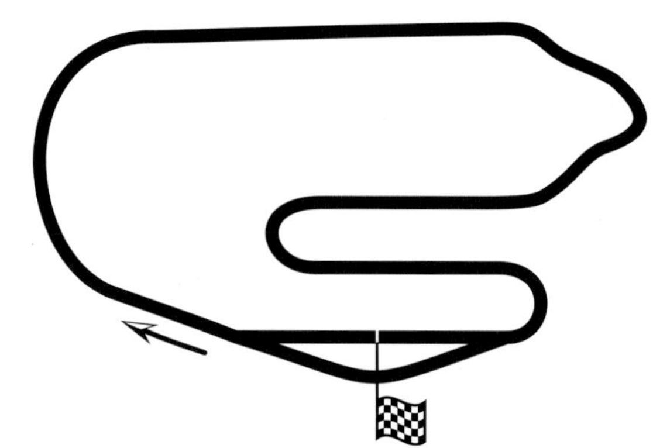

**USA**
Daytona
3.10 miles
4.98km

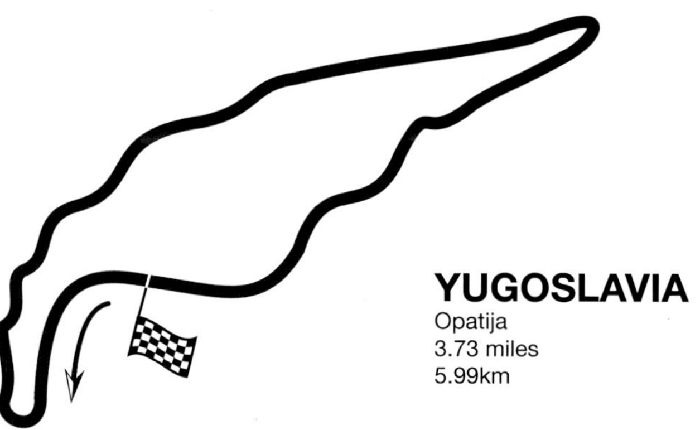

**YUGOSLAVIA**
Opatija
3.73 miles
5.99km

ALSO FROM CHRIS PEREIRA:

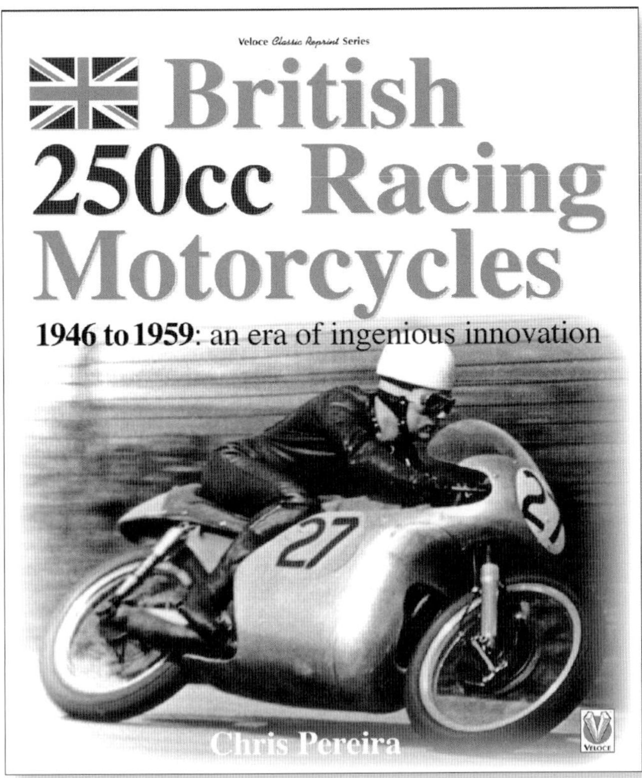


**FROM 1946** up to 1959, the 250cc class in Britain was supported almost entirely by privately built Specials and Hybrids. This book recalls the men and machines involved, and traces their history and development, in what was clearly the most technically innovative class of Road Racing in the 1950s.

ISBN 9781787113299
Paperback 250 x 207mm
80 pages

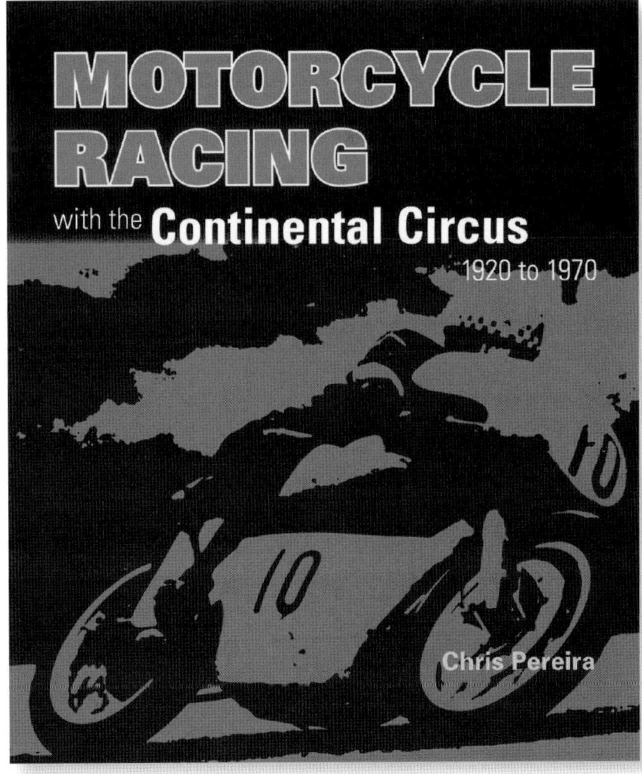


**A FASCINATING** history of Continental motorcycle racing, from the pre-war period through to the 1970s, this book details the British riders and privateers from around the world, who earned their living competing in races and events on the circuits of Europe – for the racers an exciting and nomadic existence, known as the 'Continental Circus'.

ISBN 9781787117785
Paperback 250 x 207mm
96 pages

Available from www.veloce.co.uk and all good booksellers

**THE FIRST** ever biography or World Motorcyle Champion, Gary Hocking. Exploring his life in Rhodesia, the book recounts how he was helped to become a World Champion, his dedication, and retirement at a young age – and the tragic accident that cost him his life.

ISBN 9781787114142
Paperback 210 x 148mm
176 pages

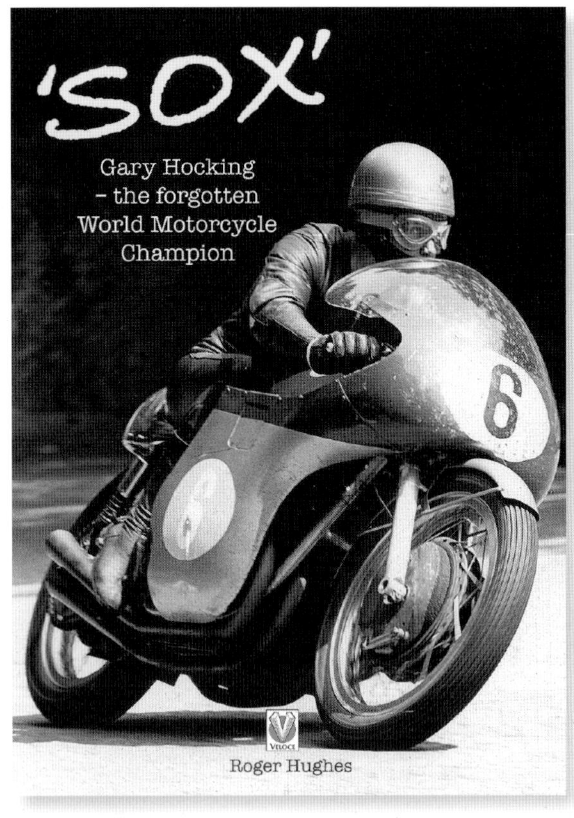

**MOTORCYCLING SOCIAL** history, as seen from the saddle. Bill Snelling's entertaining autobiography recounts a lifetime spent at the heart of British motorcycle sport, and his adventures while living on the Isle of Man.

ISBN 9781787115811
Paperback 210 x 148mm
160 pages

# Index